Who Do You Think
YOU ARE KIDDING!

Colin Bean

MINERVA PRESS

ATLANTA LONDON SYDNEY

Who Do You Think
YOU ARE KIDDING!
Copyright © Colin Bean 1998

ISBN 0 75410 499 0

First Published 1998 by
MINERVA PRESS
Sixth Floor
Canberra House
315–317 Regent Street
London W1R 7YB

2nd Impression 1998

Printed in Great Britain for Minerva Press

Who Do You Think
YOU ARE KIDDING!

Dedicated – with love – to my family,
the most understanding group of people
one could ever hope to meet.

Acknowledgements

Now wait! Now wait! Give credit where it's due!

(Professor Higgins in *My Fair Lady*)

Tom Simm, author, radio expert, doyen of academia, whose stories I have enjoyed reading for the BBC's *Write Now* programme. Only his patience, dedication and deciphering skills put my scribblings and meanderings into readable print and – wonders of technology – transferred them onto disks. I got a frosty look when I asked, in innocent ignorance, 'Tom, why do we need to put all this onto gramophone records?'

Simon Longson, expert in the mysterious world – to me – of something to do with electrical power; also on the subject of *Dad's Army*. Comedy is his absorbing hobby and he has taken on, for some years now, poor chap, the role of my personal archivist. He is also responsible for the title of this tome.

The publishers and printers for being so patient with an old 'first-timer'.

And journalist, author, photographer and friend of many years' acquaintance – Geoffrey Shryhane – for being brave enough to write the foreword to the whole shebang!

The Cartoons by Heap are reproduced by kind permission of *The Sheffield Star* newspaper.

About the Author

With the aid of sixteen volumes of his scrapbooks 'What We Did and What They Said' and comedy archivist Simon Longson, at seventy years old Colin Bean has decided to 'tell it as it was for him', thespianwise. In parts mildly humorous and sad, the story of one Wiganer (born and bred though not on the famous pier), who didn't quite make it to stardom, records a professional life he has enjoyed.

Colin Bean is a life member of the British Actors' Equity, a long-term member of the Actors' Church Union, a regular reader of poems and stories for BBC Radio North's *Write Now*, honorary production consultant to the Bijou Theatre Company, the Two-Faced Theatre Company and Palaver Productions, patron of The Barmy Army Film Club and life member (and early member) of Wigan Little Theatre.

Foreword

Curtain up on a long, fascinating and eventful life in the theatre. Stand up and take a bow Mr Colin Bean.

Colin Bean, the actor, needs little introduction. He is remembered by millions as Private Sponge of *Dad's Army* fame. The truth is that he is also remembered by armies of theatregoers all over the country for his stage performances.

In this book Colin Bean has proved himself a good writer and with his vast volumes of scrapbooks has set down in fine style just what it's like to be treading the boards for a living.

I first came across Colin Bean soon after starting my career as a reporter on the local paper in Wigan and was immediately impressed by his talents as an actor, his sheer professionalism and his irrepressible sense of humour. So it was a privilege to read his manuscript which is never less than enthralling.

There is never a dull moment in the life of Mr Bean and he successfully lifts the lid on the magic box that is the theatre and television.

The early chapters recall his determination to be an actor. The young man was not for turning despite his nearest and dearest insisting he was 'just going through a phase'.

Wigan born (and proud of it) Colin's reflections on his long working life in the world of theatre and television – in fact all aspects of entertainment – give a welcome and intriguing look behind the scenes. There is humour and pathos and not a boastful sentence, even though he has worked with the most famous in the land.

There's a nip in the pen of Colin Bean and his remembrances of his playing Pte Sponge in the still-popular and oft-repeated episodes of *Dad's Army* make fascinating reading.

It's a long time since Colin played a shepherd in the Nativity play at his Wigan school. Six decades later he still takes on the occasional part, is involved in radio and presents his one-man show of readings. His work has been his utter pleasure and that pleasure jumps from every page of his book which is peppered with facts and anecdotes.

Geoffrey Shryhane

Chapter One

When, with the help of two charming lady assistants and under the watchful eye of the wizard who had wrought this miracle, I stood up alongside my hospital bed, free of pain, the idea of 'writing it all down' first took root in my mind.

This was in 1982. I was a hip replacement patient in the pioneering centre of hip replacement, Wrightington Hospital. As I was brought to my feet for that first time, only two days after undergoing the actual replacement operation, I became aware not only of the lack of pain in my left hip and leg, but of the fact that I could stand up on legs of apparently equal length.

For some two years I had been working with a limp and in pain, both of which were increasingly affecting my work at the Octagon Theatre, Bolton, where I had been engaged as an actor and occasional play director since 1978.

The wizard who had headed the operating team carrying out this amazing change was watching very carefully. Unable to believe this pain-free sensation I believe I uttered, 'But there's no pain! Where has it gone?'

Wizard Mike (B.M. Wroblewski FRCS) said, 'I hope you left that in my theatre, but of course you slept through most of my performance!'

So elated was I at my release from agony that, I was assured later, I said, 'Well, you won't sleep through the performance next time you come to our theatre.'

So it was that, eventually, I was able to return to my work at the Octagon and some weeks later to fulfil my promise. Briefly, the play was *Charlie's Aunt* and I got tickets for Mr and Mrs Wroblewski and a friend of theirs, the doctor who had anaesthetised me prior to the operation. Playing Stephen Spettigue, part of my role involved a number of chases around the stage in search of 'Charlie's Aunt'. Mike certainly didn't sleep during that noisy romp and, when we met for drinks in the bar after the show, his wife, Peggy, told of his reactions to my caperings. One could invariably hear Mr Spettigue approaching before he actually came into view on stage. Mike, it would seem, covered his eyes with his hands each time and whispered to his companions, 'Has he made it?'

I am happy to say that, not only did I 'make it' across the stage each time, but that that operation, just two months before my fifty-sixth birthday, added another ten years to my working life. Touch wood, as it is said – actors are a superstitious lot – that left hip has never given me a day's trouble since.

The first inclinations to start recording just what I have been up to in my working life came about from being told by the stage manager as I was about to go into hospital for the op, 'For heaven's sake, got it done soon! We've used up all our extensive collection of walking sticks just getting you on and off stage!'

Thus it is that we now go back to the 1930s when I attended St Michael and All Angels School in Earl Street, Wigan, Infants School, where I was described by the headmistress, Miss Cunliffe, as 'a somewhat colourful child, unfortunately given to a rather theatrical imagination and exaggeration'. Now we know. I was a big 'ead, even as an infant!

Junior School, Mrs Wynne's class, brought my first smell of the crowd and the roar of the greasepaint when I was told that I would be a shepherd in the Christmas carol service and Nativity tableau in St Michael's church just before that year's festive season school holiday. Frank Derbyshire, Sidney Benning and I were told to bring an old sheet or some other piece of material from home so that costumes could be made. The efforts of my teachers to pin a sheet up into some semblance of a garment suited to 'watching flocks by night' did not impress this aspiring thespian. After the service when I took the sheet home again, my 'alterations', made with the aid of a pair of scissors, were not greatly appreciated.

The 'action' involving the three shepherds was to walk up the aisle with our jam jar lanterns, engaged in mimed, eager conversation and stellar-indicating gesticulation until we arrived to kneel by the manger in the stable tableau. Many years later Mr Harris, the junior school head and church choirmaster commented that my performance had been 'quite memorable'. It would appear that my progression towards the rustic scene was to be compared to a 'demented windmill' and that, even when supposed to be posed within the scene in silent, inanimate adoration of the babe, it was somewhat disconcerting to have one shepherd still in 'mimed, eager conversation and stellar-indicating gesticulation'.

The following year I was chosen for a play in the concert in the school hall, an annual ordeal during which, I'm sure, many have sat so bravely. In *Snow White and Rose Red*, my lines written out in a penny notebook I was required to supply from home, I was to be 'Jan the Huntsman', who takes Snow White to the woods. That simple fact and the added requirement that costuming was a home responsibility for all, probably brought on the first expression of parental disapproval. 'All this daft acting. Not made of money. They should be teaching you sums and things.'

Alas, parental disapproval was to continue in my case for many years to come. Added to all this, the dressmaker, engaged to make the said costume, got the dates of the two-night concert wrong. Result: Jan the huntsman had no costume for the first night and had to go on stage with his wooden sword tucked into his dad's old army belt with legs wrapped in World War One puttees and an army cap not to mention floods of tears at his humiliating misfortune. The second night's performance was, of course, correctly attired and the red and green huntsman suit served for fancy dress parties – very popular for birthdays then – for a number of years to come.

The following year brought the play *Sleeping Beauty* and the role of the king, plus the first realisation of 'what it was all about'. While the various fairy godmothers pronounced their wishes for Princess Beauty the doll representing the baby was nursed tenderly by Celia Barnes (I think!) as the queen but when the last evil fairy godmother had pronounced her curse the queen handed the baby princess to her father with a 'protect our only child' type of line.

In hindsight, was it an accident or was it a conscious effort on my part? Somehow or other – first-night nerves – I managed to got hold of the doll the wrong way round. As I 'nursed' it fairly vigorously, as had been rehearsed – that was meant to be the amusing bit – the audiences far from being merely amused, were openly laughing out loud. Looking down I realised the doll's uncovered legs were up in the air while its head was buried somewhere on my lap.

'Hello!' I thought. 'I'm doing something they like. What I'm doing is giving them pleasure.'

The damage was done; that was it. The bug had got me; the thespian virus was in my blood. The reactions of my teachers offstage in the wings were also quite animated. The scolding and the admonitions as the curtains closed could, I'm sure, be enjoyed equally by the audience. Warnings of 'dire consequences' however failed to prevent this 'terrible accident' from happening again in the second night's performance.

How very unjust, I thought, the audience loved it but amongst my tutors no praise for creativity and artistic interpretation only a reprimanding lecture from the headmaster. 'In my office tomorrow morning, before prayers.'

My father – as usual not present at either performance – was informed of my reprehensible performance, prompting further severe admonishment and hopeless prognostications for the life ahead of me.

I'm glad to say that all this worked splendidly on young Bean. Friends and relatives may have been told that 'Colin's going to be a doctor' or a practitioner of some such noble craft – but Colin knew, deep down, 'No way, José'.

Occasionally Aunt Nelly, Aunty Bertha or Aunty Annie would take me to see the pantomime at Wigan Hippodrome – a *very* special treat and not to be encouraged – or if my aunt, uncle and cousin from Newcastle had come to stay with us. My cousin went to dancing classes at home which to me 'smelled of theatre', and together we'd stage our own backyard concerts. All the usual stepladders, clotheslines with props and dust sheets for a stage – one has read it all so often.

During the second half of the 1930s I was also taken quite often to the Hippodrome during the annual repertory season, usually by a family friend or relative. This ran annually from about the end of May until September – a twelve or sixteen-week run of twice-nightly plays.

For the ins and outs of 'rep' I can do no better than refer the reader to Richard Jerram's excellent book *Weekly Rep* (Peter Andrew Co. Ltd) – with an enlightening foreword by the late Sir Michael Horden CBE. To me, at the ages of nine, ten and eleven, this was magic, the wonderful realisation of those early thoughts I'd had about the reaction to holding the baby upside down.

The first company I remember was the Lawrence-Williamson Repertory Company. T.C. Lawrence was the play director – or producer, as the term was then – and George Willamson was the general manager. T.C. and his wife, Margaret Carlisle, often played leading roles, as did our own dear Dame Lilian Braithwaite's lookalike, Bessie Osborne. Gerry Barton, as comedy juvenile, was a popular personality in Wigan. (We had our own real, local stars in those days!)

By about 1937 or 1938 the L-W company had given way to Frank H. Fortescue's Famous Players.

'Famous?' cried we younger, old rep hands. 'Famous? We've never heard of them.' Oh my small theatre world. If one hadn't played Wigan Hippodrome one couldn't claim to be famous.

By this time I had reached grammar school and was a member of the school's Play Circle – a play-reading group – and soon to be a veteran of some Scout gang shows. By the time I'd reached the upper forms in school, transitus and sixth, a few discontented members of our Play Circle formed our own company, the Tudor Players, in our out-of-school hours.

'Why Tudor?' you may well ask. We weren't a Shakespearean company and we weren't doing period plays, but family friends, with whom I holidayed on occasions in Watford, took me to theatres in Watford and London during these stays. They lived in Tudor Avenue, 'Where every house has a different design on the front' pointed out my Aunty Nan. 'Tudor'. What a grand name think I and we would be 'different' as a drama group. Don't ask me how.

Anyway, it was just before the start of World War Two. 'This new lot' have taken up residence in our local Hippodrome. First house Wednesday night a number of the Tudor Players would be in their one and sixpenny seats in the circle to give that week's production our considered opinion. If it was a nice summer evening, at about 8.15 p.m. one might have seen a group of earnest young people walking slowly through Wigan's lovely Mesnes Park, analysing almost line by line the play just seen. Often in later years I thought of this when I was up to my eyes in a long, twice-nightly rep season.

In those heady days I thought only of how wonderful it must be. Just think! A different play every week and you got to do it twice every night! All those different characters one could play, all those wigs, costumes, make-up, and so forth. It was probably a good job I did not know then the other side of the coin. Cramming lines into one's head at 2 or 3 a.m., already tired out from a morning's rehearsal and two performances and worrying about what to wear for the part. Unless it was a 'costume' or 'special' play, rep artistes had to supply their own costumes or wardrobe. In *The Stage* – before *TV Today* days – advertisements in 'Artistes Wanted' for rep seasons would often read: 'Must have good wardrobe, dress well on and off.' Quite a number of repertory companies were very wary of their own good name and very particular about how artistes appeared off the stage as well as in the plays. Harry Hanson once told a young assistant stage manager, who'd been out prop hunting, 'If you are asking a favour of someone, as a Court Player, you'll dress neat. Doesn't have to be your only good suit but I won't have "slovens" in my companies.'

Let's get back to Wigan Hippodrome and Frank H. Fortescue's Famous Players. From their arrival until my responding to call-up for national service in 1944 I became a regular patron and got backstage – that magic kingdom – to meet actual, real actors. Arthur Leslie – yes, he of the Rovers Return – his wife, Betty Morton Powell, and – names remembered – Patricia Stewart, charming Irish juvenile lead, Tony Scott, a handsome, cheekily smiling comedy juvenile, excellent as Albert Feather in *Ladies in*

Retirement, Harry Shacklock, Raymond S. Graham, F.J. Richardson, Doreen Sutcliffe-Hudson, Eleanor Patterson, Iris Dimmick, Marjorie Mee-Jonses, Ursula Hanray, Vivienne Bennet, Arthur C. Goff, Eileen Leoville and a delightful lady assistant manager (and early 'heart-throb' of mine), Hilary Dean.

Many more people who worked so hard there are re-membered but their names, alas, elude me for my collection of theatre programmes of that era no longer exists. On my first leave from the army, after six weeks' primary training, I discovered that my patriotic dad had given my huge collection to the 'help the war effort' wastepaper campaign. My make-up box, which I was able to recover, he'd given to a local drama club since, in his estimation, 'Colin won't need them any more. When he comes out he'll have got over all this nonsense and got a proper job.' How many, oh how many actors have heard that cry? To his dying day dear Dad still had a hope that I'd 'get a proper job'. Later in life he began to discover that theatre work can be very hard work. In his experienced eyes, however, it was still not a 'proper job'.

Arthur Leslie must have got fed up with this precocious sixteen year old hanging about the theatre, pestering for autographs and putting forth his views on theatre. In the end I won! He offered me a walk-on part in a melodrama called *The Face at the Window* – from the French *La Loup* – complete with rooftop chase finish.

I played a swarthy gigolo in a low den in Paris – at six-teen! My Higher School Certificate studies didn't get much attention in that week. I was fitted in at the Monday dress rehearsal and even though I played under a pseudonym, now forgotten, when my father found out 'all hall was let loose' at home. My first professional wages? Ten shillings and the offer to play a butler in a later production of *Lady Windermere's Fan*. This was wartime, of course, but everyone was assured that none of Oscar Wilde's wit would be lost except, of course, for the bits cut for twice-nightly performances because it would be played in modern dress. In other words, no special costumes but the artistes' own evening dress. I believe Arthur Leslie and one or two other members of the company fitted me out from their own wardrobes.

F.J. Richardson, a friendly Scot over call-up age, who did AFS duty as well as acting, had to enter a gentleman's room at one point to discover (Shock! Horror!) Lady Windermere's fan on the chaise longue. One evening, as he picked up the fan to exclaim to the world what he had found, he looked very puzzled, said not a word and came offstage without delivering the dramatic curtain line.

Offstage someone said, 'What's the matter, Jock? You didn't say the line.'

F.J. pulled out his false teeth swearing. 'Och! The top set's jammed on the bottom set an' I canna get 'em open!'

Before joining up in November, 1944, I had another week of 'professional experience'. The Lawrence-Williamson Company, by now resident at the Bolton Hippodrome, apparently phoned Arthur Leslie to ask if he had an actor to spare for one week for a small walk-on as an Egyptian servant. Mr Leslie had nobody he could spare but, with relief perhaps, could recommend a young man called Colin Bean. My salary soared – and my head swelled. Fifteen shillings for the week *and* two and six towards my weekly bus fares! I was an actor!

Plays at school had included, of course, the inevitable *Monkey's Paw* and that great Northern play *The Dear Departed*. 'Three One-Act Plays' was quite a popular programme in those days. Sometimes the Tudor Players would put on what we called a revue in place of a second play – our party-pieces and 'quickie' sketches as we'd remembered them from the Hippodrome variety and revue shows in the 'off-rep' seasons. Before the demise of the Tudor Players – mainly due to national service calling us – we'd tackled *Charlie's Aunt* and *The Bells*. We'd all been thrilled by Arthur Leslie's performance as Matthias, the burgomaster, two years earlier in *The Bells* at the Hippodrome of course. Guess who played Matthias? The last scene must have been ham in very thick slices!

So, into HM forces, where nothing of a theatrical nature – except seeing 'ENSA' and 'Stars in Battledress' shows – came my way until I got to India. Here I turn to a well-worn Roneoed programme sheet for 'The Force Dramatic Society' – the 'Force' being British and Indian Troops, Japan Occupation Force, or BRINDJAP force. My contribution was Sergeant Buzzfuzz QC in the case of *Bardwell v Pickwick* as a monologue – in costume! Also, a small part in a cod-drama called *Old Moore's Almanac*.

Before the mystic Orient, however, Europe had had the honour of accommodating me for a while.

Chapter Two

Service life was far removed from the theatre in 1944–45. After primary training I found myself in the Movement Control Section of the Royal Engineers. At last I was a gentleman according to a piece of regimental folklore. It's said that King George V, I think, once addressed a parade, 'Officers, Non-commissioned Officers. Gentlemen of the Royal Engineers and men of other regiments!' Thus until VE day Gentleman Sapper Bean RE served in the Shipping Movements Office in Mersey House on the docks in Antwerp.

The enemy had been 'moved out' not very long before we moved in. They'd been using the office for the same purpose. German ship names, in German script, were still written in chalk on the dock-state board, the drawers in my desk were full of forms and movement orders in German, which I had to dispose of to make space for forms and movement orders of a very similar nature in English. I can't help thinking now, what a case in favour of Esperanto! Think of all the paper that would have been saved!

The odd ENSA party caught up with us but frankly, the ones I saw were not very good. The 'big stuff' – The Old Vic, Noël Coward, Sadler's Wells and the big bands came after I'd gone.

The war in Europe ended. We actually got a day off from the office – it was a seven-day week here with one half day a week free – and Antwerp went mad.

Read about VE night anywhere in Europe and the same happened in Antwerp too. The anti-aircraft searchlights lit up the top of the cathedral with the Belgian Tricolour flying from its highest point. Its colours summed the whole thing up – black, yellow, red. 'Out of darkness into light by fire', as I'd been taught by a World War One veteran – my father.

The war in Europe now over, anyone volunteering for service in the Far East would start their transfer with a period of UK leave. What a chance to travel! While I was on my UK leave quite suddenly VJ Day came. When I reported back to my unit the group that had been the Movement and Transportation (Assault Japan) Group was now destined for India to become part of a force called 'BRINDJAP' – British and Indian Troops, Japan. This eventually became the 'BRINDIV' division of a much bigger force called BCOF – 'British Commonwealth Occupation Forces (Japan)'.

After months and months of preparation in India, in a camp seemingly 'set in the middle of nowhere' in a place called Nasik, followed by a term in an office in Nicol Road, Bombay, we of Movement Control and Transportation managed to get the whole force away to Japan, including, eventually, ourselves embarked on an old lady of the Indian Ocean called *Dunera*.

The riots in Bombay and a mutiny in the then Royal Indian Navy are recorded in detail in other books. Though hampered by them at times we were not unduly held up in our work and stories connected with them are not really part of my theatrical career.

So, with a shipboard revue called *Perchance to Scream* (you will know by that corny title what the big show in London was at that time) 'scratched up' by LAC Hatch and Sapper Bean and performed on an open, rolling deck for two nights, *Dunera* managed to reach the rather desolate-

looking port of Kure on the Japanese Inland Sea.
Eventually, settling down to new duties, new billets, new
country and suchlike, I began to find my way around in
what off-duty time I had.

We were now a much larger unit than the one we had in
India. Movement Control was an integrated, all-service
unit with its own HQ in a large building on the docks in
Kure. From here different departments, staffed by
Australian, British, New Zealand and Indian personnel
controlled and monitored movement by land, sea and air in
and around the British Commonwealth area of occupation
of Japan. Most of the country was occupied by American
forces – 'Our MacArthur which art in Tokyo' being the
SCAP – Supreme Commander Allied Personnel (Japan).

Anyway, exploration of our very large billet building in
the town centre revealed an Australian Army Education
Corps unit opening up at the other end of the floor upon
which the Movement Control sergeants' mess was situated.
A proposed play-reading group got me involved. This, with
the aid of a room transformed into what became known as
the theatrette, soon developed into an amateur dramatic
society. The warrant officer and sergeant of this unit had
been a professional theatre director and musician/music
tutor respectively in Australia.

I had my 'vast experience' of the Tudor Players, F.H.
Fortescue's Famous Players and the Lawrence-Williamson
repertory company behind me plus *Perchance to Scream*
which I had directed! Now, at twenty years old, here was I
'teaching' Glasgow tram drivers, sheep-shearers from the
outback, cattlemen from New Zealand and Bradford
woollen mill operatives – all with accents as thick as Sally
Army sandwiches. ('God bless the Sally Army,' says any
serviceman who served in wartime.) Me! Teaching them to
act!

As with all amateur dramatic societies all over the English(?)-speaking world our first effort to be inflicted upon the off-duty, entertainment/culture-seeking personnel of Kure was an evening of three one-act plays. I directed (and played the lead, of course!) in the first play *The Rehearsal*, a pseudo-Elizabethan play by Maurice Baring – costumes courtesy of BRINDIV players. Second came *Murder in the Silo*, a radio play set in a studio, well we couldn't do big scenes in our theatrette! Then *The Rehearsal II*, a futuristic version of the first play, set in the unimaginably distant 1980!

The entr'actes were, first, the Education Centre WO acting like fury in a 'mad' scene from *Lost Weekend* – and we all had a few of those during our time in Japan – and between plays two and three yours truly, giving Henry V with his troops before Agincourt. Well, if that ex-navy wallah, Olivier, was having a bash at it, why shouldn't I? Flushed with our success (I can't actually remember if we got any audiences or not but we knew how good we were!) it was natural, surely, to strive for higher things.

None of the floors in this Japanese building gave a lot of headroom for us, on the whole, taller Occidental types, so the theatrette, formed by converting two rooms into one large room, had a stage just twelve inches high. The rails for the curtains fastened directly onto the ceiling and there was virtually no room at the sides of the stage – or wing space, in theatre terms. The communal dressing room was the office next along the corridor. To 'enter' stage left one waited in the corridor until there was room to slip into the wings to await one's cue. To 'enter' stage right one had to go upstairs, cross the room above the theatrette, climb through the window, come down the exterior iron fire escape and wait outside the window until there was room to go into the wings, ready to go on. Not the easiest of activities in Elizabethan doublet and hose, cloak, hat and sword. Any ladies in subsequent plays had to be made to enter and exit stage left.

A Christmas revue was the next big attraction! The Britcom Base Singers – Britcom Base was the Kure area's telegraphic identification – were to end the show, *Bits and Pieces* (what an original title!) with Christmas carols. In a darkened auditorium with 'old-fashioned' lanterns (Japanese), heavily muffled and wrapped up against the 'cru-ell' weather they sang together with the audience – we did have a full house – then exited one by one, through the window, down the fire escape, still with flickering lanterns, still singing, going, we were told, to sing round the wards at 82 General Hospital just up the road. It's said that that was the last anyone ever saw or heard of the Britcom Base Singers!

While serving in Japan I had my first experience of broadcasting. In the Britcom Base HQ a very elementary radio station had been set up using what had been a local Japanese wavelength, all commandeered by the US forces in the initial occupation. In time this was transformed by the Australian Army broadcasting unit from a couple of bare, concrete rooms – the walls hung and the floors carpeted with old army blankets, and two standard and rather old-fashioned microphones – into a very pleasant radio station, call sign 'Radio WLKS', affectionately known as 'Radio Wilks'.

It had two small and one large studio, suitably panelled walls and carpeted floors. One studio had the turntables and controls with a microphone; its twin had a table with two or more microphones for solo speakers discussions and small group broadcasts. The larger studio, with a slightly raised platform at one end, had seating for an audience of about a hundred people and was used for concerts, recording short plays (that was how I started) and, eventually, home-grown shows like Saturday night's *The BCOF Hour* for which I was called upon occasionally to compere and contribute short sketches.

Sunday was the day for the *Forces' Favourites* recorded shows from home and the strains of a Mantovani-type orchestra sweeping into *A Pretty Girl is Like a Melody* always conjures up the introduction of one of Australia's top radio productions of those days, *The Cashmere Bouquet Show* – a programme of lovely music from Sydney, which was followed by the latest ITMA show.

There were no tape recorders or cassettes then, of course. These programmes came out to us on extra large gramophone records, in cans rather like film reel cans, by air from London and Sydney, and Wellington for the New Zealand programmes.

The Australian Education Centre personnel, with whom I'd been associated in my off-duty time, also presented a series of famous one-act plays, rather grandly called *The Midweek Play*, for a time. Alas. I had to leave it when I was posted to Okayama as chief clerk and admin. officer for that district.

However, this posting wasn't before I'd done *The Hasty Heart* – quite one of *the* experiences of my life. The director of the Britcom drama group was, it seems, personally acquainted with the play's author, John Patrick. Before being filmed with Richard Todd and Ronald Reagan in the leading roles, it was simultaneously enjoying successful productions on Broadway, in London and in Sydney as well as a number of other large cities.

John Patrick gave his permission for the Little Theatre Players – as we were now called – to present the Oriental and amateur premiere. The unique feature of this particular production was that it was virtually typecast. I played Tommy, the Englishman; Pte Ron Dear from Australia played Digger; Lt Jack McNaughton, New Zealand Army, played Kiwi; Capt. D. McKenna, education officer US military government Kure, played Yank; and a young RAF chap, LAC Stephen, played Lachy. We even had a real nursing sister from the 82 General BCOF hospital, Margaret Roberts, to play Sister Margaret. Unfortunately we had no Basuto troops with us in Japan as they obviously must have had in Burma where the play is set. Corporal Joe Collins of the Australian Army gallantly 'blacked up' for every performance, to say very little more than 'Me Blossom!' – the name his fellow patients in this hut-ward of a Burma Army hospital had given him.

The play opened at a converted Japanese, Western-style theatre which became the Theatre Royal, Kure, on Sunday 6th October 1946 at 19.30 hours. The play was very well received and seen by the BCOF General-in-Command. It was decided that it was good enough to be seen by other troops in the BCOF area.

This is how my local army magazine article 'I Have Just Toured Japan' came to be written. (See Appendix B.) The big trouble was, of course, getting people released from their units and duties long enough 'to fool around in some damned stupid theatrical balderdash' to quote one British/Indian Army Major.

Incidentally, one of my present-day oldest and best friends dates back to *The Hasty Heart*, former LAC Ron Stephen of Edinburgh who played the stubborn wee Scot Lachy. Ron worked in the RAF section and I was chief clerk in the Railway Section of Movement Control HQ, Kure, and we're still in reasonably frequent contact, sometimes in Auld Reekie, sometimes in Owd Wiggin. For almost fifty years this *tomadachi* (Japanese for friend) and I have enjoyed 'mony a wee' (large) dram – as long as we got 'oor fud!'

With my move up country to take charge of the admin. and clerical staff work at HQ Okayama, we were accommodated in Japanese-style houses not far from the large

Okayama mainline station and area offices. Japanese houses were never really meant to accommodate rather rough, tough British Commonwealth soldiers in heavy army boots! However, some of what little leisure time I managed to organise for myself included visits to the local radio station, run by Indian Army Education. Okayama was in the BRINDIV area, under the command of Major General Cowan and later Brigadier Thimayya. I worked mainly as a relief reader of *News from Britain* and *Listeners' Letters* and reading extracts from classic books, slowly, as an aid to learning English for Indian and Gurkha troops and Japanese civilians.

With regard to the tour of *The Hasty Heart* and my article in *The Gen* it should be said that the scenery was constructed by an army workshops unit. With those chaps, and the Japanese labour force under their command, there are no half measures. The scenery was solid! Eight foot by six foot timber-framed and plywood-covered with straw matting nailed on – the scene is a *basha*-type hut hospital in a forward area in Burma – each one weighing a ton. Add the six hospital beds – real ones – plus props and costumes and you will realise that 'Get in!' and 'Set Up!' followed by 'Strike!' and 'Get out!' was no picnic and as exhausting as performing the actual play.

I still have happy memories of Ron Stephen during the long wait for ferry transportation at one point, conducting a conscripted choir of Japanese baggage handlers and labourers as they sang *Auld Lang Syne* – which most Japanese seemed to know – and insisting that they learn to sing, loudly, in English, *God Save the King*. Then there was Ron Dear 'in full flight' and with rich digger lingo, lecturing said unfortunate Japanese upon the wonders and skills of sheep-droving in the wild Australian cutback. I also remember Sister Margaret Roberts keeping calmly serene through it all and, as the only lady in our little unit, often keeping the peace among all those temperamental part-time actors. An experience, which though never to be repeated, was certainly never forgotten.

During the tour we played the BCOF theatre, The Piccadilly, in Tokyo where one amazing event took place. At the huge US forces theatre, The Ernie Pyle Theatre, during our stay came the film of Olivier's *Henry V*. We as a company were invited to see it. Being the HQ of the whole of the occupation forces, as well as Japan's capital, Tokyo was full of service personal, diplomats, delegates and representatives of most of the Allied countries. The end of the film was greeted with a standing ovation by a packed audience. For some reason – as invited guests and 'actors' – we suddenly found ourselves bathed in a spotlight and the audience applauding us. We weren't even in the film but all of us, including Capt. McKenna, our Yank, said, 'We are proud to be British – just for one night!'

Chapter Three

In January, 1948, I set sail for home – Release Group No. 64 – aboard the *Strathnaver*. The Movement Control sergeants were allotted ship's leisure time duties. They ran ship's housey (bingo), the ship's daily run sweep and a daily ship's activities bulletin, for most of the journey, except in the bay of Biscay. I presented *Your Record Requests* twice daily over the ship's Tannoy system. Various welfare organisations had put about one hundred very mixed records aboard at various times. I had one very old turntable, battery-driven, and a microphone which had to be lowered to be near the gramophone speaker after I'd announced the next choice.

Lists of records available were put up in all messes and recreation rooms. A box for written requests was attached to the door of the ship's orderly room – a cupboard which was ostentatiously labelled with a large notice:

> RADIO STRATHNAVER
> Presenter Sgt Colin Bean R.E.
> 10.00 hrs to 11.00 hrs and
> 1400 hrs to 1500 hrs
> MONDAY to SATURDAY

Besides the music requests – and one or two other requests which would have proved to be physically impossible – I also started to get *Ship's Announcements*, *News from Home* (UK) via the ship's radio officer. I even accommodated one request – 'For God's sake *shut up!*' I gave a whole fifteen seconds of complete silence, and fifteen seconds is a hell of a lot of airtime in a one-hour radio show!

After demobilisation I had some demob leave due to me, most of which was spent visiting. First, London, having written to RADA, the only theatre school of which I'd ever heard. Being a sergeant, and a Royal Engineers sergeant at that, and having had both theatre and radio experience, they would of course be jumping at the chance to get their hands on me! Well, they would, wouldn't they? Boing!

I was invited to go to an audition, test paper enclosed with their letter. Learn two pieces, one classical, one modern and a very short poem or speech of my own choice. This I did, stayed at a Forces hostel and, at the appointed time, joined some fifty other people awaiting auditions, many, both men and women, in uniform as I was.

'Very amusing,' came the verdict. 'We'll put you on our list for recall in 1950 for the 1951 intakes.' This was in 1948!

That wasn't a lot of use to yours truly just bursting at the seams to be an actor. The rest of my leave was spent in visits to relatives and friends in different parts of the country – Glasgow, Edinburgh, Newcastle-upon-Tyne and Doncaster. It was time then to get back to Wigan to start seriously on the job of being an actor. Of course, nobody at home was interested. On the contrary it was a case of 'Can't think why you want to go in for this daft acting lark. You'd be better getting a proper job.'

Then, out of the blue, the Chairman of the still fledgling Wigan Little Theatre – of which I was an early member – Mr Fred C. Fairclough more or less found a key to fit the door for which I was searching. Himself a noted broadcaster and actor as well as being an expert chartered accountant in Wigan, Fred mentioned something called the Arts Council.

It seems that this Organisation – a descendant of CEMA (Council for the Encouragement of the Arts) – had opened an office in Manchester. Fred happened to know the Northern Region Director, Joseph Hodgkinson. An appointment was made. I went over to Manchester and marched into the office in Cross Street.

'So, Colin Bean,' said the genial Mr Hodgkinson, 'what can we do for you?'

To my plain statement he said, very seriously, 'Ah, you want to be an actor. You are serious about this, I can see.'

Being reassured he continued, 'Right, we'll see what we can do. You'll hear from me soon. Goodbye, Colin Bean who wants to be an actor.'

Because I didn't arrive home with an actual job 'in my hands' as it were there were many comments of 'I told you so!', 'Give it up!' and 'Get a proper job!' until about a week later, a letter arrived from the Arts Council.

I was to present myself at the Bradford Civic Playhouse at such and such a time on the given date. Would I take one short piece by Shakespeare, one modern piece and one of my own choice. Well I'd got my *Henry V* and *Bardell v Pickwick* speeches from the shows in BCOF so a piece from *Pygmalion* – the RADA audition piece – completed my programme.

Upon arrival I was to ask to see Esme Church, the theatre and professional theatre school director. The Bradford Civic is a lovely little theatre. I thought to myself, 'What an unusual set-up, a professional theatre school housed in an amateur theatre.' How this came about is a story in itself. Suffice to say that J.B. Priestley had a hand in getting Esme Church and famous scenic designer, Molly McArthur, to move from the Old Vic in London to start a much needed theatre school in the North. At this time it seemed that anything to do with serious theatre *had* to be in London. Priestley and others thought this was not so.

My audition was in late February and I was invited to become the student of Bradford Civic Playhouse Theatre School at the start of a new school year, in September. Happily in later years the name became less of a mouthful. The Theatre School and its third year students' touring company became the Northern Theatre School (NTS) and Northern Children's Theatre (NCT), more of which later.

Back to Manchester, back to Mr Hodgkinson. He never seemed to get fed up with me – I suspect he was a good actor!

'And what do I do in the meantime?' I asked.

First of all because I'd had actual theatre experience (two whole weeks, remember!) I was encouraged to apply for, and I received, an 'Interrupted Training' grant from a Government ex-services scheme. This would pay the actual theatre school fees; necessary books, equipment, living expenses and travel were my own responsibility. Good job I'd still got some of my services demob gratuity left.

What Mr Hodgkinson did next was to speak to someone in Southport. Putting the phone down he said, 'Right, Colin Bean who wants to be an actor. Go straight over to Southport now. Get a train from Victoria Station.'

Just beside Southport station, I was told, I'd find Houghton Street and Southport Little Theatre, the home of the Southport Repertory Company. This company was, apparently, the 'child' of the Sheffield Rep who'd been evacuated there during the war.

Upon arrival I was interviewed by Mr Lionel Harris and Mr Herbert Prentice and invited to start work the following Monday as the junior assistant stage manager. As we know, this is the grandiloquent title for the general dogsbody, the 'go-for' – go for this, go for that. One very valuable lesson I learned early on while helping the scenic artist, a grand old gentleman called Bill Somerville, was, 'Make the tea, make the glue – and learn the difference between the two.'

Senior assistant stage manager, Michael Miller, insisted I become a professional member of Equity right away. 'If you are serious about this profession...' I was advised by another member of the company. So I did. It was in 1948 I joined and now I've just become a 'Life Member' so no more subs to pay.

Right, back to work with a prestigious provincial – or regional as we would call it now – theatre repertory company. Hard work. Prop-making, tea making, scene changing. The fortnightly weekend changeover – an all-Saturday night job, then home to Wigan on the 6 a.m. train on Sunday morning if the set-up and lighting were finished. If not, carry on until it was. Monday dress rehearsal then the first night.

Lo and behold – unheard of before in the company – in only my second play with the rep, I'm given a small part in the production. My first really professional role as the Mayor of Bellington in an amusing, topical in its day, little trifle called *The Man from the Ministry*. I became assistant stage manager number two when our senior departed the company and among other duties came prompt corner work, which I can honestly say I've never enjoyed. During the summer break at the end of July I was kept on for two weeks to help our stage manager and scenic artist clear up and reorganise their respective props and furniture and scenery-painting workshops and storerooms.

September came and I went over the Pennines to take up residence with a number of other new theatre school male students in the Bradford YMCA in Forster Square – a 'starting point' suggested by the school in order to give one time to find digs. It remained my 'starting point' until 1950 and my turn came quite soon to be moved from a dormitory to a single room as one became vacant.

The work at school was exciting and intriguing. One loyally and enthusiastically attended performances by the senior group – the school's very first intake of students which included Bernard Hepton, William Lucas, Clifford Parrish, David Giles and the late Paul Whitsun-Jones and Dudley Foster. In my own year the students included Robert Stephens, Geoffrey Gardiner, Donald Howarth and Richard Jacques.

Fencing, ballet (at sixteen stone?), singing, speech training and swimming all formed part of our basic, first-year training, at the end of which we were allowed to put on a show in the rehearsal room with the second and third year students as our audience, improvisations and a short play, which involved everyone, called *Waiting for a Bus*. For some reason I have a fond memory of Bob Stephens charging to and fro across the stage at intervals shouting, in a very cultured voice, 'Taxi! Ay say, taxi!' and dressed, for some peculiar reason, in a gorilla suit – or could it have been a bear costume? No, we hadn't tackled *The Winter's Tale* up to then – 'Exit pursued by a bear'.

The work of being a student at what was then known as Bradford Civic Playhouse Theatre School went on. Esme Church took some of our classes but for the first year we were in the hands of other members of an excellent and highly qualified staff. The great Rudolph Laban was head of the teaching of stage movement – he of the renowned Laban system of dance notation or 'Labanotation' as we called it – the present Laban Centre of Movement being named after him. For our first-year classes in movement we were under the guidance of a young lady who was one of Laban's outstanding pupils and had become his assistant. Now one of our principal choreographers she never despaired of a group of rather clumsy ex-service types in their twenties trying to 'float' and 'glide'. The young lady was Geraldine Stephenson, still a dance creator and a director of infinite patience.

The rudiments and practice of classical ballet – aids to deportment and style especially for Restoration and classical plays – was the province of Doris McBride who also created 'country dances' for some of our more 'rustic' improvisations and later productions. Singing was under the guidance of Professor Frank Mumby and Margaret Jowatt.

Speech training was, of course, a vital part of our schedule. A lot of time was spent on breath control and projection, in practice and in theory. Don't forget, this was 1948–50 and a big innovation in the school was the arrival, with a new tutor, Mr Charles Gordon, of a thing called a tape recorder. On what looked like small film reels we could now record and play back speech and singing exercises as they were done. In the second-year 'speech class' one day Mr Gordon happened to be off sick so one of the other tutors stepped in to take the lesson.

'Right,' said Mrs Crabtree, 'let's do some breathing!'

To which one young lady called out, 'Oh, but Mr Gordon only lets us breathe on Tuesdays!'

As a final-year student I was often called upon to take over roles in productions at the Civic Playhouse. Although we were a professional theatre school the Civic Playhouse was, and still is, one of the country's most prestigious amateur theatres, and a member of the Guild of Little Theatres. They had appointed a professional 'Director of Productions', Esme Church, formerly of the Old Vic, who founded with scenic and artistic designer Molly McArthur (also ex-Old Vic) and Rudolph Laban, this training school for professional actors, stage managers and drama teachers.

Some of the plays in which I appeared at the Civic Playhouse were: *Our Town*, *Distinguished Gathering*, *The Winter's Tale*, *The Giaconda Smile* – with the lovely, talented

Olive Pandelton ('Aunty' in *Flambards*), *The Lady's Not For Burning* and *Winterset*.

Somewhere along the line I met for the first time – and I don't think I have had the pleasure of working with him since – Ken Waller, later to find universal fame as 'Grandad' in *Bread*. As with so many other actors, despite his wide and long experience, Ken seems to have got labelled with 'Grandad' as I have with 'Sponge'.

As this was our final year as students we became also the Children's Theatre Company. Specially written plays were taken out on tour, complete with scenery, costumes lighting and so forth. It was run as a touring company based in Bradford.

During the course so far I had been collecting all my notes assiduously with a view to trying to get an extension to my grant for another year in order to join in and catch up on the final year of a teachers' course, affiliated to Leeds University, with the idea of going, eventually, for that degree my father kept 'harping on' about. Father still disapproved of all this 'acting nonsense'. 'Get some qualifications and a decent job.' Even when persuaded (cajoled?) by my stepmother, who loved theatre and music, to come over to see me in a play, his opinion was, alas, typically 'Pa Bean'.

The play was Maxwell Anderson's *Winterset*. At short notice Miss Church told me that as Alan Purdy had had to withdraw from the role of Mio I would be playing it in five days' time. If you know *Winterset* you will know that Mio is not what one could call a small part! Despite my agreeable, nay (hanging my head) glowing notices in the press and, according to my stepmother, enthusiastic comments by members of the audience, what was father's comment? 'All right, I suppose, if you like that sort of thing. I'm glad you didn't forget anything. I'd have felt a real fool!'

Note that last phrase, dear reader, because I'm sorry to say that that was my father's opinion on my chosen career. Much later on in 1965, after another 'success', father's comment when asked, 'Well, wasn't he good?' was 'Oh, that's not for me to say. He's all right, I suppose. I'd have felt a fool if he'd forgotten anything!'

Chapter Four

In September, 1949, whilst working on a farm during the School's summer vacation, I was recalled to Bradford by telegram (we still had them!) a week before the start of my second year, to play Henry Straker in Shaw's *Man and Superman*, a small part which I enjoyed very much indeed. Besides students playing roles with the Civic Playhouse Society when required, they were often assigned to gain assistant stage management experience in some of their productions.

Many ex-students of the Northern Theatre School will, I'm sure, remember the redoubtable, the unique female stage manager with the most enjoyable, audible and infectious laugh I've ever heard. Dear Stella! So many of us enjoyed working with, being guided by and, always welcomed by impecunious students, the hospitality of the one and only Stella Birkett.

Even Esme Church respected her work, her abilities and her willingness to communicate with these raw, budding professionals in addition to her own commitments and other multifarious duties undertaken as a member of the Bradford Civic Playhouse committee.

Together with the Playhouse's only full-time staff, the two Toms – Tom Ward and Tom Whitwham, scenery construction and lighting – one received experience in backstage work which would prove invaluable, not only during the second year of our course, as Northern

Children's Theatre, but in years to come, out in the wide, wild world of rep.

During my first year I'd also had my first experience of filming. Oh, here was the big time! This was definitely *it*! A walk-on in the opening shot of *Up For t'Cup*, starring Albert Modley and Mai Bacon. My involvement was an early morning (literally) street scene as a mill workers' 'knocker-up' in the atmospheric Aire View, a street in Silsden. Not Hollywood, or even Pinewood but *a filum* nevertheless!

Besides children's theatre and being encouraged by our artistic director to expand my interest in prop-making and stage make-up, I had my third experience of weekly rep. Vincent Shaw was director of a successful weekly production company highly thought of among professionals, The Saxon Players, at the Hippodrome, Dewsbury. Many regular theatregoers still had their 'favourites' in 'our rep company' in 1950. A town with a company which could attract *names* to play for a week was indeed lucky.

Vincent Shaw had to direct a production of *The Barretts of Wimpole Street* starring the man who'd made the part of Papa Barrett his own – the great Wilfred Lawson. This large-cast play requires what seems like a regiment of young people, so from Northern Theatre School came Dorit Welles, David Giles, Trevor Lennon, the late Dudley Foster and yours truly to play Bella, Alfred, Henry, George and Charles. The youngest member of the family, by the way, is called Octavius – which saves you counting all the kids! That week really deserves a book to itself. Rehearsing with and playing scenes with Mr Lawson was an experience which I'm sure anyone who underwent it will never forget.

Next came the lovely role of Humphrey in *The Lady's Not For Burning*, again for the Civic Playhouse. By now I was also 'into' prop-making in a big way. I even wrote an illustrated article which was published by the *Yorkshire Observer* – oh, the nerve of this genius! In hindsight I recall clearly Molly McArthur's words. 'Colin, ducky,' (everyone was 'ducky' to Miss McArthur), 'you are so good at this, and make-up, and stage management. Why don't you make this your "line"? You'll never be out of work, ducky, but you will, often, as an actor!'

Ah, dear Molly McArthur. Who knows? My objection was partly because it sounded too much like the parental 'Why don't you got a proper job?' of very recent memory.

February 1951 brought along another part which I enjoyed playing – as I did when I played it and I directed the play some ten years later. There are four parts in Tennesee Williams' *The Glass Menagerie*. What a lovely, sad play. The 'gentleman caller' might arrive late but this young man 'who brought to the apartment house a breeze from the outside world, a fresh wholesomeness, beautifully contrived; who plays the lead in "Gilbert and Sullivan" and finds himself cast by a fond mama for the role of her son-in-law' – *vide* Yorkshire papers – is one of the parts I'm happy I got the chance to play.

Our practical experience was now growing apace. In addition to our Children's Theatre productions we still had our classes to attend and rehearsals became part of them. Movement classes now involved working with Laban himself. Though no longer young this amazing man could move like 'Ariel' and 'fill' the stage with characters purely in mime. He was very reticent to talk about his life before Mr Hitler indicated it was time he left Europe. His vast experience and his books, which were burned by the Nazis, were indication enough. He exuded vibrancy, life and feeling in a move, a gesture, or a look – just by being Laban.

Our predecessors, the previous year's second year, now decided to work together for a little longer. I have no idea what the set-up was or how it worked but under the direction of Esme Church some of them became a separate, fully professional company called Dolphin Productions.

They presented Farquhar's merry romp *The Recruiting Officer*, *Macbeth* and *Viceroy Sarah* with Esme Church as a wonderful 'Queen Anne'. At a dress rehearsal of the latter play, which we were allowed to attend, the actress playing 'Sarah, Duchess of Marlborough' missed her cue for an entrance – one of the hazards of having a quick change. She rushed on after a fairly long pause, in a bit of a fluster, and dropped a very graceful curtsey but alas instead of 'Forgive me, your Majesty, I'm afraid I'm a trifle late' the line came out as, 'For me I'm a trifle – I'm a fried egg!' *Punch* magazine cartoons would have added, 'Collapse of stout party.'

Esme looked at her, looked at us in the audience, and with a wickedly slow wink, replied, 'So I see!'

Nowadays I suppose one says, 'We fell about.'

For *The Recruiting Officer* and the Scottish drama not only were some of my year required to play small parts but, with Miss McArthur, I was also designing and making props. I was appearing as Ross as well as caring for the 'flamin'' torches – and rightly called 'flamin'' – we had made for use in the plays. They were, to say the least, temperamental torches. Miss Church wasn't in this slice of Scottish history so, thank God, she didn't witness my ignominious entrance at one performance. We were playing in a school hall where our 'dressing rooms' were classrooms quite some distance from the stage along a straight, flagged corridor. As usual Bean was having trouble with the 'FTs' as they came to be known. Hearing Ray Lindon as Duncan say, 'They smack of honour both. Go, get him surgeons. Who comes here?' I set off down that corridor at full speed to see Roy Hodges as Lennox appear at the end of the corridor, frantically waving and calling, 'The worthy Thane of Ross. What haste looks in his eyes and what speed he makes and so he should...'

I made it, almost tripped and fell on to Roy with, 'God save the King!' It got a good laugh, like my school-play baby, but stage manager Trevor had a few words to say and my name went into his stage notebook.

Those FTs were back in the studio workshop next morning – sharpish. We found the fault and I reported it to Miss Church and Miss McArthur saying, 'I'm very sorry about that but there's a screw loose.'

Miss Church put on her wonderful deadpan look and said, 'Colin, dear boy, don't run yourself down. You'll undermine your confidence!'

One aspect of the opening performance of the Scottish drama was the disturbing element of our audiences of school parties using torches and turning pages as they endeavoured to follow the text of the play from volumes of Shakespeare which, apparently, their teachers had told them to bring along.

Perhaps commendable in theory it did not create what one might call a 'theatrical' atmosphere. Before the next performance the audience was asked, politely, to put away the books and torches, save their homework for when they got home and just sit back in order to appreciate what is, after all, one of the finest horror stories ever written. Thank goodness the hint was taken for future performances, otherwise, with noses in books, they could have missed my previously related 'Ross' entrance.

For the Christmas season of 1950 Miss Church sent another student and me to the York Rep Company. Under the direction of Geoffrey Staines this two-part company were noted not only for the high standards of their all-year-round productions playing in both York and Scarborough – each company changing over so that each production played and rehearsed for two weeks – but also for their own 'in-house' pantomimes. This annual, festive season extravaganza combined both parts of the company plus a few 'extras', which is where I fitted in as Red Reuben – a miller – and Deadly Dick – one of the ogre's henchmen. It was

from this *Puss in Boots* that I learned two songs which stayed
with me in pantomime until as recently as the 1990s. 'Has
Anyone Seen My Pom' and 'The Coffee-Pot Song' were
majestically performed by character actor, Lester Barratt, as
King Bodolphus. I was so impressed with these songs that
Lester must have got thoroughly cheesed off with this eager
beaver Bean, pestering him to teach them to him. Happily I
was able to meet up with Lester years later when I was
playing in Scarborough and he was 'mine host' of the pub
next to the Theatre Royal there.

More of my time was now taken up with work under
the direction of Molly McArthur in the scenery and
properties studio. The new Children's Theatre productions
were both very 'proppy' plays, *The Three Toymakers* and *The
Two Masks*. A world of paint, wire and papier mâché. This
was in pre-polystyrene days. Making 'dancing figures',
musical boxes, a dozen practical face masks, jewels, ceremonial shields, crowns, tiaras and sceptres seemed to fill
my days. First-year students, especially those on the
teachers' course, were being sent in to watch and be told by
Miss McArthur and me just what was going on, how, and
why.

Later in the year a member of the second year left to take
up an offer he'd received. This found me taking over the
roles of King Minos in *The Two Masks* and Malkin, the
'baddy' toymaker in the other play.

The biggest national event of the year was the Festival of
Britain. It was as George VI said, 'An expression of the re-
emergence of Britain after the late war and to
commemorate the centenary of the Great Exhibition of
1851.'

The NTS and NCT played an important part in the
North of England. Early in the year we were visited by the
director of the British Drama League, E. Martin Browne,
who told us of an exciting festival project to be staged in

York. Even more exciting was the news that we were all to be actively involved in the first production for almost four hundred years of the York cycle of mystery plays.

Two more NCT productions were already in rehearsal. These would form part of the York festival also, playing at the Rowntree Theatre. A revival of the NCT's very first and very popular children's play, *The Magic Lighter*, originally *La Soldat au Briquet* from the Belgian National Theatre. I inherited the role of the Wooden Man played in the first production by the late Paul Whitsun Jones. During a very hot summer the 'wooden tree trunk' costume was, to say the least, not comfortable. Not that I complained as actors usually do. I didn't dare because I'd made it!

Looking down the cast list I find that a constant companion, 'Fido, the dog with the saucer eyes', was played by a very talented young man, Tom Bell. Let's face it. A tree *would* be a companion for a dog – not, I hasten to add, that Fido was ever called upon to use his companion as a facility.

In this play and the second play, *Smugglers' Bay*, we had a very strong programme, which young audiences obviously enjoyed. *Smugglers' Bay* is a swashbuckling tale, by William Baines, of smuggling, sword fights, and 'dodgy doings' and includes some sea shanties and dancing set in or near Robin Hood's Bay a well known beauty spot on the North Yorkshire coast, in 1734.

Tony Haigh played Black Jack who was obviously the villain of the piece because the programme described him as 'A Cockney'. Philip Anthony, the late Althea Charlton, Jennifer Wallace and a friend with whom I keep in touch still, Jon Curle, also appear in the list of players. For both plays we enjoyed working under the combined direction of Esme Church and Rudolph Laban. Molly McArthur introduced me to the making of 'prop-food' as well as goblets, wine flagons and lanthorns. One is never too old to learn.

A programme note explained some of the weird dialogue in the play: 'The Bay dialect – a mixture of Yorkshire and Danish – was actually used by the smugglers of both countries at this time.' Well now, I repeat, what price Esperanto?

Concurrently we were all doing our preliminary work for the mystery plays. Miss McArthur and myself led a small group of interested students in the manufacture of more embossed shields, belts and surcoats, monstrances, gifts of gold, frankincense and myrrh, with an exercise – 'Find out the constituents of myrrh' – thrown in for good measure. I have to confess that I have never really understood myrrh!

And the infamous 'twelve burghers' chains of office'. Miss McArthur and yours truly undertook these intricately detailed items of jewellery ourselves. They took weeks to make, keeping all twelve at the same stage of development throughout. Sorting and apportioning hundreds of glass 'jewels', setting them into sculpted settings of 'Barbola' (does anyone use 'Barbola' these days?). Gilding and waiting for the various shades of gold paint to dry took so long that I fear, after a couple of weeks, they were constantly referred to as something a little different. In our vocabulary the word 'Burgher' had changed its pronunciation somewhat. 'How are those twelve b–ggers' chains today?'

Meanwhile – back to the plot – other students had been rehearsing with E. Martin Browne and his assistant director, Henzie Raeburn, plus Rudolph Laban and Geraldine Stephenson. They were creating action and 'rhubarb' dialogue for the many crowd scenes in the production. The cycle was to be performed on a large scale before the ruins of St Mary's Abbey in York – a wide greensward to be populated by lots of 'citizens', 'countryfolk', 'soldiery' and so forth. Later in rehearsal time they in turn met up with many good people of York who had volunteered to appear as such in this great event. They disseminated what they had learned to their groups so that by the time everything came together during the final full cast rehearsals most people had a fairly good idea of what they were supposed to be doing and where.

One problem to be solved was the 'Banks of the River Jordan' scene. Our head-scratching over sheets of blue cloth, large rolls of cellophane and other suggestions was solved by Gerry Stephenson's living picture of people arriving on the 'banks' to fish, wash clothes, paddle, drink and play 'ducks-and-drakes'. This established the course of the river without any artefacts from the scenic department. 'John the Baptist' baptised 'Jesus' standing between river banks of fascinated onlookers. Among the 'angels' one cannot help but notice the name Judith Dench. Although unpublished, because it wasn't 'done' in those days, Joseph O'Connor was the beautifully voiced and handsomely dignified actor who played Jesus and our own speech tutor, Charles Gordon, was God the Father. Tenniel Evans and David Giles were impressive archangels – Michael and Gabriel. Mary Ure was the gentle Mary and John Van Eyssen a chilling Lucifer. Tom Bell, Tony Haigh and Donald Howarth were all in 'devilish' good form while Philip Anthony, James Barnes, Jon Curle and yours truly were rather ruthless Jewish soldiers. Only one performance was completely rained off during that long, sunny season. It was, truly, a lovely summer in all respects, exciting, enjoyable and full of optimism. Time for me to move on to pastures new.

Farewell, Bradford. I wouldn't be back again until 1956.

Chapter Five

At last I'm off into the 'real theatre' world. From theatre school I started with a week with a repertory company in Skipton, playing Mortimer Brewster in *Arsenic and Old Lace* – a play I was to meet again in four years' time. Mortimer has, as part of the action in the play, what used to be called 'the longest double take in the business'. Having entered at one point onto an empty scene, Mortimer, while searching for some papers, goes round the room looking into drawers, under cushions, behind chairs and so forth, and casually lifts the seat of the window seat. Having noted that the papers are not there he closes the lid, crosses the room and suddenly realises that he has seen a body in there. It's one of his dotty aunt's 'gentleman friends' awaiting transfer to the 'Panama Canal' down in the cellar. The 'canal' is being dug by equally dotty 'Uncle Teddy' – the role I was to play later – for reception of the various bodies when ready for disposal.

This double take is a great exercise in 'timing'. Just how far away from the window seat can Mortimer get before he realises what he has seen? To get the maximum effect and 'big laugh' the realisation must come just a split second before the audience 'breaks'. Happily I got it right most nights and, on a couple, even got a round of applause. Magic!

With the end of that week came a call from the Sheffield Repertory Company, one of the most prestigious of what were known, in those days, as the good provincial rep companies. Having been recommended by Molly

McArthur and Esme Church of the Northern Children's Theatre I went to see the director and stage manager. I was in! Starting 1st September, 1952, I was appointed first assistant stage manager and was to stay at the Playhouse Theatre until May of 1953. Having played many times in Sheffield with the NCT I know the city fairly well and a few people who lived there – including Mr and Mrs Chamberlain, custodians of the Montgomery Hall which was the venue for the NCT's visits to the city. They had a spare room in their large flat on the top floor of this large concert hall-cum-theatre, so I didn't have to search for 'digs'. Come October I was also playing 'walk-on' and one- or two-line small parts in addition to the stage manager work. Our general stage manager, George Fenner, also took me with him on his furniture hunts for dressing 'period' sets and explained to me the intricacies of re-covering 'button-back' armchairs and sofas.

Although, presumably, I was a competent assistant stage manager – well, they didn't sack me – my heart was still not really in it. I did gain a lot more experience in prop-making and scene painting, organising 'strikes' (to the uninitiated – taking down the scenery) and set-ups but I hated being 'on the book' and 'doing the corner'. That's prompting and controlling the lighting and sound effects. Bry Ferguson, our genius lighting expert, had to have the patience of Job when I was 'in the corner'. In a lovely, gentle play called *Lace on her Petticoat*, at the offstage sound of a horse and trap approaching on a gravel path the lovely late Ella Atkinson looked out of the window, from which she could see me at the panatrope with the needle arm lined up by cue bar over the effects record, to say, 'Oh, here he comes th'noo in the trap, spankin' doon the brae!'

Needle descended onto record and Ella pointed to her upstage ear, the one away from the audience. I took that to mean that they couldn't hear the effect so I turned the volume up a little. Ella shook her head, pointed to her ear, then put her hands over both ears at which point Mr Fenner came hurtling over to the corner and flicked a switch which, I must confess, I hadn't checked.

'You so-and-so!' quoth George. 'You've got the damned thing on front-of-house speakers. You're deafening the audience!' At the end of the scene I had quite a large audience of irate actors around me, telling me that it sounded like the chariot race in *Ben Hur*.

The director of the theatre was the dearly loved and sadly missed man of the theatre, Geoffrey Ost, a gentleman who, when occasion arose, was quite capable of expressing annoyance without raising his voice or losing his temper. Mr Ost had another occasion, later in the season, to inform me that 'he was not very pleased' with me, during *Beauty and the Beast*.

The First Born by Christopher Fry was another costume play in which, with George Fenner, I figured among 'overseers and guards'. The role of Aaron was played by Mr Henry Beckett, a mature actor of long and wide theatrical experience. When playing in a production I was ensconced in Henry's dressing room because it was a room meant for two actors. During breaks and between matinées and evening shows he would enthral me with tales of the 'old days', touring with fit-up companies in the remote Highlands of Scotland and the West of Ireland. I was to experience these Highlands myself later in life. I well remember him telling me about an advert his employer once put into the 'Wanted' column of a theatrical paper. To appreciate it one must see it written:

> WANTED weekly/nightly Fit-Up Co.
> Actor/SM/Driver
> Dress well on and off.
> Those seeking easy birth save stamps.

As 'Aaron', Henry had a particularly long speech in one scene which started upstage at the top of some steps. Looking exceptionally biblical in his long gown, long-haired wig and beard surrounding his very noble face he started his speech at the dress rehearsal in fine, resonant style. Progressing downstage, staff in hand, he arrived exactly at the last sentence at the 'floats' (footlights), shaded his eyes with his free hand and called out into the auditorium, 'Geoffrey, old boy, what the hell am I talking about?'

Soon it was Christmas when, instead of the usual two weeks, the festive season production went on for four weeks. Although this meant that the company had two weeks of no rehearsals for the next play it did mean three extra matinée performances each week.

Horror of horrors! Guess who was put on the 'book'?

Added to this, the extra performances started to take their toll on some of the actors. The play was Nicholas Stuart Gray's *Beauty and the Beast* and, after some performances, David Mahlowe found that the frequent lionesque roaring, when he was in bestial form – head and paw gloves on and off behind bits of scenery – began to play havoc with his normal speaking voice. Remembering Arthur Leslie's old trick of roaring through a lampglass in Fortescue days – ask great-grandfather if you don't know what a lampglass is – I, having been appointed to do David's roaring from the prompt corner, managed to acquire an oil lamp glass chimney and so became the 'roar of the greasepaint' for the prince's lion *alter ago*.

And so, on the last performance of *Beauty and the Beast* after six weeks' nerve-wracking attention to 'the book' – as the cast lined up for the curtain calls and I pressed the control button 'Tabs' with one hand – relief took over in a somewhat over the top manner. The other hand closed the prompt-copy and, quite spontaneously threw it up in the air and – or so my number two assistant stage manager told me – I let out a great 'Whoopee!'

Obviously I was not aware of the latent strength of my relief. Instead of going just head high, as such an action might have produced normally, the script of *Beauty and the Beast* sailed upward in a well-defined arc, over the top of the proscenium arch and landed, somewhat to the surprise of those involved, at the feet of Beauty, Prince and Wizard all taking their well-deserved bows. The director, Mr Ost, and stage manager, Mr Fenner, were not exactly overjoyed by my action and reaction to the end of the play, to say the least.

Ere long it was spring and the penultimate play of the Sheffield Repertory Company season was to be *Worm's Eye View* – the popular wartime comedy by R.F. Delderfield. Paul Eddington was a great and side-splittingly funny Porter, ably assisted by a terrific performance by the talented actor, later writer, Richard Carpenter as Taffy. For an assistant stage manager it was unusual but, again, I was given an important role (after the finale of *Beauty*, too!) as the 'like mother' pompous, officious son, Sidney, of that harridan landlady, Mrs Bounty.

In those days if one mentioned the play by name it was hugely popular – the immediate reaction was 'Oh yes! Peggy Mount, Mrs Bounty!' I had seen the West-End production. Miss Mount gave what many admiringly and punningly described as a Vesuvius of a performance. Almost as famous as Dame Edith Evans' 'Handbag!'

Darling Ella Atkinson was anything but another Peggy Mount. Ella was quite petite, a lovely, gentle lady and a very good actress. Her 'Mrs Bounty' also brought the house down night after night, not by her vocal and physical powers but by the audience's approbation. Scurrying, sharp, incisive movement, deadpan face and a clipped, monotonous, grating voice soon reduced all these servicemen to jelly and was a vivid explanation of why the poor, under-dog husband – played feelingly by Henry Beckett – was as he was. To Mr Bounty retirement from work must have been a cruel blow – work of importance, as he assures us, 'There's a lot in drains!' I have to confess that when some years later I came to play Porter myself, memories of Geoffrey Ost's house-packing production of the play were never far from my mind.

During the run of the play the Sheffield Lyceum came again to its annual summer season of twice-nightly reper-tory with the very popular Harry Hanson's Court Players. The standard of this weekly repertory company was universally considered in the biz as being high. Led by the imaginative director Douglas Neill, the settings built by Eric Osborne and painted by Robert Pitt, were universally received by the audiences with enthusiastic applause.

The two companies enjoyed a good and cooperative relationship. We'd lend them props and they'd lend to us. If we had a charity 'do' on they would turn up; we were invited to any of their social occasions and the like. It appeared that Mr Neill and his stage manager, Mr Clarke, popped into the playhouse, usually on matinée days, as I believe Mr Ost was always welcomed when he slipped into the back of the Lyceum stall seats for each new production.

Next thing, Mr Ost called me into his office. I had been with Sheffield Rep for a whole year. He had found my work, apart from a couple of stage management lapses, very satisfactory. Mr Neill of the Court Players, having seen me in *Worm's Eye View* and as Dr Gathorne Wetherby in N.C. Hunter's *Adam's Apple* (another wig and nose job), the final play of the current season at the Playhouse, invited me, through Mr Ost, to visit him at the Lyceum. Mr Ost thought I should go and see Mr Neill.

At this time the Playhouse Company were to move to the much smaller Library Theatre while extensive alterations and decorations were carried out at the Playhouse. They'd be playing on a reduced scale, on an away ground, until November or possibly Christmas. He knew I was really interested primarily in being an actor rather than a stage manager. (This echoed Molly McArthur, 'Pity, young Colin, but if that's what you want to do...') Mr Neill wanted a young (this was 1953 remember) man to play leading roles. Angela, my number two assistant stage manager, lived in Sheffield and wished to stay on. She would be assistant stage manager number one with the Playhouse Company and was, I think, pleased withal.

I visited Mr Neill. He spoke on the phone to Mr Hanson. Outcome – I was to play 'guest artiste' at the Lyceum in the following week's play, *Romance* with well-publicised best wishes from the Sheffield Repertory Company, and then join Mr Hanson's company of Court Players at the Pier Theatre, Hastings. Read Richard Jerram's fascinating book *Weekly Rep* to learn more about this amazing theatrical entrepreneur, Harry Hanson. Sixteen companies on the go at one time! Joke of the day was: 'For heaven's sake, don't leave your garage/garden shed/outhouse empty. H.H. will put a repertory company in it!'

Chapter Six

A major year. Despite being told how good I was and being advised by many much more knowledgeable people to follow that line of work, I was glad to released at long last from the job of stage management. Oh boy! Now I became a full-time, professional actor with, in those days, one of the best weekly repertory organisations, Harry Hanson's Court Players. Perhaps I didn't aim high enough in my ambitions. I was then, and have been so in many companies since, happy in my job and enjoying the local kudos that came with what I hope was a job done to the best of my ability. With hindsight perhaps I should have followed that advice. Perhaps *this* represented the heights of my abilities – a young (?) keen actor playing in a variety of character roles week after week, and enjoying the challenge presented by each part, be it large or small.

This was the start of five years of almost constant work, first as a juvenile character man, then as a leading man and, eventually, a play director (we called them producers then). And Mr Hanson gave me two weeks' paid holiday each year, another feature not encountered in many of the weekly commercial reps in 1953.

The Ticking Clock came next at the Pier, Hastings. The crux of this play, set in a pub called The Ticking Clock in the Derbyshire Dales, was a rather large, ominously ticking grandfather clock. The work was described as a 'murder mystery' which turned out for me and a young actress, the charming Peggy Sinclair, to be one of the most hilarious experiences we'd had in our then short careers,

'Broad effects rather than subtlety', as the local paper reported, rather summed it up. Among the odd people turning up at this inn was a variety act called Delaware and Leroy – our lovely old 'character' lead actors Mabelle George and Keith Lorraine – who, among other things, had an accordion in their act (which neither Mabelle nor Keith could play). The sound and sight of one of them playing this thing was, somehow, essential to the plot. (The plot? Ha-ha!)

To achieve this, the compromise was Keith standing outside the inn as the front door was flung open dramatically holding this wretched instrument, with me crouched down on his right trying to keep out of sight except for my right hand trying to finger 'Three Blind Mice' on the keyboard while, I think, Peggy helped Keith support it and Keith tried to finger some of the buttons. Why couldn't it have been a tin whistle?

The play was supposed to become very tense when it was discovered that the sinister purveyors of murder, dope and smuggling were gaining access and egress, despite all security, via the ticking clock! As Delaware, of Delaware and Leroy, discovered and explained very carefully to young Anne Pritchard and Brown (Peggy and myself), when the brass weights and chains inside the clock were pulled in a certain order and manner the back of the clock opened up to reveal a passage which eventually led to the caves below – caves are famous in Derbyshire.

Yes, dear reader, we too found this hard to believe and our faces must have reflected this on the first night. The audience was in hysterics of laughter when Keith suddenly looked up and said, 'I do wish you'd take this rubbish seriously!'

The Daughters of the Parsonage brought a country vicarage and a son called Bramwell – maybe it was supposed to be a modern allegory about the Brontës. In one scene I, as 'Bramwell the son of the parson, not of much account except as a kind of "Greek Chorus"' (local paper), had to sit in a low armchair, downstage right, while smoking a pipe. I had only one line to say in this particular part of the action, which was quite a long passage. The Pier Theatre at Hastings was not a big theatre – fairly low stage and no orchestra pit – consequently the front row of the audience was quite near to the front of the stage. Dear old Bob Woollard was 'holding forth' as the Rev. Herbert Lovell in fine flow when I became aware, gradually, of a persistent 'Sss... Sss... Sss...' noise below me, to my right – the audience side. Concentrating on the action of the play and waiting to contribute my own pithy comment to this very important scene, I tried to ignore the noise. Alas, it became louder and even more persistent. Even the other actors became aware of it but carried on in true pro manner. A sudden sharp push to my right arm was, however, just too much. As quietly and as unobtrusively as I could I turned my head away from the action – may Esme Church and Rudolph Laban forgive me – to find a little old lady, one of our regular Tuesday-night front-row patrons crouched down in front of the stage by my chair making 'Sss... Sss...' noises. Upon my eventual reaction she whispered hoarsely, 'You were very good last week!'

With what, I hoped was the faintest of smiles, I turned back to the play. The action was still in full flight – Bob looking like thunder, the rest of the cast looking questioningly at me. As I tried to facially indicate my own horror at what had happened there it was again – 'Sss... sss...' I won't swear to it but I think Mr Woollard uttered a rather audible aside, *sotto voce*, as I turned to our fan who then said, 'Tell Mary she was good, too!'

Incidentally, I missed my one and only pithy comment line in that scene.

In one of our plays during my stay in Hastings the very talented leading lady, Mary Gauntlett, had a long dramatic speech which she delivered, as can so often be effective if done well, with her back to the audience. Mary was versatile in that she could be very quietly strong and powerful in highly emotional scenes and killingly funny as old maiden aunts, prudish vicars' wives or prissy spinsters. In this play she was a Mrs Danvers type, quiet, menacing, draped in black.

For this speech we, the rest of the cast, were standing or sitting upstage of Mary, she with her back to the audience, hanging on to every word. Atmosphere tense, building up to her climactic, measured paces at the end and exit through double doors up centre, invariably getting a great round of applause from the audience. On Saturday night as she walked past me in royal manner, tears streaming down her face, she looked me straight in the eye as I heard her whisper, 'Who writes this tripe?' Thank goodness her exit brought the curtain down – it finished us!

Headline (nearly made the front page of the local paper!): 'Popular Court Player to leave Hastings!' Not exactly a shock-horror story but it felt good to have it announced that Mr Hanson was transferring 'this talented young character actor' to his number one touring company, the company destined for a long, mid-year season at a number one theatre – the Lyceum, Sheffield.

First, however, the new Sheffield company was to assemble at the Olympia Theatre, Dublin. 'Now why,' a number of us asked ourselves, 'should one of Eire's number one theatres, the one which took in shows transferred from the West End, lock, stock and barrel – and stars – suddenly book an English rep company for six weeks?' Dublin was famous for theatre companies of great prestige and world-wide fame – The Abbey, the Edwards-MacLiammoir Company and others.

We realised, eventually, that we were booked for the season of Lent. I don't know how things are at present but in 1955 we were told that people in Ireland tended not to indulge in theatregoing during Lent! Still, the Illsley-McCabe management assured us, at a reception they were kind enough to give for us, that they were proud to be presenting us, so come what might we had six weeks work ahead of us in this fascinating, historic capital.

One aspect of my stay that I found amusing was 'spot the postbox'. All street postboxes, even some of the older ones with the 'VR' insignia on them, were painted green. Not easy to see at a distance, being used to red ones.

The season opened with a great tear-jerker of the day, *Johnny Belinda*. The Court Players were noted for stage sets of a standard and quality which, certainly for weekly rep companies, was generally agreed to be quite remarkable. As with his artistes and stage staff, Mr Hanson would not tolerate 'tat'. Bob Peet was the scenic artist and Eric Osborne was the master carpenter with our company, noted for stunning, realistic stage sets. The set for *Johnny Belinda* was certainly that! 'Black McDonald's Grist Mill' was quite an achievement, added to the realism of our director, Douglas Neill, and it became memorable for a number of reasons. I'm not going to plough through the melodrama's story, suffice it to say that at the dress re-hearsal one rooster 'got his notice' before we even opened. Oh yes, besides real straw, pulleys, wheels and ropes we had real poultry on the set.

'Scatter the seed well upstage, at the back of the set, then they won't get in the way, but they'll look terrific.'

Alas, at the rehearsal, the said rooster didn't realise what he was supposed to do. Perhaps he was an envious, frustrated actor. Downstage Locky (a wonderful performance by Ivor Salter) was about to 'have his way' with Belinda (Sorell Carson) on an old sofa. This interested the rooster much more than pecking at seed upstage. He took up a stance on the head of the sofa, crowing triumphantly as he watched the action. 'Sack that bird!' came the cry of director Douglas Neill, from somewhere mid-stalls.

Another aspect of realism was a goat, tethered to one leg of a table for an act of the play. This was the act in which Black McDonald – played by yours truly 'with rather too much hair on his face' (Dublin Evening Herald) – after his death is laid out on the table with everyone gathered round while the Rev. Peter (Harry Bowers) recites the Lord's Prayer over the corpse. And 'corpse' everyone on stage did. The audiences on the other hand, laughed until they cried and applauded our performance when, at 'Forgive us our trespasses' the goat performed both his natural functions simultaneously. Even the 'dead body' must have looked as though it was going to rise again for, although my eyes were of course closed, I could hear the noise of said 'functions' over the clergyman's intoning of the prayer and a very *sotto voce* 'Bloody hell! Right on my shoe!' from another actor.

On the whole Dublin wasn't exactly mad about our season and our best came last, according to the general opinion. In *Arsenic and Old Lace* I charged up and down a very long staircase, blowing a bugle and shouting, 'Ch-arge!', when I wasn't digging the Panama Canal in the cellar. (See play for explanation. It's a very funny play.) Our season finished with Somerset Maugham's *The Letter* for which, I'm happy to say, I collected some excellent reviews for my contribution as Ong Chi Seng – an inscrutable Chinese clerk – in the national press and on Radio Eirrean. Mr Hanson was very pleased and told Mr Neill to tell me that my salary would go up by ten shillings when we got to Sheffield.

Ah, Dublin. Exciting, enjoyable, unusual, classical, historical capital city. As we were only once nightly at the Olympia there was time for sightseeing and visiting the surrounding countryside between rehearsals and evening shows (no matinées). Soon though it was back to Dun Laoghaire for the journey to Holyhead, Sheffield and the Lyceum.

With experiences of a season in a capital city in a number one touring theatre and now about to start a season in another number one date, I began to feel that I had 'arrived'. The height of my Court Players career was about to be achieved, starting with 'the headmaster' (played by Alastair Sim in the film) in *The Happiest Days of Your Life*, a role I was to repeat some years later in Ayr. For *Me and My Girl* – the straight play version with the 'Lambeth Walk' finale – the programme announced that I designed and made the banners on the wall of Hareford Hall. Again I wondered briefly, 'Was Miss McArthur right after all?'

In *Lady Look Behind You* I received an accolade when I was given my very first solo curtain call at the end of a play and in *Black Coffee* – where I 'doubled' as murder victim and police inspector – the *Sheffield Star* reported, 'Newcomer Walter Plinge acts superbly in the important yet small role of the murdered man.' Poor Inspector Japp, who has all the work to do, didn't even get a mention. Anyone who has played an Agatha Christie 'Inspector' will know what I mean. A somewhat truncated *Pygmalion* figured in our twice-nightly season as did the old melodrama *Smilin' Through* (with real garden!) and ended with one of those rep plays of the day, of which one has never heard since, called *Jackie*.

It had been a successful season, with plays both good and bad, and parts played ditto. There was one 'stinker' I will name because (a) it was so bad and (b) both Sheri Grant and I found it impossible to learn and we were both reckoned to be 'good studies'. The authors (?) were given as Maurice Kemp and Lane Madic. Their effort was *Black Magic*. I'm surprised the famous chocolate manufacturers didn't sue them! Mr Neill reported the play back to Mr Hanson and, I believe, no other company of Court Players was required to do it.

For *Double Door*, described as 'a strong mystery thriller', Mr Hanson in his wisdom thought that it 'would be good experience for me' – mainly a character player – to undertake the straight juvenile role for one week, i.e. the romantic young man. Me! Old nose putty, wigs and beards Bean! Ah well, nothing ventured nothing gained. During Monday's first-house performance who should appear on one of his occasional surprise visits but H.H. himself. While on stage I caught sight of him watching from the stage management corner, stage right. After playing the particular scene the 'young romantic Robert Van Brett' made his exit stage left to be assailed by the disembodied but unmistakable 'carrying' whisper of Mr H. from stage right. 'Mr Bean! Mr Bean! Come here!'

'Oh Lord, what now?' I thought. 'Will I go to Court Players Penge or Keighley or somewhere next week?' But no. I had taken care with my appearance as the young Van Brett, including my juvenile make-up, five and nine, eyeshadow, well-shaded lips and so forth.

'Good evening, Mr Hanson,' said I.

He *looked* at me. 'That make-up, Mr Bean, that make-up is awful. Make it more rugged, more rugged. Who're you trying to attract, the girls or the boys?'

Well, at least it wasn't a transfer to Keighley!

My next port of call was to the Court Players in Crewe, opening in *Meet the Wife* – Lynn Starling – the Monday after *Jackie*. For a whole week I commuted between Sheffield and Crewe via Manchester by train. To be in time for a ten o'clock rehearsal with director David Ashe's company in

Crewe I had to leave Sheffield at six each morning. David had instructions from Mr Hanson that I must be released at twelve noon promptly in order to be back in Sheffield for the first-house performance of *Jackie* in which I, as the butler, played the opening scene. Second house finished at about ten o'clock so, for that week, no 'après-le-show' pints for me. Back to my digs, eat, study for next morning's rehearsal. Tuesday, read through and plot moves; Wednesday Act One; Thursday Act Two; Friday Act Three; Saturday whole play – usual Court Players pattern. Try to sleep and be up in time to get down to Sheffield Station for the 6 a.m. to Manchester stopping at every halt and crossing the Pennines en route!

The five-week stay in Crewe included my second encounter with *Vice in the Street* – which was *for adults only* – by Ian Stuart. In Sheffield I'd played Gilbert, a young man given to 'coshing' people, but this time I was Gilbert's disapproving stepfather, Bert. An interesting aspect was playing the noisy and violent scene from 'the other side' as 'twere.

The season also brought my first meeting with Max Reittmann's play (where did these authors find these names?) *Love on the Never-Never*. In subsequent productions I was to play both of the two male roles in it. Today I cannot remember a single word of this epic which filled theatres with laughter in 1955.

December came and I was heading back to Sheffield Lyceum to be stage director and play 'King Wolf' for John Beaumont's spectacular *Red Riding Hood* with a strong cast headed by Ken Dodd and with Rex Jameson as Mrs Shufflewick, both the newest national TV stars of the day. On Boxing day evening, live, we presented excerpts of the show at 7.30 p.m. for BBC TV. This was possibly the first panto broadcast on this fairly new medium. Geoffrey Wheeler, of BBC Radio fame, was the commentator. For this very long pantomime season I had the additional duties of taking understudy rehearsals, 'covering' both Mr Dodd and Mr Jameson. What it was to be young, keen and 'eager to get on'!

"BECAUSE I AM BLACK"

COLIN BEAN 1955 LYCEUM

Chapter Seven

The by then traditional pantomime companies' party, held during the final week of both shows, took place as usual with great success. Blowing my own trumpet, I can say that quite recently I met a former dancer who still remembers and still laughs, she says, at the double act of Molly Veness and myself. Molly was playing the witch in the Empire Theatre's pantomime, whose cast was headed by Charlie Chester and I was King Wolf from the Lyceum. Next day we had a lovely letter from Charlie to say how much he'd enjoyed it and six of the ladies from our chorus of dancers received a very large bouquet from him as thanks for the great 'Crazy Charleston' which they had contributed to the entertainment. That was Mr Chester, one of theatre's gentlemen.

Now we come to what the papers may have called 'Shock-Horror!', 'Disaster in Sheffield!' and suchlike. The then perennial production of *Peter Pan* was out on tour again and this year Sheffield was one of its 'dates'. Peggy Cummins was this year's Peter and I had some friends in the cast. One very good friend, James Gill, was playing Mullins, one of the pirate band. It had been my intention to see the show on the Monday night and then go for a drink with the members of the cast I knew. During that afternoon I received a phone call – I think it was from James – asking me if I could go down to the Lyceum as they had 'a bit of a crisis on hand'. Actor Ayton Medas, who was playing the role of the Black Pirate – now politically unacceptable I suppose – had suddenly been taken ill and been rushed back to London by a specialist. The theatre manager had, it seems, told the now somewhat distraught company manager about my performance in a recent Court Players production of the play *Because I am Black* – a very controversial play in those days. Outcome? I was taken backstage, told of my one and only line, 'De Doodle Doo has killed dem all', to be cried out as I emerged onto the deck of the pirate ship upon cue from an assistant stage manager. 'Then', I was told, 'just stick with Jimmy [Gill], Lionel [Wheeler], and Geoffrey [Fredrick]. They'll shove you around and whisper what to do next.'

What did I say earlier about being young, keen and 'eager to get on'? I certainly had 'got on' this time. It was a scary experience. Having been asked if I'd stand by next day, in case the Daniel-Mayer Company hadn't sent an actor to replace Ayton, I went to the theatre at ten o'clock next morning – I think the others had an understudy call – to be told that following company manager Peter Banks's report to head office the part was mine for the rest of the tour and would I please carry on. Thinking back, it was all like a *Carry On* film! Thus did I continue with the company to Leeds Grand Theatre, Manchester Opera House and Newcastle-upon-Tyne Theatre Royal.

At the and of the run we learned that Ayton was indeed ill and wouldn't be working for quite some time. Presumably I must have impressed someone because in the autumn of 1956 I was asked if I'd play the part again, in London and on tour. More of this in its proper place – it's quite a saga in itself.

The festive season well and truly over, early April found me in Stockton-on-Tees for three weeks with that company of Court Players for *Mad About Men* – a 'Miranda' play by Peter Blackmore – and *Widow's Might*, which I was to meet again when I returned to Sheffield. On the opening night back at the Lyceum on 7th May, 1956, it was announced, 'by Harry Hanson himself', according to press reports, 'We're here until November.'

Yes, a season meant a good long period of work in those days, providing, of course you knew and could do your job. When newspapers made references to 'Harry Hanson, himself' being present one couldn't help but feel that there must have a been a divine descent from Olympus – or Brighton! Read Richard Jerram's interesting book *Weekly Rep* to find out what it was like to work for H.H. whether you were in his 'good books' or his 'bad books'. The director and stage director, Douglas Neill and Derek Clark, were friends from the previous year. Douglas' wife, Carol, rejoined the Court Players, following family production, as stage manager. In the acting company I was with one associate from last year, that very underestimated actor and gentleman the late J.W. Terry. Mr Terry, in his own quiet way, and without 'teaching and preaching', had enabled me to learn an awful lot about working in repertory. This time the company was also to have the strength of J.W.'s wife, Diana Glynn, a delightful leading and character lady, who could be as frightening as 'Mrs Danvers' as she could be uproariously funny as 'Mrs Bounty'. Agatha Christie plays were always a popular attraction and with all due respect to David Suchet, Sir Peter Ustinov and Albert Finney I must state that, in my humble opinion, J.W. Terry was the finest of all Hercule Poirot portrayers I have ever seen.

Working with Mr Terry, rehearsing and playing, usually as Captain Hastings, I could during the rehearsal week see him become Hercule Poirot. The appearance, the walk, the voice, the meticulous mannerisms were all there. Costume perfect – and don't forget that in 1956 actors in weekly rep still provided their own 'modern, everyday' costumes.

'Must dress well, on and off. Good wardrobe essential'. How many times have older actors encountered that phrase in advertisements in *The Stage*? In many contracts of the day there was even a 'Minimum Costume Requirement' clause of what the artiste was expected to bring to the engagement. Only 'period' costume came from hire firms or other theatre companies. As Court Players didn't carry luxuries such as wardrobe departments one wore what came as best one could.

En passant, the other 'luxury' you would not find in the Court Players was that of a prompter. Mr Hanson expected everyone to follow his dictum that he paid us to learn the parts and he wasn't paying someone to keep reminding us of what we should have learnt. DLP – Dead Letter Perfect. This was the criterion, the ideal, and if you got into 'a mess' on the stage you got yourself out of it. Fortunately at Sheffield you often had the help of others on stage with you at the time.

For such a long season (weekly, twice-nightly) one respected Mr Hanson's other great principle – 'Troublemakers are out. Everyone must got on well together in my companies.' Any ex-Court Player could tell you, I imagine, of very talented actors sacked by H.H. because they 'upset the company'.

My Crewe experience of the previous year must have remained in Mr Hanson's memory because in June it was announced that I would be playing in the Bradford Prince's Theatre Court Players for two weeks. I think they were having a change of leading man in the company.

In retrospect, I cannot remember how we all found time to do all we did in those weekly, twice-nightly days. In my scrapbook for about this time appear pictures of me giving a stage make-up demonstration to a drama club, reports of members of the Court Players being present at and sometimes opening garden fetes, fashion shows – usually our leading ladies – manning stalls at charity events and the like. How *did* we find the time?

After the two plays in the city where I'd been at theatre school, still going strong in 1956, I went back to Sheffield and another 'Poirot' play, *Alibi*. This time I was Dr Sheppard, of which the Sheffield Star reported in a very complimentary 'write-up', 'Acting honours go to J.W. Terry, Colin Bean, and Diana Glynn as a shady sort of housekeeper.' It was always great to play scenes with Mr and Mrs Terry, even first house on a Monday! There seemed to be a mutual confidence when we three were in a scene together. I was to experience this 'feeling' later on in my career with one or two other actors. Nona Williams, Lesley E. Bennett, Victor Graham and the two Dereks, Wright and Tobias, spring to mind just now.

Confidence in follow artists in the hectic work of weekly rep was indeed a bonus. By the way, the price of a Lyceum programme (1956) was fourpence. It had scandalously gone up from thrupence! I can see a cartoon of Mr Terry and me as identical twins in *Out of the Frying Pan* (yes, that was the name of this epic) and a warning to subsequent audiences for Edgar Wallace's classic *On the Spot*: 'A front-of-house speech most effectively delivered by Colin Bean as the chief detective commissioner triumphantly overcomes the handicap caused by latecomers taking their seats. Future patrons please be on time.' (*Sheffield Star*)

The week commencing 8th October saw us presenting the soccer farce *The Love Match* with the press, having headlined the write-up with 'Football is Funny Business' ending the piece with: 'And the love scenes between Rose, Eugenie Cavanagh, and her Goon Show boyfriend deservedly hold up the action for hilarious laughter. What man but Alf Hall, Colin Bean, could postpone an ardent embrace with "Please don't breathe on my specs, love".'

In the same week also came the call from the Daniel Mayer Company inviting me to appear in the production of *Peter Pan* at the Scala Theatre in London and on the national tour to follow, a condition being, 'You can't have one without the other.' To me the prospect of a long period of work and in a tour of number one theatres ensured that I accepted with alacrity.

Chapter Eight

'Peter' in the 1956/1957 production was a charming young lady called Janette Scott, whose family I was to get to know later. John McCallum was Mr Darling/Captain Hook, the role being taken over later when John had other commitments to fulfil by Barry Sinclair. This time it was an enjoyable experience and an exciting interesting tour. 'De doodle doo' certainly 'killed dem all' with confidence in that production. Part of my costume was a very large real sheepskin cloak. On extremely cold days – this was of course, the Christmas/New Year season – as we arrived on stage to await the curtain up there was a fairly long orchestral overture and the petite Janette, shivering in her very flimsy 'Peter' costume, would come to me to be wrapped around in part of my cloak. A small cartoon was to appear later – in the theatre only, I hasten to add – of a large sheepskin cloak supporting two heads and four legs. I think the caption was 'Another cold day!' or something equally inane.

Being in a long run we enjoyed many after-the-show parties both in London and on tour. Playing in Nottingham we met and enjoyed the company of Janette's mother and father, Dame Thora Hird and the irrepressible delightful gentleman, Scottie. I was to work with Miss (as she was then) Hird again in three years' time. I'm happy to say that, to date, we still exchange Christmas cards and occasional 'Best wishes' messages.

At this point however, summer season 1960 is still some way off in the future. The tour of *Peter Pan* ended, would you believe it, in Bradford! This time we were at the much larger, famous Alhambra Theatre. From this point on life took another dramatic – in both senses of the word – turn. Following the last Lyceum season, during a company last-night reception that Mr Hanson gave, apparently at the end of a good run of business, I was taken aside by Mr Neill. 'Mr Hanson wants a word with you before you go.'

'Ha-ha,' I thought, 'but what?' The 'word' was that both Mr Hanson and Mr Neill felt that after five years with the firm, it was time I spread my wings. 'Otherwise,' said Himself, 'you'll be in the Court Players for the rest of your life. You are capable of other things.'

'Like prop-making', crossed my mind.

I was given an extra week's salary (note to Inland Revenue: duly and properly recorded on my tax return for that year!) and a very fulsome letter of reference and told to make an appointment with the George and Alfred Black office in London. Mr H. it seems had spoken of me in very favourable terms and he'd been in managerial partnership with them in the past.

This was not to 'pay off' immediately but in the not too distant future I and the interview were remembered, resulting in two G. & A. Black summer seasons. Being an ex-Court Player also served in lieu of an audition when eventually I appeared at the Palace Theatre, Watford, many years hence.

By the end of *Peter*'s sojourn at the Alhambra, Bradford, we were well into April, 1957. During the final week I was visited by Victor Graham, another ex-Court Player, who had now started his own company for summer seasons in the lovely Scottish resort of Ayr, 'the toon o' honest men an' bonny lassies'. During the last week of May I was to start on my new career with The Graham Players, week by week, once nightly. Utter bliss! I was to share leading roles and direction of the plays with Victor.

I count myself very fortunate in the number of 'adventures' I've had in my life. It must be a case of 'who I know', not 'what I can do'.

The Civic Theatre in Ayr is a delightful, small playhouse and, in those days, the facilities were somewhat limited. A very cooperative and obviously far-sighted town council did however start on great improvements. One 'tower of strength' in the whole set-up was the gentleman in charge of the building, Mr Tommy Faulds. A 'driver'? Yes, to a degree – Tommy didn't suffer fools gladly. If he thought you couldn't do your job then, in his book, you were 'fit for pettin' oot an' nae let in agen'. (Or for the uneducated, 'a waste of time, not worth consideration'.)

Being a relatively small company it was hard work. We all 'mucked in' to strike the set each Saturday night and take it across the road in any weather (oh shades of plastic sheeting and mackintoshes!) to the shed which was the scenic studio. The new set was brought back and set up before we departed, sometimes in the not-so-early hours of Sunday morning. Victor, Tommy and myself, often with assistance from young Frank Small, would come in later on Sunday to rearrange the lighting, particularly if the play had a complicated plot. I am never very happy on ladders. I don't like great heights but I managed to learn to take a ladder up into the 'circle' – our gallery seating – to change positions and colours of front-of-house spotlights. No medals for bravery here. 'Ah, gerron wi' it!' was Tommy's comment and 'Ay, no' bad' if it met with his approval, for Mr Faulds was – as we later insisted he be named in the programme and credited – our 'excellent resident stage manager'.

Not that all was plain sailing by any means. A 'difference of opinion' could put a halt to operations on rare occasions.

Mr Faulds had served and cared for the Civic since it first opened and justifiably he was, quietly, very proud of it as a building and equally concerned about 'what went on there'. A bonus was that having been in the employ of the royal burgh's council for many years, including the position of the provost's officer, Tom knew 'council thinking' and was able to advise us of what we would and 'what we wouldnae get awa' wi'.

Now we come to the 'funny bit'. In addition to the season at the Civic, Victor had also negotiated a contract for the summer with Butlin's Holiday Camp – very pre-Wonderwest days, more like prisoner-of-war days – to provide an alternative to entertainment by the camp's resident revue and variety company. Each Wednesday evening we presented a 'version' of a famous play, lasting about one hour and a quarter and on Thursday afternoon a play lasting for just one hour. Please remember, we were still playing a new play each week – Wednesday evenings excepted – and rehearsing the next week's play at the Civic.

Some of Butlin's happy campers were in the habit of staying there for two weeks so we had to provide four different plays. Week One: Wednesday night, *Night Must Fall*, no more than one and a quarter hours (there was a film to follow) and on Thursday afternoon *All For Mary*, played as a farce in one hour exactly. Week Two: Wednesday night, *High Temperature*, a comedy, and Thursday afternoon Acts One and Three of *The Veil*, a drama. The one-hour limit was achieved in this case by omitting Act Two, which was a flashback scene. By very judiciously 'nudging' the dialogue in Acts One and Three the storyline followed through quite clearly, except that is (there's always one performance, isn't there?) on one day when Victor Graham and Gillian Francis as Father Wade and Molly Martin were playing a scene in which the lady was to be persuaded to atone for her misdeeds by confession under the cloak of darkness.

'When I put out the light, speak your mind, my child,' said Victor, going over to the light-switch by the door on the all-purpose, every-play, beam and plaster set. 'Confess, my child, *as I put out the light*,' said he with a little more volume. Nothing! '*and when I put out the light*,' cried a now desperate 'clergyman' it was discovered that the electrician had been called to the Chandelier Ballroom to replace a light bulb. Although not supposed to touch the switch-board, one of our company, who had some stage management training, managed to throw the master switch, which blacked out the whole of the theatre, until 'Molly' had made her by now hysterically laughing confession.

It has been my good fortune to work with a number of people who have, in later professional life, achieved great heights of fame. A young lady just starting out with The Graham Players was a local lassie, one of Ayr's 'bonny' ones, Gwyneth Guthrie, later to find fame for herself and her hats as Mrs Mack in Scottish Television's *Take the High Road*. Jean Parker, descendant of an old, long-established theatre family well known in Scotland, was another of our indefatigable merry band. Jean was, I believe, related by family to Henry Parker of my Sheffield Repertory Co. days.

Thanks to Victor Graham I now had my first opportunity to direct a professional company of actors in a play. The week commencing Monday, 17th June, except on the Wednesday, The Graham Players presented Sir Noël Coward's *Blithe Spirit*, a very enjoyable experience for all concerned. *Wuthering Heights*, *The Cat and the Canary*, *Peg o' My Heart* with the charming Gwyneth as Peg, and *Reluctant Heroes* were the first plays in this long, very hectic season.

For *The Cat and the Canary* the press said, 'Colin Bean scores another success as a villain but only in the later stages of the play did he receive his opportunity to go berserk.' As anyone who knows me will tell you, I love an opportunity to go berserk!

Another 'Christie', *Murder on the Nile*, a non-truncated version of *Pygmalion*, and *Worm's Eye View* with Derek Wright as a marvellous Taffy followed, and *Doctor in the House* brought us to the end of the season with yours truly enjoying himself as Sir Lancelot Spratt and directing this mad caper, including the lovely 'bleeding time' line. The headlines in the *Ayr Advertiser*, 12th September, 1957, read: 'Their Last Production was the Best of the Season' and continued, 'When the curtain closes on Saturday night and the laughter of *Doctor in the House* dies down they will get a rousing ovation.' We did!

What a note upon which to venture forth into pastures new. The hardliner regulars – minus Gwyneth who had already been snapped up for other commitments – headed for the Pier Pavilion, South Shields. Here, it was thought, we could establish a winter season in a theatre which had suffered significantly with lack of success, until the Ayr summer season opened again in 1958. Successful we would doubtless be – look at our outstanding success in Ayr! Alas, disaster loomed on the horizon. Even with programmes costing only thrupence we didn't make a success of lethargic South Shields. This long narrow venue, which was like an aircraft hangar, defied heating, weather and audiences during the cold September, October and November months of 1957. Finishing in the week commencing 23rd December, with a company of just six people, we managed to end our unhappy experience in this seafront shed on a note of laughter with Kenneth Horne's *Love In a Mist* and, as a gesture of defiance (we will not be defeated), an afternoon seasonal show for children which we concocted among ourselves, *Children's Christmas Pudding*. As the *Shields Gazette* reported, in our obituary review, it was 'a Christmas gesture rather than a source of income'. Some children –

and parents – did brave the elements and come to see it but my grandiose plans of passing the balloons over your head to the people behind became 'Pass the balloon along the line and see who's got it when I shout "Stop!"' Oh dear, oh dear. Nice place, South Shields, but in 1957 not a theatre town. I'm sure Victor Graham will not mind me saying that, at the and of this experiment, he was far from being 'in pocket'.

Unbeknown to me, Douglas Emery, the director at Tynemouth Repertory Theatre on the opposite bank of the Tyne, had been in to see some of our shows. Even though we were working on a 'try not to spend any money' basis he was, it seems, impressed with our standards. For the last surviving members of Victor's company Christmas day and dinner was courtesy of a friendly, supportive publican and his wife who had done their best to help and promote us. I can only reiterate the opinion of an old friend, David Williams. 'One does, occasionally, meet some nice people in this business.'

The Graham Players parted company on 28th December with Louise Ralston, our excellent 'character lady', Jean Parker and myself scheduled to return to Ayr for the next summer season. In the meantime I found myself 'across the water' at the Tynemouth Repertory Company from early January until March of 1958.

Chapter Nine

Leaving behind news headlines such as 'Repertory Fails Again' and 'End of Shields Repertory is not the Players' Fault' didn't exactly make one feel comfortable at the work prospects. I was fortunate to be taken on by Mr Emery. He had already got a fairly large resident company so I was indeed lucky. Looking into the Tynemouth Rep programmes I find well-respected repertory actors such as the late Carl Paulsen, Bernard Severn, Nona Williams and, way down among the 'wines and spirits, i.e. among the assistant stage managers, a very young, eager and willing worker, Dennis Kirkland. I wonder if he dreamed then of directing famous comedy actors such as Benny Hill on TV? *Subway in the Sky* was a particularly enjoyable production. Nona Williams played Dinah, both she and I getting glowing reviews in the local rag. Finishing my stay there with *Double Image*, in the week ending 31st March, 1948, I prepared for the return to Ayr Civic Theatre. 'On the Hayhill Bus Route' said the posters, in case anyone didn't know where to find us.

After the traumas of South Shields we put on our bravest smiles to reopen The Graham Players' summer season in Ayr with *The Happiest Days of Your Life*. I was the headmaster again but this time I decided against an 'Alastair Sim' bald wig. The 'encounters in battle' between Miss Whitchurch – Louise Ralston – and Mr Pond played by myself had, I think, a little more edge to them than the Rutherford/Sim version. Victor directed but was soon due to absent himself from the weekly workings of the company due to other commitments occasioned by our recent Tyneside season. Jean Parker and I were, as co-directors, left in charge.

Owing to the fact that Butlin's Holiday Camp was undergoing a complete reorganisation we didn't have the second, modest income from plays in their theatre this season. It was missed financially but in view of what the Civic season had in store for me – was I glad? You bet I was! Read on!

This season was to be notable, firstly because amongst our company was that talented and delightful actress Rosemary Leach, and secondly because of the imaginative and beautifully painted settings of Jimmy Robb. Victor started us off on rehearsals of play number two of the season, *Subway in the Sky*. It was a good thing I had played Baxter recently at Tynemouth because this allowed me to concentrate on solving the problems presented by the next play, *Charlie's Aunt*, on our very small stage with very limited wing space. To add to my directional problems I played Lord Fancourt Babberley as well.

From mid-June until *Sailor Beware* in mid-August I directed and invariably played the 'heavier' leading male while Jean played both major and minor roles and cared for the company administration and finances. During those seven or eight weeks we covered plays such as *The Man Who Changed His Name*, with a very good leading performance by Christopher Owen, and *Harvey* in which I had a whale of a time as Elwood P. Dowd. There was a lovely set by Jimmy for the first Agatha play of our long season, *Spider's Web*, yours truly doing his 'Walter Plinge' bit again as the one who gets murdered, returning in another guise as Inspector Lord.

As I mentioned earlier, actors who have played Christie detectives and police inspectors know what it's like. I solved our problem of the invariable 'See you in the library one by one' scene by asking each actor who was playing a suspect to be questioned to stand offstage where I could see them quite clearly as I opened the door – just to give me a moment to remember which set of very similar questions I was required to ask each time. Louise, bless her heart, who'd played in countless Christies, would take out a hanky and very gently touch her nose and remind me, *sotto voce*, of the next question if I 'dried'.

It's a Boy by Austin Melford is the basis of the musical *Blue for a Boy*. We, however, decided to stick to the original but with musical numbers interpolated at various points – The Graham Players' occasional 'let our hair down' week!

Hectic week followed hectic week and trouble didn't desert us entirely. Before the dress rehearsal of the next play, *Dry Rot*, Bob Francis our stage manager was also playing Albert Polignac, the French jockey. Poor Bob, sometime over the weekend, was hit by a massive and very nasty attack of influenza. Not only could he hardly stand up or see properly but in the theatre he'd have been a danger to the rest of the company. With Bob, on doctor's orders, confined to his digs and his bed, what the hell were we to do?

Fortune showed sympathy in the form of Mr Andrew Milroy. Besides being a good actor and a prominent member of the main local drama group, Andrew was also a councillor and, as a member of the Leisure and Entertainments committee had, naturally, a continuing interest in the Civic and The Graham Players. A wonderful bonus was that Andrew spoke fluent French. At dress rehearsal he studied and marked all the moves on stage and got a rough idea of what he was supposed to be saying in broken English. In the evening, with guidance and gentle 'nudging along' from the rest of us on stage, he sailed through the play, all in frantic, volatile French. As I had to cope with the

Brian Rix role of Fred Phipps and I was learning Dr Sloper for next week's *The Heiress* I decided to leave Polignac to his own devices. Mr Milroy proved to be one of the highlights in a very well received production.

By the time I'd got through directing and rehearsing *The Heiress* I was, to say the least, tired and exhausted. Jean Parker was to give a beautiful rendering of the part of my daughter Catherine and during the week of *Dry Rot* she and Victor decided I needed a bit of a break. Not easy when it's a small, hard-working, tightly scheduled and not very affluent company. Again Dame Fortune was to hand in that an old friend of Victor's had been in Ayr making a guest appearance in *Dry Rot* and was persuaded to take on the directing of *Sailor Beware*.

My week of less pressure helped me recharge the batteries because we still had *Towards Zero*, *My Wife's Family* and *The Corn Is Green*, part of the celebrations of 'Fifty Years of Rep' and tribute to Miss Horniman's famous Manchester company. How Jimmy Robb was able to achieve some of his scenic effects I shall never understand. His very unusual, sharply angled drawing room for another Christie play and his exterior backcloth gave one the clear impression that 'Gull's Point' was indeed right on the edge of a steep cliff on a wild Cornish coast. For *My Wife's Family* the set 'made the news'. This was the first time that the quite small Civic stage had been graced by a divided set, showing a living room and a garden. Add to this the problems presented by having to 'blow up' an outhouse and one can see that in addition to coping with the role of Dr Knott I had my work cut out.

The Corn is Green was almost a haven of quiet during the next week with lovely leading performances by Michael Arden and Louise Ralston as Morgan and Miss Moffat, and admirable support from the rest of the company. With the following week's 'frivolous finisher', a lightweight comedy called *Bob's Your Uncle*, the third season of The Graham Players closed on 20th September, 1958, happy to be able to say to our patrons, 'See you next year.'

By the time the *Bob's Your Uncle* set was struck and stored away, arrangements made for borrowed props to be returned to our always willing and helpful town centre stores and local dramatic societies, I was, as one might say, 'fit to drop'. Tommy Faulds was kind enough to say, 'Aye, yer fit tae drop but ah hope ye'll be comin' here again.'

What eighteen-week season, especially such a hectic season, could go through without the odd hiccup or disagreement? Whate'er befell, in the end Mr Faulds was there at his post, usually on the lighting gantry, ready, willing and very able. To see – and hear – him come down that steel ladder, if and when a scene change was required during a play, was a study in the art of aerodynamic descent. Hence the oft-heard cry from his own stage crew, 'Watch oot! Tommy's aboot!' We had been warned!

Friends one has in different degrees. I'm fortunate in enjoying and having enjoyed the friendship of some great comrades-in-arms in this precarious 'showbiz' of ours. One such is James Gill (Mullins in *Peter Pan* – remember?). Probably because he was aware that I'd had a very heavy and tiring season, James had phoned me during our final week. He, too, had had a busy season as a Court Player and was ready for a holiday. 'Get your passport up to date,' said James. 'I've got us a couple of vacancies on a Millbank package holiday to a small, quiet seaside town in Spain.'

As at that time I hadn't even got a passport, again through the good offices of Mr Faulds I was able to gain access to the Provost of Ayr, whose influence presumably was able to make speedy arrangements on my behalf with the Glasgow passport office. The following Monday I was off for a two-week holiday in the lovely and then still 'untouristy' town of Callella, just a train ride from Barcelona.

During the year I had been contacted by the Lyceum Theatre, Sheffield, and invited to be assistant director and stage director of John Beaumont's new production of *Goldilocks and the Three Bears*, devised, written and directed by Douglas Neill. Part of the job, also would be to play the villain of the piece, Captain Gruber, and to understudy Mr Peter Butterworth as Dame Rose Ringler. This was to be another long engagement, made even longer by the fact that, in preparation for the extravaganza, Mr Neill required my presence in Sheffield for production meetings and to appear as guest artist in the last two plays of the current repertory season. They were only very small roles, thank heavens, but what a reception I got when I walked on on my first Monday night back! One actor on stage said, 'Well, we might as well all have a sit-down.'

And so to the pantomime which was to be 'The Biggest and Best Pantomime Ever!' West-End transfer was being bandied about even before rehearsals started. But, where do I start? What do I say about *Goldilocks and the Three Bears*, opening Christmas Eve, 1958? Do I open Pandora's box or just pass by and say that it was not without its troubles? That is, perhaps, kinder to all concerned.

When handed the initial script, which was about as big as a five-act play, I felt that even as assistant director I was going to have some slight problems. Sleepless nights, some very unpleasant rehearsals, a complete overhaul after the disastrous first night when the show ran for four hours, and having three jobs at once to do managed to obliterate the benefits of my earlier holiday in Spain.

One good thing to emerge was my first meeting with a very talented artist in all senses of the word with whom it gave me pleasure to work again in years to come. Young and at the time, I believe, new to 'the biz', in the stage management corner was John Inman. From experience I can say don't be fooled by the precious, dilettante Mr Humphreys of *Are You Being Served?* John is an Artist with a capital 'A'. Artistic and very practical, his knowledge of props and costumes, especially appertaining to pantomime, is phenomenal. For our dame he made the first 'steaming kettle' hat I'd ever seen; in later years I was to see pantomime costumes and props which took my breath away. It has been a privilege to know John. Incidentally, he's also the best re-creator of our famous (infamous?) North Country comedian, Frank Randle. The first time I saw him in the role my subconscious automatically registered, 'It can't be. Frank's dead.' He was Frank Randle to the nth degree in voice and appearance, and a supreme Mother Goose to boot – elastic-sided, of course. As for *Goldilocks* – best let sleeping bears lie!

Chapter Ten

Clearing up after pantomime season was quite a hectic and sometimes unpleasant business. Like discovering that one of the twelve 'mobo-horses', which had been borrowed but never used, was missing. The firm which made a six feet high and wide steel snowball frame meant for the dame's first entrance didn't wish to collect and remove same.

Nobody – including the resident theatre stage manager – could entertain huge cane and canvas wearable models of a teapot, a milk jug and a cup and saucer! As a simple little ditty, to get the dame, Simple Simon and our top-of-the-bill star singer together just once, I had suggested the kiddies' favourite oldie *I'm a Little Teapot* as a short frontcloth during one of sixteen very heavy and sometimes noisy, scene changes.

Two days later these two great things arrived at the dock doors 'ordered by the director personally'. Besides occupying most of our available wing space off stage, one would have needed to strike part of the set or take cloths out just to get them and the snowball onto a full set. Fat chance they had of being used on a 'frontcloth'!

All these items, including 'mobos' and six tricycles, occupied space in the understage storage space and part of the orchestra room for the rest of the show's troubled run. My stage manager, Tony Rowe, and I had the job of getting rid of all this mess.

In a way I was grateful that, although it would mean quite a long period of 'resting', my next definite job wasn't scheduled until the end of April. Then I was due to return to Stockton-on-Tees Hippodrome to take over direction of productions for the Court Players from Richard Dale. Richard was to remain in overall management of the company from his new post as director of the Bridlington Court Players' summer season.

So, returning to London where by now I had acquired residence in a very nice small rented flat just off Holloway Road, I got settled in and decided to decorate the staircase walls up to and including the landing of my first-floor home. The first week of April found me up a ladder, paint brush poised, when the phone rang. Any actor who is 'resting' automatically reacts to a phone bell. So did I, coming down the ladder rather more quickly than I had intended and, dammit, no audience to appreciate the result.

Instead of applause I discovered a very dear friend on the line, speaking in a very distraught manner. Derek Tobias was having his first experience of playing major roles in weekly rep with the New Elizabethan Repertory Company in the seaside resort of Cleethorpes. No, not a classical or Shakespearean theatre company, the NERC had presumably been formed in or around Coronation year, 1953, by Miss Edith Carter (previously of the Frank H. Fortescue Management). When the 'Fortesks' – as they were known in some quarters – closed down, the stock of scenery and such like was apparently split up amongst the surviving members of the management. Miss Carter's NERC share was at the Empire Theatre, Cleethorpes, where, on the first night of a play, disaster had struck.

This call was coming through at approximately 10.30 p.m. Derek told me that, due to an accident, the leading man and the play's director, Frank Marlborough, was in hospital. 'Edith's going berserk. We don't know what to do. Can you come and help us?'

'Gobsmacked' is a fairly new word; had I known of it in April, 1959, I feel quite sure it would have described my stunned state admirably. It was like *Goldilocks* again – another sleepless, hectic, panicky, nerve-wracking night. No dear Clive Dunn as yet to comfort me with the immortal words, 'Don't panic! Don't panic!'

I phoned British Rail and eventually caught the first available train to this east coast seaside holiday spot, to grab the script about an hour before the curtain was due to go up, and to go on to read the leading role of Peter Thornton in *Proof Before Murder*. In the final scene the Police Inspector's pistol *did* go off on this night, thank goodness. On the previous night, I was told, in lieu of the failed gunshot the inspector made a physical attack upon Peter Thornton and, unfortunately, literally knocked him out. Poor Frank, in falling, had cracked his head on a window sill on the set. An ambulance, I believe, was whisking him off to hospital as the rest of the cast were taking the final curtain call.

Miss Carter thanked me and asked if I'd carry on for the rest of the week as Frank was quite seriously injured and, when he got out of hospital, would be going 'on leave' for a while. I agreed to carry on reading the role for the four remaining performances. It was a very long part so I wasn't going to attempt to learn it. I hadn't even found anywhere to stay in Cleethorpes! When that question had been resolved by Derek and another friend, Barbara May, Miss Carter then handed me the script for the next week's little drama, *Stolen Waters*, by Lionel Brown. 'Oh, you'll be Lord Quinton,' said Miss C. as she vanished into the shadows at the back of the auditorium.

'You will stay, won't you?' asked various members of the still assembled company. They were such a nice crowd. What else could I do? Jean Rimmer, Bruce Bennett and Eunice Mann were all very good actors with whom I was to meet up in later years. I like to think that 'the drama of Cleethorpes' helped us to work well together at our next respective meetings as, I remember, we did.

Earlier in the year Victor Graham had invited me to go to the Civic, Ayr, for another season. Unfortunately I had already accepted Mr Hanson's offer of Stockton. This season, I am sorry to say, had a sad ending. For some time previously, despite the standard of production – Richard Dale was an excellent director and Clive Pickerill an inventive and meticulous set designer and painter – the Stockton Hippodrome audiences had been reducing in size. We were a good bunch, we all got on well together but, as people left the company, I was not to replace them. As a consequence I found myself playing in four of the seven plays left to us. Actors who went on to greater things were members of the company – Freddie Jones (then rather grandly programmed as Frederick), a cheerful young 'likely lad' called Rodney Bewes and a gentleman who had been, and would be for many years, a stalwart in any company, Nicholas Brent.

Once I was told 'officially' that the notice would be going up on the board, I told Victor Graham who informed me that I'd be welcomed in Ayr because patrons had been asking why I wasn't there! I got the dress rehearsal of the final Stockton play over (*Simple Simon's Baby*), made a quick dash back to London – mainly to tidy up after the unfinished decorating – and then overnight, with all my wardrobe, off to Ayr.

This started my third season at the lovely little Civic Theatre in one of the nicest holiday resorts in which I have worked. Another of Victor's well-chosen programmes of plays kept us busy, with 'House Full' boards out on occasions. The indomitable Tommy greeted me with a quietly disguised enthusiasm. 'Aye, so yer back! Ah kent ye would be!' Never one to go over the top, our Tommy Faulds.

Friend Derek Wright had already been greeted back to The Graham Players by audiences remembering some of his fine performances the previous year. My return persuaded Victor that as Derek and I had gone down so well as Taffy and Porter in *Worm's Eye View* (extra matinée on Saturday afternoon to accommodate demand!) in a previous season, this year its sequel would be in our schedule.

And so in the week commencing 3rd August, audiences (and I must confess Derek and I both) enjoyed the mad capering and the mayhem of Delderfield's *Wagon Load of Monkeys*. Besides *Major Barbara* the season included *Alibi* and *Black Coffee* to satisfy an insatiable appetite for Agatha Christie plays, and *The Diary of Anne Frank* – a very moving experience for us all. This season ended with a play by another old friend and ex-Court player, Austin Steele. Described by the press as 'a rumbustious laugh-a-minute farce', it proved a perfect finale and was the aptly named *Friends and Neighbours*.

During the season one actor had left the company so Victor and I agreed to recruit a young man with whose work we had been impressed when he first started with Harry Hanson's company – Derek Tobias. Ashamedly I have to say that Sebastian Green, as played by Derek, 'corpsed' me at every performance!

Friends and Neighbours has always been an enjoyable if hectic play to perform. Its only minor fault is its ending, to which even then Austin said he had not found a perfect solution. In a subsequent production which I directed some years later (for those who know the play), I brought the final curtain down slowly on a frantic barricading of all the doors and windows on the set.

As I said earlier, there are some actors with whom I have enjoyed a particularly good rapport when on stage, one of them being Mr Victor Graham. In *Cup of Kindness*, a Ben Travers farce, two particular moments come to mind. During one performance, in a scene during which Victor and I had a long and, I hope, amusingly acrimonious dialogue which I think we both enjoyed playing, we were to be interrupted by the entrance of actor Bill Auld as Ernest. 'Himself' (Victor) and yours truly were in full swing with our verbal tennis match, possibly improvising a little (for shame!), when Bill threw open the Aldwych farce essentials, double doors upstage centre. As he opened his mouth to speak, Victor and I yelled together spontaneously, 'Get out! We haven't finished yet!' Exit Bill to hover behind said double doors because the audience had 'cottoned on' by now and were obviously enjoying it all – until I said, 'Right, Ernest. You can come in now.'

In another scene, at another performance, a fairly long scene had to be interrupted by the phone bell, manually operated by the assistant stage manager in the prompt corner. We got to the cue – nothing! Louise improvised, Victor improvised. I edged towards the prompt corner to find our young lady assistant stage manager busily examining some presumably new shoes that she had on. 'What's next?' I whispered hoarsely.

'Oh,' said the flustered assistant stage manager consulting the script. 'Er, the phone rings,' and looked at me with a charming, seraphic smile.

At which I heard Tommy's not so seraphic voice, from the lighting gantry, saying, 'Well for God's sake ring the bloody thing, girl! Otherwise we'll be here aw nicht!'

Another outstanding presentation of that season was the old melodramatic classic *The Chinese Bungalow*. The role I played had been made famous by the late Matheson Lang in years gone by, another of my 'enigmatic Chinese' roles in a beautifully colourful setting by Jimmy Lovell. One scene was a particularly difficult one to play. It covered two facing pages in French's edition. Alas, the last line on the right-hand page was almost identical with the first line on the left-hand page. On at least two occasions Victor and myself, being sole occupants of the scene at the time, found ourselves back where we started and our stage manager, dear little Anne Lee, having taken over the prompt corner, tearing her hair out and trying to follow us. In the end I called for the 'thinly disguised Chinese manservant' – Derek Tobias, who was already doubling this with another part in the play. I said, 'Bring some champagne and a fan for Mr Marquise,' implying, 'Tell me what the next line is.' The champagne and fan line wasn't due until the next scene. The look on Derek's face! Meanwhile, during this diversion, Victor, bless his heart, had picked up where we were supposed to be from a whisper by Anne. Who says weekly rep was boring? Never a dull, or predictable moment!

After the season in Ayr I was able to establish myself in my London accommodation, 'resting' courtesy of the labour exchange when not doing odd days of 'walk-on' and 'extra' work for my first ventures into television. With other actors, many known to me from various rep companies, I started doing the rounds of agents and film casting directors' offices.

Most of my 'bits an' pieces' came my way via the Eric Blyth agency. Everyone went to see 'Uncle' Eric, a very astute, not so young gentleman who, when and if you got into his good books, could be a friendly and helpful adviser to those who would listen. How very pleased I was, later in life, that I'd followed 'Uncle' Eric's number one priority advice. 'Even if you do only one day's work in a week – stamp your insurance card.' A number of his young clients, who probably felt that they knew better, would omit to tell the labour exchange if they had had only one or half a day's work for a TV or film company. They'd save the cost of a weekly insurance stamp (one stamped one's own card) and claim a full week's unemployment benefit.

'Madness, Colin. Sheer madness,' said 'Uncle' Eric. 'They think they're smart but it will catch up with them eventually – probably when they most need some financial help.'

The daily rate for extra and walk-on work was by no means princely, and the purchase of an insurance stamp for that week could make quite a hole in the fee received – after Eric's agency commission – but I stuck with his advice, even when told sometimes by other agencies not to bother.

Emergency Ward 10 was made in the old Islington studios which, conveniently, were situated not far from the flat in which I lived. Thus on days when Victor and another old friend, Tony Mayne, were also on the set (they were on 'Uncle' Eric's books too) we'd all go back to my place for some lunch instead of hazarding our chances in the fairly primitive studio's rather limited canteen.

Programmes went out live in those days and I can recall watching with amazed horror when, in one transmission session, I saw a camera being tracked backwards through the doors of our ward, being due to swing round and move up the corridor to pick up another scene there. Instead of encountering the two actors playing hospital staff who should have been preceding towards it, the camera met another camera heading in its direction. Presumably someone in the control box must have plunged a 'panic button' or something as the whole studio and, I imagine, the homes of all who were watching resounded to a very clear and very loud expletive! Thankfully the chaos was sorted out very quickly, so much so that when I told some neighbours about it in my 'local', for I know they were regular '*EM10*' watchers, they hadn't even noticed it.

My professional life was now to undergo some changes. Being based in London was making a difference. Different managements and agencies began to get to know me. With some, my long association with Mr Hanson's Court Players was a good introduction. This festive season was not to be pantomime for a change – the shades of *Goldilocks* still gave me nightmares – and my next steps were in the direction of a company called Theatre Outlook, with whom I worked from 1st December until 23rd January, 1960, in two plays which were both most enjoyable experiences, as well as being my first experience of acting in a 'play area' rather than on a conventional pros-arch stage with tabs and footlights. I had to go back to t'North again for *Mine Hostess, Mirandolina* (Goldoni) and *How He Lied to Her Husband* (Shaw) but what artist could complain at playing in the beautiful setting of Liverpool's Blue Coat Chambers?

I was very happy to meet up again with Frank Marlborough, now recovered from his Cleethorpes catastrophe, and Jimmy Lovell, now a stage director. Ray Lonnen, later to become known as a TV policeman amongst other roles, was the other newcomer to this small company.

These charming plays provided a very pleasant change – for an actor anyway – from the usual 'Festive Fayre', as Fabrizio in the Goldoni and the incidental pianist (mimed I must confess) in the Shaw. I thoroughly enjoyed my short season with Theatre Outlook.

Chapter Eleven

Next, and very reluctantly, I returned to stage management. By means of various contacts I had managed to get an interview with The Noel Gay Management. This, to me, was moving in upper echelons. Alas, my backstage abilities were known to NGM who were about to launch a new 'high-class with West-End artistes' repertory company, in Lowestoft. I agreed to go as stage director 'to get them started', as the first two plays had already been fully cast. Tony Rowe, still suffering from shades of *Goldilocks*, was again my stage manager. Having set up, supervised and worked through the first production, *Sabrina Fair*, which was my commitment, I returned to London for a short 'rest'.

During March and April I managed to fit in a short spell as an admission point supervisor at the Ideal Home Exhibition and some more television 'extra' work for ATV and GUILD TV. In May, following a week's rehearsal in the upstairs room of a pub somewhere off Shepherd Market, my next port of call was the Empire Theatre, Edinburgh, in Carl Clopet Productions' presentation of David Kirk's *Love Locked Out*. I was to meet the play again! Ex-Court Player Sylvia Melville and I played the leading roles in this 'modern-day North Country Lysistrata comedy'. Gillian Francis, former Graham Player, and Jeanne Cook (ex-Northern Theatre School) were in the company so I was among friends. As I had already been interviewed and engaged by Messrs Alfred and George

Black (that initial recommendation by H.H. came to fruition) to play in a long summer season in Scarborough, it was in a way fortunate that the Edinburgh visit was a 'try-out' weekend and not a tour.

July found me in rehearsal, back in London, under the direction of David Leach (ex-Court Players stage manager in Hastings) in Walter Greenwood's *Saturday Night at the Crown*. The cast, headed by Miss, now Dame, Thora Hird, rehearsed in (must be a favourite venue in London) the upstairs room of a West-End pub. I was playing Sam Cross, one of the two regulars who sit with Ada and her husband every Saturday night in the snug of The Crown. My table companion, Charlie Butler, was played by a gentleman whose work I've admired many times, Harry Littlewood. Thora referred to us as her 'corner men', the supporters off whom she could bounce her sharp, funny comments. Jeanne Mockford, 'in a symphony of red raddle', bounced around as the flashy Eunice Sidebottom. Thora could make me laugh at every performance as she confided to Harry and me, with that 'knowing' look so typical of ladies in my 'north countree' which confidently implies that 'she's no better than she should be'. 'That's Eunice Sidebottom. Calls herself "Siddy-Bow-Tome" y'know.'

Despite some foul weather it was, on the whole, an enjoyable season, Thora and her husband 'Scottie' arranged a couple of outings, we had picnics, tea and sandwiches backstage courtesy of Harry plus, as next door neighbours, *The Black and White Minstrel Show*.

Let me explain, for those who didn't know Scarborough in 1960. The 'Minstrels' were appearing at the Futurist Theatre and we were literally next door at the Arcadia. So closely connected were the two that one stage door served both. The probable consequences of taking a wrong turn and making an entrance onto the wrong stage was often discussed over sociable 'get-togethers' between members of the two companies.

Like so many people, myself included, Thora loved listening to the George Mitchell Singers, a major part of the B and W show as we referred to it. On occasional mornings I sneaked into the Futurist when their company was rehearsing or learning new numbers, just to hear them sing – and invariably found that other members of the 'Crown' company had done the same.

Their season was scheduled to close a week before we did, and don't forget, they were literally next door neighbours. During Act Three on our penultimate Saturday night Nick Haigh dashed on, as rehearsed, to give us all some more 'earth-shattering' news. Instead he said, 'Someone to see you, Ada.' Well, it was time for that heavyweight feather to come into play!

In trooped all the gentlemen of the B and W show, in complete make-up and immaculate white tail suits and toppers, in line, hand-on-shoulder-of-the-one-in-front fashion and, to the tune of 'Ida, sweet as apple cider' in perfect harmony, they were singing, 'Thora, oh how we adore her.' I can resort only to the old cliché that it brought the house down. In at the door of the snug bar (upstage centre left), downstage, crossing and exiting through the door downstage right. They moved so smoothly that one can think only that they must have rehearsed it. They were very fond of Thora and the last gentleman in the line was the late, gloriously voiced Tony Mercer who, as he passed 'Ada', raised his top hat and kissed her on the cheek before making his exit. Nothing was said, just the singing and a simple salute from a great gang of great fellas!

After that it was a case of 'meanwhile back at the ranch' or 'and so back to the plot' but not before Thora gave us another 'gem' which I treasure. Frank Pettitt, playing the landlord of The Crown, said, 'What about that then, Ada?'

and she immediately replied, finger to where Tony had kissed her. 'Most touching – and I have no colour prejudice.'

Well, customers, Harry Littlewood and I nearly choked on our pints of dandelion and burdock, the audience didn't half show their appreciation. I wonder what the 'show timing' read in stage manager Martin Anderson's logbook for that night. Talk about over-running! Messrs G. and A. Black must have approved when eventually the book went to head office because, I'm happy to say, they did employ me for another summer season which we'll reach in due course.

Now I don't want to be maudlin but I do need to pay a tribute at this point. Without going into all the details I'll say only that the final week, after the 'Minstrels' had gone, was a sad one for me. My dearly beloved stepmother died after a long struggle with the 'big C', making Father a widower for the second time in his life. What upset me most was that, try as I might, there was just no way I could get from Scarborough to Wigan and back in one day to attend the funeral and appear in the first house of *Saturday Night at the Crown*.

To Thora and Scottie I owe sincere thanks for kindness, understanding and the lengths they went to trying to help me get there and back in time. They were a great comfort to me. As one door closes another opens, so they say. This sad happening prompted my first conscious contact with the ACU – that's the Actors' Church Union. From the theatre noticeboard (I'm not sure but I think it was Thora who pointed the card out to me) I got the address and phone number of the Scarborough Theatres' ACU chaplain. The support I got from all those friends enabled me to get through playing in this riotously funny play until the end of the week. But we won't say goodbye to *Saturday*

Night at the Crown. I was to meet up with it again twice, in Watford and in Bolton. More of that anon.

Most of October and November was spent on tour again – this time in my first venture into 'the commercial world'. Donald Masters, a director with whom I was acquainted but hadn't worked with before phoned to ask if I was free to undertake 'something a bit unusual'. The Frigidaire Company (a division of General Motors) had commissioned a short play to be written about the three new models of their latest refrigerator called the Sheerline. The play, *Home in Three*, was to be toured by three small companies of actors, each with its own portable set-up (a bit like the wartime ENSA outfits with stage, lighting and so forth) each directed by Donald. The engagement was for some six weeks at a reasonable salary (fifteen pounds per week) plus hotel bed and breakfast and transport provided. Quite unheard of in any theatre company I'd worked for but considered essential by Frigidaire which one appreciated when one discovered that their 'dates' were one or two-night stands all over the country.

We performed Monday to Friday, usually in large hotel ballrooms (staying in the same hotel overnight) or at a nearby hall. Picked up at home in London on Monday morning by a Vauxhall car courtesy of GM (no train calls, even when playing Scotland!) and delivered back late Friday night. Each company was warned that there would be one weekend in their schedule when it would not be possible, because of distance (our company's was Scotland: Ayr on Friday, Edinburgh on Monday) for us to get home. For that weekend full board would be provided at the hotel by the Frigidaire Company.

It was not a difficult play to perform and there was always a reception to which we, the actors, were invited (free buffet supper!) because our audiences were not of the general public. This was a promotion aimed at the local

Frigidaire stockists, dealers and agents to introduce these three models for the 1961 sales. We were, very diplomatically, requested when we were at the after-show reception to talk about the Sheerline if approached by audience members and not about ourselves as actors. Not an easy thing to ask of any actor! I resorted to restating what was said in the play. I must have been convincing because I was approached by an area manager and asked if I would not prefer the security of a 'proper job' with Frigidaire instead of a precarious one with the theatre. I do hope he wasn't too offended when I declined the invitation.

"Goldilocks & The 3 Bears"

COLIN BEAN

LYCEUM

1958

Chapter Twelve

Early in December I was off back to Wigan again. I felt that certainly for this Christmas I should be with Father. I'd managed to get a small part as one of the two broker's men in F.W. Entertainment Ltd's *Cinderella*. This was to play Crewe and Southport so I could commute and be at home in Wigan all day each Sunday. Not the most outstanding pantomime but memorable for me because it introduced me to, and allowed me to study at close quarters, the art of playing the dame. As I said, I was only a bit player. Jackie German, the other broker's man, had a speciality unicycle act which he did in the ballroom scene, loosely under the disguise of 'The Entertainment'. As he had to change into his own specialist unicycling variety act costume to perform, it had nothing to do with the story of Cinderella at all! That would never happen in a Perry panto or, in later years, any panto of mine.

My 'other' job was to act as dresser and understudy to the ugly sisters. I am fortunate in that I have worked with some lovely people during my career. Brother and sister Max and Maisie Norris became not only friends but the first people to recognise and encourage my interest in the art of playing pantomime dames. I watched, listened to and heeded Max and Maisie both when I was on stage or in the dressing rooms. I also learned a great deal about the sheer artistry of a good clean costume 'quick change'. In later years Max, who was a noted pantomime writer/director as well as a renowned dame, was to direct me as dame in a panto, again in dear auld Ayr at the famous Gaiety Theatre, but that's yet to come.

Obviously the Christmas at home hadn't much feeling of festivity about it. Father, I think, was still in something of a state of disbelieving shock. It most certainly wasn't a merry Christmas and patience was stretched on both sides. Enough said.

1961 was the year in which I was again managed by someone who, subsequently, was to put quite a lot of work my way, Mr David Kirk. In those days David was what one might call a leading light of the touring dates. The dates might have been widely scattered, involving long Sunday train calls but, like Mr Hanson, if Mr Kirk liked one's work and one wasn't a disruptive influence in his company, one worked.

I had, of course, worked under his direction the previous year in his own play *Love Locked Out* at the Empire Theatre, Edinburgh, now the Festival Theatre. I was to meet the play again this year for a long summer season in Morecambe after I'd toured in such 'classics' as *Forbidden Flesh* and *A Girl Called Sadie* (both by Eugene Hamilton, it says in the programmes). The latter *for adults only* drama had, I gathered, originally featured a very formidable, attractive and talented actress known then as Patricia Hamilton but better known later as Pat Phoenix. Sadie in this production was an equally charming and, if she'll excuse me, buxom blonde bombshell called Sidonie Bond. Sidonie was later in the year to play the seductive wrecker of domestic harmony in the Morecambe summer season production.

In *Forbidden Flesh* I played a young Anglican vicar. During the week we were at The Pavillion Theatre, Glasgow, I was on my way to the stage one evening. I turned a corridor corner to meet another 'grey-suited, black front and dog-collared' gentleman. 'Funny,' I thought.

'Hello,' he said, 'I'll see you when you come off stage. I'm the RC chaplain.'

Somewhat taken by surprise I indicated my own dog collar and replied, 'Well, snap Father! Same firm, different branch.'

A great favourite, particularly in his own native North Country, was a very funny, quiet, gentle comedian who has made a name for himself on Radio and TV as well as on the stage, Ken Platt.

Back to London for two weeks of rehearsal in the inevitable upstairs room of a pub in Glasshouse Street where assembled to support Ken in his first straight play were Barbara Miller, Olga Regan, Rita Franklin and Sidonie Bond, together with Messrs Jackie Lester, Benn Simons and yours truly. Ken is noted for his wonderful facial expressions and one of the biggest laughs in the show was at the delivery of Ken's own famous opening line to his solo stand-up comedy routine, 'I won't take me coat off. I'm not stoppin'. Ken was very insistent that this was a play and that he was not going to interpolate any comic gags into the script. However his famous 'intro' was not lost upon the audience when, upon my very first entrance in raincoat and bowler hat I announced, 'I won't take me coat off. I'm not stoppin'.' The look on Ken's face brought the house down and quite spontaneously he said, 'Now where've I heard that before?' Another even bigger laugh! I don't think there was a performance in the whole season which lacked those two laughs among many others in the play.

Most of that summer enjoyed pleasant weather so Father was persuaded to come to Morecambe for a week to stay at the hotel next door to the Alhambra Theatre where *Love Locked Out* was playing. Both are on the seafront and the company used the hotel bar regularly for midday snacks and after-show drinks. Father was introduced to all and sundry and actually came to see the show! The company was wonderful. Even when I wasn't around those who were in the hotel would sit and chat with him, and at lunchtime and after the show he was included in 'the company'. I think it was Jackie Lester who said, 'Keep him occupied. It's the best thing. I've been through all that with my mother.'

Father went back to Wigan feeling, I hope, that he had a whole host of new friends who 'knew and understood'. I found comfort also in working with such a team.

During this same season I met another gentleman, a Lancashire author with whom I've kept in contact ever since and who was responsible for a lot of the material in my 1980/1990 one-man recital *A Gradely Neet*. Cliff Heyworth, writes under the nom de plume Bill o'Bows. Read his fascinating *Nobbut a Thought fro' Lancashire* to find the story behind his 'nom' and a wide selection of his great Lancashire dialect poems and essays.

The end of the season in Morecambe saw us back 'on the road' again as *Love Locked Out* visited the Opera House, Seaton Sluice and the Empire Theatre, Oldham.

By now it was almost the end of September. We made a quick return to London and back to the upstairs room in the West-End pub to rehearse a new production – again with David Kirk directing – of Austin Steele's *Friends and Neighbours*. As in the earlier production I did in Ayr with The Graham Players I played Albert Grimshaw with the author himself playing the gormless Sebastian Green, played in the film version by the late Danny Ross. At this time Austin had a gruelling schedule since he was one of the principals of Tyne-Tees's daily *One O'Clock Show*. To facilitate matters (after all, it was Austin's play!) we continued rehearsals at the Newcastle YMCA before opening for the week of 9th October, 1961, at the Empire Theatre in Newgate Street. Twice nightly in this hilarious but exhausting romp meant I was certainly ready to 'rest' for a while, a rest interrupted by my first television speaking part, as opposed to the televised excerpt from the Sheffield pantomime. British film star, Dermot Walsh, was 'Richard the Lionheart' (Danziger Productions for ITV) whilst I appeared among the 'wines and spirits' with my two lines as a yeoman for the princely sum of fourteen pounds (less 'Uncle' Eric's commission) for one day's work.

Made a bit of a change from fifteen pounds per week and pay for digs and so forth on tour, playing twice-nightly for six days a week. Twenty pounds per week was considered to be a good salary for theatre work unless, of course, one was a *star* or an up and coming TV 'name'. Still, I'd progressed one step up the ladder. I was now on record as a 'speaking artiste' in TV terms.

I carried on doing extra and walk-on work through the efforts of 'Uncle' Eric until in time, after I'd done a longer role in *Z Cars* in 1963, a decision was made. The Blyth Agency would henceforth submit my name only in consideration of speaking parts to which I added, 'However small the part may be.' Shades of Pte Sponge with his, 'Yes, Captain Mainwaring', 'No, Captain Mainwaring' yet to come?

By now it was almost panto time again and via my contacts with David Kirk, Carl Clopet Productions and G. & A. Black I was put in contact with F.W. Entertainments Ltd again. I had decided I ought to try to be near to Wigan again so that Father would not be alone. Not that there was any lack of good friends in Wigan. I felt that he might wish for more personal company for Christmas Eve and the midnight Communion service and for Christmas Day. So the outcome of all this 'fixing' was that I was booked to play the grand vizier in a fairly spectacular production of *Aladdin* at one of the premier number two touring dates, The Theatre Royal, Bolton.

The show, written and directed by West End theatrical producer and agent, Al Heath, starred two very popular artistes, Clinton (*Fanlight Fanny*) Ford as Widow Twankey and TV presenter Billy Raymond as Wishee Washee. A real magician, Benson Dulay, was a mystical Abanazer. I was understudy to Clinton and Billy – not an easy task as Clinton had never played in a 'book' show (i.e. scripted lines to be learned and spoken) before and Billy, with his irrepressible Scottish sense of fun, could 'bubble over' and ad lib at any given moment sometimes saying some of Twankey's lines as well as his own. Being used to TV game shows, this presented no trouble to Billy even if it 'corpsed' the rest of us. Now director of a theatre complex in Australia (would you believe it, *Ayr*, North Queensland!), Billy and I still exchange Christmas Greetings more than thirty years later.

To do his solo spot – and I don't think this had occurred to the management – Clinton had to change into, as they say in the contract, 'act as known', in his case a very dapper light-grey suit, bow tie and straw boater, by which he was well known when he sang. What to do? He couldn't really sing 'Fanlight Fanny, the Frowsy Nightclub Queen' dressed as Widow Twankey, could he?

Hello! Bean shoved in his 'fourpennorth'. Outcome? From offstage on a microphone, a mysterious voice (the old lamp-glass again) made the excruciating announcement. '*And now*, ladies and gentlemen, boys and girls (we hadn't even heard of sexist political correctness in 1961) Abanazer, with a magic word, turns Twankey into *Clinton Ford!*' And through the centre of the number two tabs stepped the immaculately dressed Clinton, as his fans knew him, to sing their favourite songs whilst the stage behind was set for the sumptuous 'willow pattern plate' finale.

As his was the penultimate 'walk-down' ('Boy' and 'Girl' *always* come last in a panto walk-down) of a large cast he had time to do a quick change in the wings before he was due at the top of the steps under the blue and silver lovebirds on the 'willow pattern' backcloth.

It most certainly was a 'value for money' show. Besides Clinton and Billy's own 'spots' we also had a magical interlude from Benson and an aerial trapeze act by the Chinese policemen, aka the Sensational Skylons. The genie and the slave of the ring, alias Shari and Dahl, also got their Eastern adagio acrobatic act into the cave scene. 'Princess' Pat Jagger and Aladdin, Mimi Pearse, both had time for a solo each as well as their duets. There was not a lot for the emperor and the grand vizier to do really but it was good fun, a happy season and twelve pounds per week, once nightly with no 'digs' to pay – I was commuting next door to Wigan.

Chapter Thirteen

Next important stop? The Palace Theatre, Watford, and the start of my long association with Jimmy and Gilda Perry.

After panto in Bolton I had a week in Wigan with Father, who was by now finding it difficult to work because his arthritis was getting worse, as was his general health. Still a very independent gentleman he would not even consider early retirement. How would Pendlebury's exist without him was, I think, his sincere belief but they managed somehow two years later! Nor would he give up the three-bedroomed semi-detached with gardens back and front for something smaller and easier to manage. Any mention of a flat, a retirement apartment or sheltered accommodation merely provoked the angry retort, 'If you'd give up this daft acting lark or get married there would be someone to look after me!'

I was thirty-six years old, keen to get on, carrying, I believed, the goodwill and recommendation of every management for whom I'd ever worked.

I returned to London with a heavy heart and spent a couple of months when, I have to admit, I made little effort to find work while I tried to 'sort myself out' in my own comfortable little flat in London. 'Uncle' Eric had a few TV 'one-liners' and a day at Shepperton Studios saying, 'Mr Someone will see you now, sir' in some film whose name I have forgotten.

Then on my birthday in mid-April, I received a phone call which cheered me up and 'bounced me back to normal'. Ivan Butler, a playwright and former Court Players' director, was now resident director for Jimmy and Gilda Perry's weekly repertory company at the Palace Theatre, Watford. Through the organisation of the said Court Players, it appears, they had heard of me and of my work with them for a period of five years.

As usual on these occasions one was asked, 'And what are you doing now?' Sounds an innocent enough question, doesn't it? Not in this business, especially when asked by agents and managements! It can be 'loaded'. If you are working you are probably not free for what they have to offer. If you are not working, why not?

Carefully I explained that after a successful pantomime season 'up north' I'd done a couple of TV parts and a film. Well, I'd said, 'Mr Someone will see you now, sir,' hadn't I?

Mr Butler obviously knew his ex-Court Players well. He replied, 'So you're free at present?' He went on to say that he'd spoken to Gilda and Jimmy about me, the outcome being an invitation to appear at the Palace Theatre, Watford, for a week, in a comedy called *Hot and Cold in All Rooms* by the mysterious Max Reittmann again. Did anyone ever meet Max Reittmann, I wonder?

Again, it was a company of experienced actors, some of whom were 'regulars' and very popular with both audiences and management. I discovered that instead of going into Town and out to Watford by underground I could reach Watford on the North London British Rail lines from Highbury Corner rail and tube station. Some trains went through direct, others required one change at Willesden Junction. On the whole it was easier and usually less crowded than the morning underground journey. The last train from Watford at night was invariably a no-change train so there was no need to find digs in Watford.

I played Basil Clutterbuck in this very amusing little epic. At one point Basil is required to open a tin of baked beans. During 'plotting' Ivan said, 'Any ideas on this, Colin, as you're a Bean?'

'Not at this moment,' I replied, 'but give me time.'

'What does he mean?' said another member of the cast.

Ivan (bless him!) replied, 'Ladies and gentlemen, for those who haven't met him before, this is Colin Bean, a fellow ex-Court Player. I think we can leave the tin of beans in his hands – but for no more than half an hour. Colin, I've heard all about your improvised comedy "business" from Dougie Neill.'

Suffice to say, in performance, I managed to open the tin of beans in a matter of one and a half minutes in an escapade which took me from cupboard to table, flourishing the tin-opener, round the table, under the table and finally on top of the table until at last – in triumph – the tin was opened.

Jimmy and Gilda were not appearing in *Hot and Cold* but one or other would watch the dress rehearsal. I wonder if they thought, 'Oh my God! What have we got here?'

Anyway, I wasn't sacked. In fact I worked for them fairly continuously – odd breaks here and there – until the advent of *Dad's Army* in 1968, but 'Don't panic!' I'm not going to jump the gun. We'll stick with 1962 for the present.

My first stay at the Palace lasted until September, appearing in most of the productions, which included more Christie in the form of dear old *Towards Zero, Simple Spyman, The Big Killing*, the charming French frivolity, *Don't Listen Ladies*, in English of course, and an interesting revised version by Ivan Butler and the author of Clemence Dane's *A Bill of Divorcement, The Amorous Prawn* and, for me, a re-visit to *Saturday Night at the Crown* with June Garland as the irrepressible Ada and the role of Sally being played by a very talented young lady of whom I'd heard, but never met before, called Glenda Jackson.

Hay Fever, Doctor at Sea, George and Margaret and *The Man with a Load of Mischief* also figured in the season. Perhaps *Hocus Pocus* and *The Devil Was Sick* could now be left to their own devices; they weren't actually record breakers! One of my favourites was Thomas Swinley in Hugh and Margaret Williams' *The Happy Man*.

In his review of the play in the Watford weekly paper E.F.G. confesses that he/she ventured backstage to examine the drinks used in the play. 'I presume the bottle of whisky Colin Bean was drinking from in *The Happy Man* is the same bottle I tried. Cold tea. If it is, Colin Bean perpetrated one of the finest drunk scenes in a long time. If it is not and is the genuine article, then I must congratulate him on his ability to hold his drink.' Rest assured, it was indeed cold tea. 'Pte Sponge' hadn't even been thought of then!

After the colourful production Ivan directed of Ashley Duke's classic *The Man With a Load of Mischief* I went back to Cleethorpes for a week. Fear not, nobody else had been knocked out. As I was not cast for the next two Palace plays I was able to undertake an engagement for an old friend of mine. Tony Mayne had for the past few years compered fashion shows very successfully. Now he was to join – and eventually direct – the team of 'voice-over' artistes for the Wembley Christmas Ice Show. The Cleethorpes date – for three days – clashed with his starting on a very long season with *Round the World in 80 Days on Ice* and so I took over the first of two fashion shows which I was to do for the Cleethorpes co-op society.

My welcome back to Watford in October was a re-meeting with the most Polish pianist of all Polish pianists, Jan Letzarescou, in *Dear Charles* by Alan Melville, which I had played in Hastings After an affectionate and very well received revival of Wynyard Browne's *The Holly and the Ivy* we were in trouble! For the week of 29th October we presented a play called *Open Verdict*. The headline in that week's review? 'The Verdict: Unwise!'

Oh dear! After some credit for effort on the part of the actors the writer 'could almost sense their discouragement at the task ahead'. I won't embarrass the others with what was said about them, suffice it to quote the last line of the review. 'Leopold Wilkes: Ua-h! Bad luck, Colin Bean.' It cheers one up no end.

Thank goodness we were soon back into the 'good books' with *Young Wives Tale* and an elegant production of A.A. Milne's *The Dover Road*. In reviewing it the former columnist E.F.G. was to write at one point, 'The other couple were played by Colin Bean and Jill Simcox. Over them I have enthused so often that I fear I am becoming boring, but if I thought readers would take any more I'd do so again.' No, E.F.G. is not a relative of mine. To this day I still don't know what his or her name is.

Being near to London this was the sort of company where artists could and would be happy to appear in just one play or occasionally on a non-regular basis. Besides Ivan Butler, the other play director, who was a fine actor too, was Richard Dare. I have never met anyone who spoke of Richard with anything but kindness, affection and admiration. He, too, would occasionally 'pop off' to do the odd TV or radio show. He was, however, one of the mainstream elements of the company. It was also pleasing to have occasional visits, to play a variety of roles, from my dear friend, Derek Tobias, Although he wasn't with us for Richard's next production which reacquainted me, beard and all, with Black McDonald in *Johnny Belinda*. Belinda herself was played very sensitively by Hazel Burt and Jimmy Perry was Locky. This time, I'm happy to say, no real cockerels or goats on stage. Perhaps one or two members of the audience – considering themselves sophisticated – found parts of this melodramatic play somewhat amusing, the majority, however, seemed to appreciate this 'drop of drama' in full measure.

Mid-November, and this, it seemed, was the customary time for the Perrys to announce the subject and cast for their annual, highly acclaimed Palace pantomime. I held my breath. Would I, wouldn't I got my chance? I did. Jimmy and Gilda Parry gave me the opportunity to open up a new and greatly wished for direction in my career. With character actress, Adele Strong, I was to be an ugly sister. The sagacious planning and experience of Jimmy and Gilda cast me – as my first dame in my own right and not an understudy – with someone well experienced in playing an ugly sister. Adele and her by then retired husband, Tom, had been noted ugly sisters in *Cinderella* for many years. On the number of occasions I was invited to their home for tea and a chat I learned a great deal from these two about the art – because done properly it is an art, and hard work – of playing the dame.

The Perry pantomimes were very popular because they were 'book' pantomimes. They had a story and no twenty-minute gaps for a pop singer, a group or a troupe of trampolinists to do their own act. Most of the Palace regular rep players were in it and I got the impression that they all looked forward to it each year. Being my first 'proper dame' I was, at the start of rehearsals, apprehensive to begin with. Having taken a chance on me would the Perrys be happy with Dame Bean? I think they were because I was to do two more for them before they finally left the Palace and two more after that on their recommendation.

Performances twice daily and three times on Saturdays, with ten changes of costume meant that I was happily busy in this production. Adele's character was named Quinine and I was Chlorodine.

During the first week I realised that Adele, who was by no means as young as me, was gradually changing the emphasis of our roles. I was becoming the one to get the laughs while she took over the 'baddie' nature. For a couple of our own comedy routines she said, in private, 'You take over the comedy lead, darling. I'm finding it a bit tiring at my age with so many shows each week.'

With Richard as Baron de Pawn I was able to say, 'Well, I've been his son, his father, his nephew and his grandfather this season – but never his daughter before this!'

Among the smaller roles and on the list of stage management credits appeared the name of TV director, Pieter Morpurgo, an efficient assistant stage manager who had accompanied me in a number of police officer duos in the seasons of mystery or murder plays earlier in the year. Diana Dove and Karen Andrews were, respectively, the Prince and Cinders, with an equally dashing Diane Holland – later of *Hi-De-Hi* – as Dandini. Jimmy himself was the cheerful chappie Buttons, and Jill Simcox a very graceful and purposeful fairy godmother. Gilda Perry and Bill Smale were probably the craziest broker's men I have ever seen, certainly superior to 'Smash and Grab' in Bolton the year before and not a unicycle in sight! It was a very happy if exhausting three weeks.

Before the end of the season I was called 'into the office', i.e. the number one dressing room, to be given a pleasant shock. My work had been watched closely, it seemed. Jimmy and Gilda asked me if I'd like to play Widow Twankey in the next pantomime. I'm a bit heavy to 'jump for joy' but I think you've got some idea of how I received this invitation. Although it wouldn't be announced until the traditional time during the next season I could keep it under wraps that the next pantomime was to be *Aladdin*, one of my favourite pantomimes, so full of colour, characters and comedy opportunity.

Chapter Fourteen

The first week in March found me back at BBC TV playing an antique dealer whose shop had been burgled in an episode of *Z Cars* directed by Michael Leaston-Smith. By 18th March I was back at the Palace Theatre playing Richard Kinsale in Sir Peter Ustinov's intriguing play *Photo Finish*, and judging by the photo I've got, it was another 'nose and mutton chop whiskers' job. My theatre school training in stage make-up certainly made life in weekly rep interesting for me and my fellow cast members who, or so I'm told, were prone to say at dress rehearsals when we assembled in full costume and make-up for the first time each week, 'What on earth will he come as this week?'

Interest? Desperation? Boredom? I leave judgement to those who had to put up with it – and you.

Another quick trip to Cleethorpes to compere the spring fashion show, Tony being still tied up supplying the voices for Phinias Fogg and others at the Wembley Ice Show. The next play back in Watford, *Joy of Living*, might have been symptomatic of my attitude to my career at this time. It's a pity I've never heard of the play since. More Agatha Christie, *Alibi*, plays by R.C. Sheriff, *The Telescope*, and Martin Doyle's study in insanity, *Signpost to Murder*, which later I was to direct in Ayr.

After *The Seventh Veil* and *Miss Pell is Missing* I was missing from the Palace for a while as I headed back north of the border for my fourth season with The Graham Players at the delightful Civic Theatre, Ayr.

'Craigie Road on the Hayhill bus route' was a line added to our publicity at my suggestion, not because the good folk of the royal burgh didn't know they'd got a gem of a theatre but for the benefit of holidaymakers, of which Ayr entertained great numbers during the summer months. The choice, even in a resort which I don't think would call itself 'large', catered for all tastes in theatrical terms alone. There was the famous Gaiety Theatre with its world famous summer show, Popplewell's *Gaiety Whirl*, a revue show full of colour, music and invariably a top-star Scottish comedian. On the other side of the town, a bit 'off-centre' – hence the bus route direction – there was a now well-established repertory company with, in 1963, Victor Graham offering his sixth summer season. Both theatres changed their programmes weekly and, though different in nature of production, worked in an amicable relationship of cooperation and, at times, assistance.

To get the season under way, and to give us time to get organised practically and financially, we opened with a small cast play, André Roussin's *The Little Hut*. A charming, funny and colourful piece which gave plenty of work to Victor and myself as Henry and Philip with the season's new leading lady, Jill Tanner, making an instantaneous success in Ayr as Susan. As the rest of the company would not be joining us until rehearsals for *The Big Killing* started, my old pal Ron Stephen – he of the *Hasty Heart* in Japan – travelled over from Edinburgh daily to help us out in the small but essential part of the stranger.

Both Victor and I, and the audiences, loudly applauded 'a desert island somewhere in the South Seas, but you won't find it in an atlas' as created by our new scenic artist, Audrey Bellwood. She and the irrepressible, indestructible Tommy Faulds had a very healthy respect for each other and each other's work. That whole season saw some wonderful settings which made full use of our quite small stage. I don't think a week went by but both the local papers' theatre reviews commented favourably, and sometimes in unashamed admiration, on the staging of our wide selection of thirteen plays between June and September.

I had played Charles Barcher before in Watford so *The Big Killing* was my first production in the 'director's chair' for this season. The formula, roughly, was that Victor and I would direct alternate productions thus giving each of us more preparation time. We were both playing quite hefty roles each week, but that's weekly rep!

Plaintiff in a Pretty Hat led us on to *The Touch of Fear* by Dorothy and Campbell Christie in a truly amazing 'garden room' in Michael Stanhan's house, painstakingly produced by Audrey and Tommy. Being a seaside resort and a great favourite with day visitors during the 'Glasgow Fair', Ayr Civic opted for the sea for a couple of weeks with Leslie Sand's comedy *Beside the Seaside* and *Doctor at Sea* by Ted Willis.

'Two hours of nerve-tingling suspense at the Civic Theatre' was the press review headline for *Signpost to Murder*, another play I had met before and again I played Dr Forrest and enjoyed the challenge of directing this complicated 'mystery of twists and turns'. For our small stage the setting again was a technical, physical and artistic achievement which well merited the applause that greeted it as the tabs opened each night and warranted the gasps of surprise when the upstairs inner rooms lit up to be seen through what appeared, at first sight, to be ordinary painted 'beam and plaster' cottage scenery.

Who's Your Father? provided some light relief the next week as did the 'ghosty' comedy *The Poltergeist*. *Affairs of State* ran smartly and elegantly up to 31st August.

J.B. Priestley's works fascinate me to this day so imagine my delight when Victor said, 'I think *Dangerous Corner* is your cup of tea.' An added attraction(?) was that I was not appearing in it, thus I was able to enjoy directing without having to remember lines myself.

Private Lives and *Bell, Book and Candle* were the plays to wind up the season. Alas, I could not participate because of an urgent phone call from my downstairs-flat neighbour in London. Briefly, the person to whom I'd rented my flat, for a very very modest sum per week in exchange for 'house-minding' for me, had 'done a bunk'. For a couple of days, it seems, my front windows looked unusually dirty and were open quite widely at the top. A persistent odour of burnt wood finally persuaded them to go up to my floor where they found the doors closed but not locked. There appeared to have been a small fire, apparently originating in a wooden wastepaper bin which stood next to my teak fire-surround. The fire had been put out by means of water being thrown over it.

Victor insisted that I return to London, bless him. Derek Wright undertook what would have been my final 'direc-torship' of the season. I returned to start on the sad task of cleaning up my home. No sign of the lodger of course, no forwarding address and, when I searched my personal correspondence file, the two letters of reference, which had been brought in the first place, had been torn out. I know! I know! I should have checked them out before I went away. In hindsight one could say I fell victim to my own story's title, *Who Do You Think You Are Kidding!*

Word, fortunately, had reached the Palace, Watford, that I was back in town earlier than scheduled. I soon had Ivan Butler on the phone, inviting me to play in the Perrys' next production, a play by Dodie Smith called *Amateur Means Lover*. Not, perhaps, one of the great plays of the twentieth century but delightful enough and introductions and reintroductions to people who figure, and had figured, in my career: Michael Knowles (*You Rang M'Lord?*, *It Ain't*

Half Hot, Mum and a number of episodes of *Dad's Army*)
and his charming wife, Linda James; Mavis Pugh (*You Rang
M'Lord*) and husband John Clegg, (*It Ain't Half Hot, Mum*);
Diane Holland (*Hi-De-Hi*); and newcomer Alan Foss who
scored a considerable success as 'the actor, Courtney
Kemble'. I never worked with Alan again but we kept in
contact over the years until his untimely death, mainly
through our respective interest in and work for his Catholic
Stage Guild and my ACU organisations. We'd meet for a
drink and a chat in the Salisbury or the Green Man &
French Horn, in St Martin's Lane, or meet up with friends
Ray Mander and Joe Mitchenson to go to a show.

Come Blow Your Horn followed and allowed E.F.G. of
the Watford weekly newspaper to write, 'Colin Bean's quite
outlandish performance as the father was a delight.' I enjoy
being outlandish as much as I enjoy my 'opportunity to go
berserk', as was said in another write-up.

During the week of 24th September and Philip King's
How Are You Johnnie?, it was time to announce the subject
and cast of that year's Palace panto. At last I didn't need to
keep under wraps the knowledge I'd had since *Cinderella*. I
was to be Widow Twankey. Before getting into skirts and
eyelashes again, however, there were still plays to be
appeared in, ranging from Agatha Christie's *The Unexpected
Guest* – in which Linda and I caught E.F.G.'s particular
admiration because we were 'left alone on the stage with
the body for a good half-hour at the beginning, without
interruption to "rig" the murder. This I found completely
fascinating.'

R.C. Sheriff's *The Long Sunset* was an interesting expedi-
tion into England of AD 410 and the withdrawal of the
Roman occupation. A young Australian actor, Frank
McNamara, with whom I'd appeared at the Palace in a
number of plays, impressed me by his playing of Otho to

my 'rough diamond of a fighting man', to quote E.F.G., or King Arthur known simply then as Arthur.

Contrast Otho with his role as the eponymous Norman in Frank Harvey's play the following week and one had a fair idea of his range of characterisation. John Clegg was suitably mysterious as the fanatical house guest in *The Lodger*, with its all-pervading atmosphere of Victorian London, real gas jets and all! An outstanding performance by Gilda Perry as my wife, Ellen Bunting, added terrific intensity to this exciting and macabre play.

My presence was not required for a couple of plays so I got down to repairing fire damage and creating costumes, eyelashes, earrings and outrageous hats for Widow Twankey. Back on parade in mid-November for the 'company-let-their-hair-down' last play of this rep season – Philip King's *See How They Run* in which I escaped a lot of the very complicated comedy mayhem by popping in as the intruder. Linda, Gilda, Jimmy, Michael, John and myself were getting some practice in for the coming panto season which was to follow an excellent amateur production of *Rose Marie* by the Cassio Operatic Society. An operetta, one imagines, is difficult to put over nowadays since the Monty Python team got their hands upon the RCMP (Royal Canadian Mounted Police)!

After the pantomime full dress rehearsal on the 23rd December, a train from Watford Junction got me to Wigan in time to spend all of Christmas Eve and Christmas Day until the very early hours of the 26th with Father. (We had trains which ran at Christmas then!)

Before 2 a.m. on Boxing day I was en route for Watford Junction and was greeted by the ladies cleaning the theatre foyer, about 8 a.m., with hot tea and a bacon and egg sandwich.

The first of the day's three performances was at 2 p.m. so dresses hung in order of appearance, hats ditto and there was time for an hour's rest on a backstage prop sofa before everyone else began to arrive to open a show to which, I think I can honestly say, we were all looking forward with great pleasure. Rehearsals, under the direction of Jimmy and Gilda, besides being efficient and concentrated, had been great fun; the run of the play was to prove likewise.

Aladdin and Princess Badroulbador were Margaret McDonald and a young lady with a fantastic voice who looked and sang like an angel and was to find much wider fame later as *Hi-De-Hi*'s campers' friend, Gladys – Ruth Madoc. At the bottom of the cast list in the very colourful programme are '1st Guard', played by the stage manager, Bryn Ellis and '2nd Guard' by one Charles Mainwaring. One wonders if, even as early as this, James Perry was already conjuring up phrases such as 'Don't panic!', 'Permission to speak, sir?' and 'Do you think that's wise, sir?'

Michael Knowles and Chris Gannon provided lots of fun as 'Ping' and 'Pong', the policemen. Gilda played Wishie-Washie in her inimitable style – the children loved 'him' – and Jimmy was Abanazer in le grand style, i.e. very effectively way over the top in a manner everyone enjoyed, the rest of the cast in particular. John Clegg was an impressive Emperor with Bill Smale back for panto as the Grand Vizier – much funnier than I had been in the part a few years previously, but then I didn't have this very funny script.

Chapter Fifteen

In *Aladdin* I was able to use for the first time in pantomime – and subsequently on quite a number of occasions – a song which I'd been saving since I first heard it sung by Mr Lester Barratt in the York panto in theatre school days, an old Florrie Ford number called 'Has Anyone Seen My Pom?'

Now I don't know about other artistes who love pantomime but I find it galling when the introduction of the traditional audience participation is badly and crudely handled. Young TV personalities in panto for their first time, ignorant of how to play it will say, 'Oh, just get the kids screaming. That's all they want.'

I ask myself, 'Where's the enjoyment in having one's intelligence insulted in such a manner?'

It's also traditional, in response to the audience's first attempt to respond, to feign sadness and say, 'Oh, that wasn't very good!' or 'Oh, I'd never hear that!' Then some commit, to me, the unforgivable, 'I'll go off and come on stage again.' Oh dear, oh dear, and we've just spent all the scene trying to pretend the scene is set in Old Peekin'.

Sorry if I'm old-fashioned and upset the modernists and the politically correct but 'frankly, I couldn't give a damn'. Even worse are those who sing chorus songs about 'being in pantomime'. For heaven's sake! The audience aren't imbeciles, they know they're in a theatre but we're supposed to be creating magic here, not telling them that because they've paid seven and six or whatever they're stupid!

This is why my 'Pom song' – and the very similar descendants of it which I have written – satisfies my own awareness of tradition. Part of my storyline is that when I introduce Widow Twankey in Scene One I explain that I've just lost my little dog. 'Aaah! He's a little Pomeranian dog – I call him Pom-tiddly, because he is!'

Then I enlist the help of the audience to find him, the last line of the chorus being, 'Oh has anyone anyone, anyone seen / My Pom-tiddly-Om-Pom...' and without any prompting from me audiences have never failed to respond with a rousing, 'Pom Pom!' Throughout the pantomime on every entrance I 'look' for my dog, calling, 'Pom-tiddly-Om-Pom and from out there comes the reply 'Pom Pom!' And at the finale 'walk-down' there, in my arms, rests my little 'Pomeranian' – a stuffed pyjama case.

Two other songs of a similar nature come up later. 'How Are You Keeping? All right?' and 'Well Hallo There! Well Hallo!' Another panto *bête noire* is having too many catch phrases and audience responses. One pantomime in which I appeared – not my own, this would not have been allowed – five principals were scheduled to play for audience responses. They complained sometimes to the audience in an unorthodox manner of lack of reaction. I pointed out that there were too many principals requiring responses. By the time the poor audience had recalled what they were supposed to reply to a particular 'character' the moment and the spontaneity of the moment was lost. The comedian, who'd never done a panto before, insisted that as he was 'top of the bill' his catch phrase and response was the most important. For the sake of the audience, not for his benefit, I dropped my own 'response-seek' for the rest of the run. The other three refused to cut so confusion continued for the rest of the season, to a decree, and didn't make for a totally happy pantomime company, unlike Jimmy and Gilda's pantomimes which were very happy experiences for me.

We worked hard, I believe, because we enjoyed the show ourselves even if two daily performances and three on Saturday did keep one on the move. Pantomime is, of course, a complete contradiction by tradition, women playing men's roles and vice versa. Thus it may come as no surprise to find that despite my little 'soapbox sermon' about playing this type of show another fairly old tradition is that of the 'last-night gag'.

In many panto companies strict instructions have been handed down to the cast by the management that, merely because this was the final performance of the panto, no variations or departures from the script and direction would be tolerated. 'Please remember, this audience has paid as much for their seats as audiences on any other night.' A strict reminder indeed! But, oh dear, how often have 'little mistakes' crept in, for years and years, until now, I think, the patrons expect the final performance to be 'different'. Over a long period of time this has developed into a trend similar to that in a long season of repertory or touring show – the 'company-let-their-hair-down' syndrome.

At the Palace, Watford, the then theatre manager and old friend, Frank Godfrey, could assure us that for most Palace regulars, the final performance was probably their second visit to the show, usually this time without the smaller children.

By the time I did *Cinderella* for them the Perrys had that last day of the season well organised. Between the end of the 5 p.m. and the beginning of the 8 p.m. performances the principals would be invited to sit in the stalls to watch the juvenile dancers present their version of the pantomime and their own playing of the principal roles. Quite a revelation, believe me. Apparently when playing dame I tend to wag a disapproving digit quite frequently known in some circles as 'the Bean finger'. The little girl playing my part had, so I'm told, observed me very closely during the run of the show. Even my noted long 'dame eyelashes' were so beautifully exaggerated that the dear thing could hardly see anything and kept bumping – on purpose – into the others. The young lady playing Adele's role of the ugly sister spent her time walking across the stage with a cup in her hand saying, 'You carry on. I'm going for a cuppa and a lie down.' Yes, even the young dancers had noticed the change in emphasis of the playing of those roles.

In 1964, some of the dancers in *Aladdin* having been in *Cinderella*, the juvenile interpretation of the dame was even more acutely observed and had me in fits of laughter. Talk about 'out of the mouths of babes...'

After the juveniles' half-hour version, which we thoroughly enjoyed, it was the 'half-hour' before the final performance, and one or two furtive 'looking over the shoulder' movements in and around backstage by various members of cast and staff. In the previous year's *Cinderella* we had, of course, the inevitable football boot left on the ballroom staircase, because 'nobody can find the glass slipper' it was alleged. The Prince and Dandini in their 'change of status' scene decided, for once, not to exchange coats, hats and the princely sash of office, to the complete confusion of the rest of the cast and the amusement of the audience who were, of course, in on the joke. When Gilda tried to sing 'Take a Pair of Sparkling Eyes' in the singing competition scene a huge cut-out of blue, glitter-studded spectacle frames – now well worthy of Dame Edna – suddenly appeared, hovering over her head.

The final performance of *Aladdin* is one I shall certainly remember for ever. First let me explain a point about 'last-night gags' in Jimmy and Gilda's pantomimes. As I said earlier, we were well aware of the fact that the audience for the 'last night' third performance were, in the main, friends of the theatre, most of whom had already seen the show. Everyone in the cast, and each technical department were allowed just one gag. One was required to 'clear' one's gag with Jimmy and Gilda, in confidence.

Rightly they were proud (and careful) of the fine reputation and respect their years of running the Palace had built up. Anything offensive, distasteful or not quite obvious to the audience was definitely 'out'. I concur by reiterating my own firm and strongly held belief that 'in' jokes on the stage may amuse fellow actors (or annoy them) but are very unfair, if incomprehensible, to an audience who has paid good money to see the show.

But what if your idea for a 'gag' involved either Gilda or Jimmy? A natural question, and in that case you 'cleared' your idea with the one who was not involved. It was fun for all in the pantomimes I did with the Perrys – I'd another to come in December, 1965 – but I could well imagine it would be woe betide anyone who didn't stick to the rules!

Thus the 8 p.m. performance on the 18th January, 1964, got under way. My own 'gag' had been in the opening 'behind-a-gauze' tableau, held while Abanazer (Jimmy) did the prologue. Instead of our normal pose of Widow Twankey holding up a reproving digit to Wishee-Washee I sat upon a stool with Wishee on my knee, putting a large 'comforter' (a dummy) in Gilda's mouth while Wishee mimed a yelling baby. Maybe not the greatest gag but it made Abanazer a little amusingly uneasy in his dramatic monologue.

Once into the opening and I was an early victim. After my spectacular first entrance, flying in on a centre fly-rope (Yes, the line *was* 'I've just come in on the Central Line!') I came down to the floats for the traditional dame introductory chat before launching into the saga of my lost Pom. At the point on widowhood – 'Yes, I'm a widow, own hair, own teeth, own knife and fork, if any handsome young man is interested' – four gentlemen (hadn't time to see just who) in raincoats and slouch hats rushed up to me from the wings crying, 'I'm interested! I'm interested!' They then picked me up, bodily (no wonder it needed four!), turned me round, carried me upstage to the backcloth of the scenery, plonked me down on my backside on the floor – and left me there! When I recovered and got back to the front and the script all I could think of as an ad lib was, 'Talk about getting carried away!'

The first 'big scene' or full-stage set in a pantomime is often referred to as the plot-setting scene and thus is invariably a bit longer than the others. All the characters have to be introduced and explained, dancers, singers and juvenile dancers all have their 'bits' to do. At the end of the scene in this production all the characters and villagers, guards and peddlers are all on stage – a build-up to the Scene One closing musical number. Abanazer suddenly appears and fiendishly puts a curse on all except Aladdin. We are all frozen into immobility while Aladdin's wicked uncle entices our hero away with a tale about an old lamp and untold riches. As they exit Abanazer snaps his fingers and gives a fiendish laugh. Right from the first rehearsal, when Jimmy allowed me to add the line, I blinked at the audience and yelled, 'Oo, who put the lights out?'

At this point, in this performance, the swiftest, smoothest and quietist set-strike I've ever witnessed occurred. As I said my line the lighting designer and effects operator, Penelope Charteris, in working bib and brace overalls, with a large coil of electrical cable over her shoulder (so that nobody could doubt who she was) appeared downstage left and shouted, 'Well, it wasn't us!'.

She immediately blew a very shrill whistle and (taking a line from Miriam Karlin in a popular TV show) ordered 'Everybody out!' Simultaneously the backcloth, overhead scenic borders and book-wing pieces which had depicted Dorning Hibbert's lovely, traditional 'Old Peek-ing', all literally 'shot out of sight'. Principals and chorus were left on a totally bare stage – right up to the bare brick back wall of the theatre – upon which to try to sing our Scene One final chorus. The audience roared with laughter and applause.

Sidney Crooke (piano), Maurice Bromley (organ) and Mike Pullen (drums) must have been taken aback too for the accompaniment stopped and three heads appeared up from the orchestra pit to find out the cause of the uproar. Mercifully a kind stage management (for this was their 'gag') lowered in the next frontcloth scene, once this huge joke had been appreciated, as we hysterically tried to carry on with our rousing chorus, unaccompanied and in complete chaos. Who thought it up? How and when did they – the stage crew rehearse this instantaneous strike? Someone must have noticed. This was one very well-kept secret.

In the Twankey's Laundry scene, Grand Vizier Bill Smales – sounding suspiciously like Peter Sellers' Indian doctor – came to collect the emperor's laundry from my Twankey 'super-duper-dipper' machine which was supposed to eject clean, dry clothes as and when required. When Bill usually said, 'There's a sock missing,' he looked into the machine and out flew a solitary red sock, which matched no other in his washload. This night, as he looked into the machine, he got a large and very wet handtowel right across his mouth. Somewhere, at one point, someone (I forget who) in the middle of a scene or duet, was handed a telephone handset as he or she came near to a wing flat. The natural reaction is, of course, to hold it to ear and mouth and say, 'Hello'. Tonight this was answered by a cloud of (I found out later) talcum powder. The scene carried on with our white-faced clown character, all of which, of course, the audience could see and appreciate.

The last performance overran of course. In the 'haunted bedroom' Gilda (Wishee) and I (Twankey) assumed we wouldn't get through it without something happening – at least a collapsing bed. In the final ghost chase – we'd done the ghost gag earlier in the scene – we found that we had run out of pillows with which to bop these ghosts on the head as they appeared through the revolving wall panel. We'd one ghost too many and no pillows left! Pulling off the ghost sheet, lo and behold there was our friend and front of house theatre manager, Frank Godfrey.

The ladies who helped in the auditorium had their moment when, as in a cinema, with trays and torches, they came round with ice creams right in the middle of a love duet, letting the customers know what was on sale in the customary manner.

By 10.45 p.m. a truly enjoyable pantomime season, a good show with a lovely company, was over. I know I felt sad over a post-show drink we all enjoyed before going our various ways. I would have been even more upset had I realised that in two weeks' time I was to learn of the untimely and sudden death of Richard Dare, a rare talent indeed, snatched away at only forty-one years of age.

Chapter Sixteen

There now followed a long period of 'resting', not even a TV or a film walk-on came my way. For some reason the general view seemed to be, 'It's dead everywhere.' From 18th January to 9th March absolutely nothing and the bank manager's letters were becoming less cordial! Again, the formula of 'knowing someone' came to the rescue as one evening a phone call from ex-Court Players colleague, Harry Bowers, set me off on an enjoyable, if at first daunting, adventure which was to last until 4th December, 1965.

By now Harry had changed direction in his career and, despite being one of the best light-comedy actors with whom I had ever worked, was now a stage manager. An even bigger surprise was the fact that he was stage manager with the then current show at the Theatre Royal, Drury Lane, *The Boys From Syracuse*. He phoned to tell me about auditions taking place there for a number one tour of the great musical, *My Fair Lady*.

The production which had played at 'the Lane' was going out on tour but H.M. Tennent Ltd had decided to mount a second national company of the show – new sets, new costumes and new company. The stars of this production were to be Tony Britton as Professor Higgins, Jill Martin as Eliza and Bert Brownbill as Doolittle – full chorus and orchestra as in the original and Herman Levin's original direction of the show to be recreated by Honor Blair.

Harry had learned that there was a slight problem, in that with rehearsals due to start in a few days' time the role of understudy to Alfred P. Doolittle – who would also play three small roles in the show when not 'Doolittling' – was still unfilled. With a quick revision of 'With a Little Bit of Luck' and 'Get Me to the Church' from my cover version (Woolworth's Embassy Records) I was at the stage door of that famous old theatre at 9.30 the next morning, Harry having suggested my name to the company manager.

In the past I had been to see shows there but to stand on that great stage and peer out into the vast auditorium was, one could say, 'quite something'. The rehearsal pianist asked for my music. I said I hadn't got any. She said, 'Fine. You start. I'll pick up from you.' I asked which song I should do. She said, 'Whatever you like as long as we get an understudy for Doolittle. We've heard some awful people.'

I thought to myself. 'Oh, we are making a good impression, aren't we?'

On such a stage the distance to the centre seems like walking to eternity. Out there – somewhere in the darkness – a female voice said, 'Good morning, would you like to start?'

This was it! No messing, straight into 'With a Little Bit of Luck', my naive thinking being, 'What the hell! I'll probably need all the luck I can muster!'

I got as far as 'the Lord above...' of the first line when the pianist 'picked me up'. When we got to the end of one verse a male voice – from 'out there' – cried, 'Well, that's one version. Try "Get me to the Church".'

The pianist looked 'out there' and said to whoever it was directed, 'Perfect C pitch!'

With the next number I got two verses out before I became aware of people coming down the centre aisle saying, 'Thank you, Mr (a look at the clipboard) Bean!'

The pianist interposed, 'Perfect G pitch that time!'

I was asked to phone the office of H.M. Tennent after 2.30 p.m. As I went off stage in something of a haze I got a thumbs up and that infectious grin of his from Harry who'd been in the stage management corner, ostensibly doing a report on the previous night's performance. I can't remember now whether we went across the road for a drink – he had a matinée that day so couldn't go far away but I went on to the Salisbury and phoned from there at 2.35 to be told I'd got the job, contract in the post, start Monday 10 a.m. at Drury Lane. The tour was to start with five months in Bristol, at the previously unheard of salary, for a long-term job, of thirty pounds per week, eight performances per week, one-eighth extra for more than eight per week.

Rehearsals in various rooms and on stage at Drury Lane were fascinating. For the first few days those of us who had never worked there before had a tendency to get lost occasionally. One or two of our singers and dancers had been in the original Drury Lane production and been assigned to this new production because they had been 'leaders' or understudies before. Invariably Ruth Walters or Bob Crane had to come on a 'search' to guide us to where we should be. The size of the stage may be imagined when I tell you that, before leaving for Bristol, we were able to have a full set and costume rehearsal on the Drury Lane stage behind the set for *Boys From Syracuse* which itself was not actually small.

The summer of 1964 was to be a glorious summer. Our first night at the lovely Bristol Hippodrome went well, understudy rehearsals got under way and, despite being such a large company – 'Cast of over sixty, full chorus and augmented orchestra' – for the most part we all got on well together as we got to know each other. As summer approached we even had rehearsals with the famous

Hippodrome sliding roof open and the auditorium bathed in sunshine.

Father was persuaded to come down for a week's holiday and stayed for two. He was amazed to find that so many daytime rehearsals took place and watching the ballet master, Lionel Luyt, put the dancers through their limbering sessions and hearing the singers doing warm-ups certainly changed a few of his previously held ideas about theatre people. The company manager allowed him to sneak in at the back of the stalls one morning to an understudy call and when we all went up for lunch he avowed we 'trained like athletes'.

This became a very friendly and sociable company. By now Tony Britton (a Lords Taverner) and the properties master, Nigel Fernihough, had formed 'the M.F.L. Cricket XI', in support of which assistant stage manager, Sandra Ireland, and I started up a supporters' club called the 'Doolittle Club', complete with its own stage door noticeboard illustrated news-sheet, membership badge and so forth. Together we all enjoyed many off-duty outings and social events. And we managed to raise quite a bit of money for charities such as Mencap as we did it.

At the cricket matches we attended Father was, of course, much more in his element. Until he died he treasured an affectionately signed picture taken of himself with Tony, in cricket whites, and 'Eliza', the very pretty Jill Martin. As one may read in *The Doolittle Gazette*, it was with great regret that we left what had been a most enjoyable stay in Bristol. Whether or not it is still there I don't know but the Grapes, opposite the Hippodrome stage door, was presented with an illuminated certificate before we left, nominating it as the Doolittle Club's Bristol HQ. (The one in Ma Egerton's in Liverpool is still there, but Liverpool is a long way off yet.)

Now it was time to head for Birmingham to open on 17th August for a stay at the Hippodrome where, as the posters later screamed at passers-by, 'It's now *My Fab Lady* – extended until 20th February. So we all knew where we'd be for Christmas that year!

Brum is a big place so finding digs was not easy and, in 1964, I feel sure some of the worthy citizens of that city had not sorted out the layouts of some of the pedestrian underpasses and overpasses, shopping malls and so forth. There is a note in the first Birmingham issue of the *Doolittle Gazette* which says, 'One of the younger members of the company went shopping on Monday last in the Bull Ring. Her next of kin have been informed.'

Birmingham found us enjoying a couple of late-season charity cricket matches and lots of off-stage sociable activities both charitable and pleasurable. Visits to watch cars being built in Longbridge, chocolates being made in Bournville, aqua-suits being tried out at the *Birmingham Post* Boat and Holiday Show and a cathedral-packed Christmas concert in aid of the *Birmingham Mail* Christmas tree fund. This concert, arranged by Tony and conducted by our MD, Jan Cervenka, involved most of the cast in readings and choral solos and ensembles. According to the Bishop of Birmingham it wasn't so much a concert as a 'wonderful experience'. Friends from TV's *Crossroads* and the other Birmingham theatres were there in good time to get seats at the front and to express congratulations afterwards.

During the Birmingham season I was able to arrange a weekend visit home and present my old school, Wigan Grammar School, with a Theatre Trophy in celebration of the Shakespeare quatercentenary. This was awarded annually during a school theatre production until the sad demise of that worthy, ancient seat of learning (founded 1597).

Alas, unlike the school song, 'And for three hundred years and more / the school all storms has faced', it didn't weather the storm of so-called educational reorganisation. It became 'reprehensive' and, trophies and suchlike apparently being frowned upon and not 'politically correct', were to be disposed of. The Theatre Trophy was rescued, at a much later date, and is now in the custody of the prestigious Wigan Little Theatre, of which I have the honour to be a Life – and very early – member.

The month of March was the time to move on again, further north, to the great city of Liverpool. Having attended so many performances at the theatre when young it was now very exciting for me to tread the boards of the vast Empire Theatre stage for five months. A major change for the company was the departure of Jill, to bring forth a sibling for little Karensa. Jill's understudy, Wendy Bowman, succeeded to the role of 'Eliza' so Rosemary Lyford became my new 'Eliza' at understudy rehearsals each Thursday morning.

Cricket and other social and charity events proceeded with an eagerness and Company support which, a Liverpool newspaper commented, was certainly unusual in theatrical touring companies of its experience. Highlights? A Sunday match versus Liverpool City Police, in aid of Mencap and other charities, at Lewis' Sports Ground in Aigburth. 'Grand Charity Match. Enormous Doolittle Club Prize Raffle: Over 50 Prizes! First ball of the match to be bowled by Mrs Bessie Braddock MP.'

Thank goodness that wonderful lady's constituency secretary saw this advertised in the *Liverpool Echo* because the officials who had undertaken to organise invitations to Mrs B. and the Lord Mayor of Liverpool forgot to fulfil their duties. The Lord Mayor, alas, had already a prior engagement. Mrs Braddock, however, was on the phone to the Empire on the Saturday night. Instead of being annoyed or even angry (one remembers how resounding 'Battling Bessie' could be in Parliament) she affirmed that she would be there and also that she was now going to phone 'the nationals' to highlight Mencap and the other charities we were supporting.

Dawned the day, Sunday, 16th May, 1965, and we organisers were about our 'organising': tents, prizes, refreshments, tickets and the one hundred and one other requirements before we even got round to cricket. Due to bowl the first ball at 11.30 a.m., Mrs Braddock with husband, Bill, and entourage appeared at 10.30 a.m. wishing to know what she could do to help. As some press representatives had now appeared on the scene and our eleven were 'in their whites', Mrs B. led everyone out onto the pitch where she insisted on donning cricket pads and gloves and with Tony as wicketkeeper, plus other cast members of the team around, gave the photographers a series of aggressive cricketing poses which made most of the daily papers next day.

The *Liverpool Echo* became even more interested in this 'M.F.L.' which seemed to be so unlike any other company. Long feature articles about the Doolittle Club and our other charity efforts appeared on Friday and Saturday the 14th and 15th of May. This publicity helped tremendously with subsequent efforts to support good causes. A letter on House of Commons notepaper – and written in her characteristic red ink – from Mrs Braddock graced the theatre noticeboard and the *Doolittle Gazette*. There we had proof for all to see that she had enjoyed her 'day out' with us.

Another of 'this crazy company' occasions was when we learned that the Liverpool Everyman Theatre was, to say the least, having problems. The Doolittle Club, and other company members, organised and performed in a one-performance-only production called *Everyman's Theatre*, given on the afternoon of Sunday 13th June in the Everyman Theatre. The company dancers and singers in particular seemed to enjoy an opportunity to practise their other skills and talents in short plays and sketches. Whether we did actually help the Everyman in its difficult time I don't know but it was an experience to meet and cooperate with such a keen and dedicated young Everyman company as Terry Hands, Peter James, Michael Freeman, Susan Fleetwood, Karin MacCarthty, Sarah Rivington, David Bailie, Paul McConnochie and Bruce Myers plus visiting friend and cabaret artiste, Dennis Burrows. The 'M.F.L.' musical director, Jan Cervenka, gallantly accompanied at the grand piano throughout the almost two and a half hour performance, yours truly arranging, directing and appearing in the show. The party we held after the show was quite something and, because our effort had had the blessing and full-hearted support of H.M. Tennent Ltd, once again the 'M.F.L.' National Tour Co. made most of the national dailies.

Time to hit the road again came in July; a strange move for a company whose official appellation was the Southern National M.F.L. Co. because we went further north! In the 'romantic' headline of the *Doolittle Gazette* we moved from 'Coast to Coast' – or was it 'One Great Seaport to Another?'

'M.F.L.' was indeed a big production. Striking, moving and resetting took a few days, time for the cast to head off to their homes for a break. I managed three days in my flat in London before heading back to Wigan to spend a couple of days with my father and to give him the good news that his 'favourite' show was off to the land of his birth, Tyneside – the Theatre Royal, Newcastle Upon Tyne, to be precise. For father this was 'something like a theatre!' And it was in 'God's Country'. A holiday would most certainly be on the cards because we had family relatives there. Father and my late mother both claimed the banks of the Tyne as their birthplace. Dunston for mother, Wylam for father. Was I ever forgiven, I wonder, for being late on my very first entrance onto the stage of life and not appearing until after they'd arrived in Wigan in 1926?

'A foreign land, hinny. A foreign land.' I can hear him now, describing his first impressions of Lancashire.

Chapter Seventeen

During the break between Liverpool and Newcastle, a few days at home in London and a call from Jimmy Perry settled the rest of the year for me. After all the usual enquiries such as 'How's it going?' Jimmy asked for how long I intended to stay in *My Fair Lady*. 'Hello! Hello!' I thought, 'Something in the wind? Do I sniff the scent of new interest?'

Now, as the saying goes, 'on the grapevine' it was thought that the Newcastle date could be the last of the long-stay dates as the next date, Oxford, was for four weeks only and with some even shorter 'return' dates – Bristol and Birmingham – to follow. We were due in Oxford in November (we were now in early July) by which time the show would have been on tour for almost two years. I had a feeling that by then I would, perhaps, have had enough, enjoyable though the show was.

The outcome of all this cogitation? Jimmy and Gilda were about to start work on the script for this year's Palace panto *Babes in the Wood*. As the theatre itself had now been taken over by the Watford Civic Theatre Trust Ltd, this, their tenth Palace panto, would be their last. Before writing the show they wanted to know if I would play the dame for them again. Eager to expand my career in that line I said, 'Yes, please'.

The Perrys had given me my first opportunity to play a dame in my own right and my last appearance with them had been in that colourful and popular production of

Aladdin. I notified the H.M. Tennent head office that I wished to leave *My Fair Lady* during the second week of the Oxford stay in November, thus giving them ample time to find a replacement. I'm happy to report that they were kind enough to send me a letter of understanding and appreciation that I had given them plenty of notice. I remember that early in the tour a singer had departed suddenly without warning, because he was 'fed up', causing the hiatus of sudden rearrangement of parts of the show which concerned him. Needless to say neither H.M. Tennent nor British Actors' Equity were at all pleased with the said artiste. I doubt he ever worked for H.M. Tennent again!

With all this arranged it was now time to head north to – according to Father – 'The finest city in the world'. (I have relatives there still so I make no comment on Father's views!)

After the usual period of rehearsal and two 'as per' full dress rehearsals the show opened to a packed house on Saturday 10th July. Why open on a Saturday? Because at each new venue it took almost a week to move the large, complicated sets, the two-revolve stage and the special lighting. Not to mention the Newcastle musicians who were to augment the basic touring musical staff. The theatre's own backstage staff and lighting staff all had to familiarise themselves with a fairly long and far from easy to operate show. Besides trying out entrances, exits and access on and off stage, usually in a blackout or, at most, working lights, we artistes had to familiarise ourselves with a new location of dressing rooms, staircases and toilets and so forth. All this takes time if the show is to open as the *Newcastle Sunday Sun* of the 11th July was to headline: 'Happy audience joins in chorus as *My Fair Lady* glitters at Royal'.

Another important job for the members of the cast was to get to know our new dressers. 'John Public' will often pooh-pooh the mention of dressers as 'sheer affectation and supercilious nonsense' – believe me, dear 'John', a dresser who doesn't know what he or she is doing spells disaster. I speak from experience, both as a dresser in the past and having suffered a critical hiatus because of a dresser's inattention to the job in hand in a future production. We'll come to that in time – I nearly wrote 'in good time' but on reflection there was nothing 'good' about it, believe me!

My Fair Lady had kept its reputation for its magnificent appearance ever since it opened because of careful, meticulous and detailed staff work. For instance, one hazard, which could be located in a different place in each theatre visited, was the Tent. This was a carpeted, canvas-covered corridor, rather like an open-ended marquee, in which all the ladies' fabulous, Cecil Beaton-designed, Ascot scene and embassy ball scene dresses, hats, shoes and gloves were stored, under wraps, on hanger-racks and shelves. Although the gentlemen's costumes were in their dressing rooms the rules were equally strict and heaven help anyone who broke said rules.

In Ascot or Embassy costume an artiste must not sit down, unless required to do so on stage in the action of the play, or take drinks or confectionery of any kind. The wardrobe mistress, the fabled 'Watty', and her staff examined every costume, hat, shoe and glove every day. For each performance the gentlemen had clean, white formal shirts. The ladies' costumes were brushed carefully and hung up after the scene and woe betide anyone who had a mark which should not be there!

There were many quite dazzling scenes in this 'glittering' production and it was largely due to such dedicated work by wardrobe and scenic staff that the sudden blaze of white light onto the 'living tapestry' of the opening of the Ascot scene never once missed its instantaneous roar of spontaneous applause. I may add that 'we artistes' also 'had our work cut out'. The stiff, stylised and exaggerated movements and singing of the 'Ascot Gavotte' with a long scene to follow were quite difficult to sustain. As Lord Boxington I had to sit on a banquette in a very straight-backed, nose in the air pose holding a cup and saucer up in the air, and cope with silver-topped walking stick and grey gloves for some time before I could move when the cues came for my few lines. Having had to change make-up as well as costume from a 'gorblimey cockney' to aristocracy, one then needed to change back again for Act Two. And were we ready for an interval by then!

In August it was announced on the noticeboard (next to the *Doolittle Gazette*) that from 25th September until 9th October the part of Alfred P. Doolittle would be played by yours truly. Bert Brownbill was the only principal artiste who hadn't had a break since we opened in April 1964. H.M. Tennent Ltd (so I was told) finally persuaded him, apparently somewhat against his own wishes, to take a break before I left the company. The second understudy, so it seemed, was in the 'emergency' category.

For the week previous to Bert's holiday daily rehearsals of the Doolittle scenes were the order of the day, initially with the other principals' understudies, Rosemary, John and Gavin, and then a dress rehearsal with Wendy, Tony and Patrick.

After this final DR the company manager came to number three dressing room – Mr Brownbill's – as I changed out of my own 'Doolittle' wedding suit. Number one understudies did not, of course, have to wear the costumes worn by the principal – duplicate outfits were made in my own size. From the look on his face I thought, 'Oh dear!'

'Miss Blair [Honor Blair, our production's director] has had to rush off to catch her train back to London to report to head office,' he said. Pause. 'I'm to tell you that you are no longer understudy "Doolittle".' My heart plummeted.

'You are now to be classed as "deputy Doolittle" and will be announced as such.' I don't think I quite took all this in at the time.

Across the road from the stage door was a very congenial pub – trust M.F.L. to find good pubs! At lunchtime this hostelry had on offer the most delicious boiled ham and pease pudding barm cakes. Two of them and a bottle of Newcastle Brown and, believe me, dear reader, one had had a banquet. Any road up – as we tend to comment in the posher parts of Wigan – whilst imbibing with my regular cronies the significance of what the company manager had said became clear. Thus, when I took over on the Monday of the next week, the audiences didn't find that disappointing slip of paper in the very 'swish' programme or a small postcard in the box office window to announce the usual 'At this performance the role of Alfred P. Doolittle will be played by…' Oh dear me no. Outside the theatre, for my two weeks, the large posters had an almost indistinguishable sticker over Bert Brownbill's name and the title page and cast list of the programme had been reprinted and there I was! My name, along with Tony Britton's, above the title of the show! So that, I discovered, was what being made 'deputy Doolittle' meant.

When I got into number three room, Bert's dresser was there to say, 'Mr Brownbill's left a message for you under the table.' Under the table? You may well ask. A crate of twelve bottles of Newcastle Brown ale (very much Alfred P., I think you'll agree) and a card which said, 'Well done, lad. Keep up the good work! "Brownie" [his wife] and I slipped into rehearsal on Saturday: hope I'm still in the part when I get back. Enjoy it. Best of luck, Bert and "Brownie".'

All the other principals and the musical director visited me (Tony gave me a bottle of Bristol Cream – 'for the throat') and I trembled with first-night nerves as I don't think I'd ever trembled before. In the wings all the dancers and singers wished me well. Some were even kind enough to say they'd enjoyed rehearsing with me. Now that *is* some compliment, especially from those who had been in the Drury Lane production and with the show ever since then.

At the age of thirty-nine I suppose I must have been 'in pretty good nick' healthwise for nowadays my next shock would give me heart failure. On cue, in Scene Two, I 'fell' out of the pub with Harry (my own understudy Don Lawrence) and Jamie to lead up to 'With a Little Bit of Luck'. As I approached the floats musical director, Jan Cervenka gave me a big smile and a discreet 'thumbs up' (and a long introductory note – 'just to get you in on the beat') and then it happened. I saw them! There, in the house seats (about three rows back in the stalls), my Uncle Bill, two aunts and a cousin and my father! I've never known how a feather could possibly knock down someone of my size and weight but I certainly know now what the expression 'knees like jelly' means.

I realise all this has taken some time to recount but, of course, it all happened in an instant and away we went with 'The Lord gave man an arm of iron' (in C). I was hoping the Lord above would give me 'a little bit of luck' and would stay with me. Believe me, I am very proud of a signed photograph I have of Tony Britton, given to me before I left the company in November, which has the inscription 'Best Wishes to a Great Doolittle' above 'Tony' and after 'To Colin'.

Chapter Eighteen

Father knew, of course, the period for which I'd be at the Theatre Royal. If I didn't get a chance during any week, Sunday midday was reserved to have a phone chat with him no matter where I was. By now his arthritis was very severe but, determined man that he was, he still managed to get himself around the house unaided. He made sure he had the phone near to hand every Sunday at lunchtime.

From his previous visits to Bristol, Birmingham and Liverpool he knew and was known to most of the company. Knowing just when I was to play Doolittle he must have contacted his brother-in-law, Uncle Bill, and made his own arrangements afterwards. I learned later that, once it was arranged, he'd then phoned the company manager, Tom Elliott, a fellow cricket 'M.F.L. Eleven' fanatic. The result of all this scheming you now know.

After my first performance an assistant stage manager brought a message that Father and aunts and uncle would meet me in the foyer. Whilst the relations were, happily, 'over the moon' (and not just about their nephew; they hadn't seen the show before) Father's comment was his usual, 'Not bad. Not quite as good as Bert, though'. Fat chance of getting a fat head with my somewhat taciturn parent!

By 12th November the dreaming spires were set to be graced by the *Fair Lady* and Co., with yours truly in his original roles of Selsey Man, Harry and Lord Boxington. The 1st December saw the last issue of the *Doolittle Gazette* and by the 4th my own understudy had taken over the roles plus carrying on as a chorus singer. Bert would be 'covered' by someone to be decided if and when necessary and I was on my way back to London to get ready for *Babes in the Wood* with Colin Bean ('recently in a record-breaking tour in *My Fair Lady*') as Nurse Daisy Dogood. Get the analogy? 'Doolittle, Dogood' – oh the subtlety! Blame Jimmy and Gilda!

Another spectacular fun-and-music-packed Perry panto. As usual, a 'book' show – no speciality acts or twenty-minute 'pop star spots'. All story and comedy with a Part One finale of what appeared to be a whole phalanx of knights in armour giving a glorious rendition – courtesy of the gentlemen of the Watford Choral Society – of 'Rose of England'. No, I'm not going to give away Jimmy and Gilda's secret of how we 'filled the stage with knights'. Let's just say it was very impressive and ensured a storm of applause to bring the curtain down for the interval.

Jimmy himself was a great Sheriff of Nottingham and Gilda again treated us to her irrepressible, irresistible 'perky little boy' character, this time as Cuddles 007 (ex-court jester and secret agent!). Friends Michael Knowles and his charming wife, Linda James, were there as Little John and Maid Marian. Director/actor Bill Redmond enjoyed himself as Friar Tuck and the lovely Diana Landor was Robin Hood. An inspired comedy teaming by the Perrys brought us the antics of Chris Gannon and Peter Birch as the Sheriff's henchmen, Titchy Fred and Slimy Sid. There were more friends in the orchestra pit, all very talented musicians in their own rights: musical director and organist Esme Hand; playwright, actor and cabaret star Hugh Hastings on piano (and in later years to turn up with me in the Walmington-on-Sea Home Guard); and the multi-talented Mike Pullen was 'amongst the pots and pans in the kitchen' as the percussion department is often so rudely referred to.

The song which I had written, 'How Are You Keeping – All Right?', made its first of many pantomime appearances and I'm happy to say that the 'audience response factor' soon caught on. When out in Watford High Street, shopping or coming from the station, people who'd obviously seen the show would shout across the road to me, 'Colin, how are you keeping – all right?'

The nursery scene included my battle with a bookcase which would persist in coming away from the wall as I tried to climb up the shelves to get the babes' teddy bear from the top of it. Not easy, either for me or the six strong blokes behind the scene who took the weight on ropes to pull the bookcase up to the wall again with me hanging onto it, red bloomers and striped stockings (yes, you've guessed, 'I've got another pair like this at home'), one red and white and one blue and white stripe on view for all to got a good look. It was a great and enjoyable pantomime running from Boxing day (2 p.m., 5 p.m. and 8 p.m.) until 26th January, 1966. Of course I haven't forgotten! After all it was a Parry panto, but I won't try to enumerate them all. I'll tell you of just one 'last night' gag.

In the nursery scene, before tucking the 'babes' into bed, we did a rather nice little song and dance number called 'Me and My Teddy Bear' (see moving bookcase gag above). So, as always, I said to Esme when they started up with a 'full orchestral' intro, 'Oi! Hang on! What's that?'

Voice from orchestra pit, 'Your intro.'

Me, 'What's all that noise? I'll never got them to sleep. As an orchestra you're "Band!"' Segue into 'Me and My Teddy Bear'.

Oh, they got their own back that night! Oh boy, and how! They embarked on a wonderful rendition, beautifully and heroically arranged (by Hugh I suspect) of 'Teddy

Bears' Picnic'. Well, as that late, great radio character, Syd Walker, used to say, 'What would you do chums?'

Brave young Barbara Randall (boy babe) and Julie Clough (girl babe) and Nurse Daisy battled on, creased up with open laughter, doing our best and the audience loved it. I'm here to tell you that the words of 'Me and My Teddy Bear' don't fit into 'Teddy Bears' Picnic'. Try it for yourself.

The last night of the panto was on the Saturday and I was back in a West-End pub upper room at 10 a.m. on the Monday morning to start rehearsals with another repertory company. The Perrys having now left the Palace, Watford, this company, the Intimate Theatre Co. of Palmers Green, was nearest to my home in Islington. As Palmers Green is in North London, and members of the company came from both sides of the river, rehearsals in Central London were felt to be more generally convenient. Michael Knowles had appeared with the company before and I met director, Douglas Emery, in Tynemouth so it wasn't a 'lions' den' feeling.

For this stay I was to be with them for four weeks – one had to travel out to Palmers Green for the evening show – and Mr Emery decided that I was the type of actor who should tackle a Charles Laughton role. After two easily forgotten dramas the next attraction was Benn Levy's dramatisation of Hugh Walpole's *The Man With Red Hair*. A local hair coiffeur had a great time on the morning of St Valentine's Day transforming the Bean dark brown thatch into a bright, bright ginger and believe me, the 'character' greasepaint went on, not with a trowel but with a shovel. One feature of the Intimate productions each week was the always excellent set, with limited space and resources, created by David Vickers.

Hey ho, and would you believe it? The first week in March found me back at the Palace, Watford. ('He certainly gets around after a fashion,' I hear someone cry.) Directed by Giles Havergal, the Watford Civic Theatre Trust opened a new season of plays with *Henry V*, my first meeting with the Bard of Avon since theatre school. I enjoyed playing Gower in this very robust and energetic production, especially with the prospect of playing a wonderful role in the next production, Robert Bolt's *A Man For All Seasons*. In my humble opinion it is a truly great play in which I had 'a whale of a time' ('tempered with humour and sensitivity' according to the local paper's review) as the 'Common Man'. What a role. I wonder if Leo McKern enjoyed playing it originally as much as I did recreating it in Watford?

Victor Winding's performance as Sir Thomas More was, I think, an inspiration to us all. A strong cast, under Peter M. Elrington's direction, gave it a sensitive and effective simplicity. The *Watford Observer* on the Thursday said, 'The whole plot was pieced together by an extremely hard-working Colin Bean, playing both storyteller and just about every other minor role in the play.' He also carried on and off all the furniture and props which the sixteen scenes required while doing his storytelling but the paper didn't go into details!

The 'Hampton Court' scenes were indicated by a trellis screen covered with foliage and dozens of flowers. Someone (naively in my humble opinion) suggested that these be got from the florists over the road. I suggested, 'They'll all be dead before the show opens once the lights get onto them.'

'Okay, big-head,' someone kindly remarked (jokingly, I hope), 'what's the answer?'

'Crepe paper and florist's wire,' I muttered, which is how I came to give myself even more work, giving classes to all the assistant stage managers in how to make paper roses on stems. Why can't I keep my gob shut? More importantly, which theatre school had they been to?

There's nothing like a bit of variety in life, is there? I was invited by Mr Havergal to stay on with the company. As I was committed already to appear as a leading actor and director for my fifth season with The Graham Players in Ayr my stay had to be limited to the following two Watford presentations. It is amazing how friends keep on 'turning up' in my life. In *Semi-Detached* I met up again with Jean Rimmer (New Elizabethan Rep) and Jane Lowe, another very talented actor from my home town of Wigan. My current Palace season concluded with my first venture into the world of old-time music hall (No, I didn't say, 'Olde Tyme Musick Halle'!) called 'A Victorian Evening'. As local papers and parish magazines are wont to say, 'A good time was had by all'. Reviewer K.H.G. in the local press reports at the end of his atmospheric account of his visit, 'and about the only item which was not transferred back to the good queen's period was the bar tariff, which remained realistically 1966!' (In 1996 one could hear the cry all over Britain, 'Oh for a bar tariff realistically 1966!') Apparently even I, as the stalwart Mr Chairman, was observed dabbing away the odd tear during the heart-rending rendering of *East Lynne* – 'Item ten in your programme, Ladies and Gentlemen, with interval.'

The adapter, Mr Elrington, had done his work well. Until then I had not realised that Mrs Henry Wood didn't write, 'Dead, dead, and never called me mother!' That was introduced by some other perfidious adapter in bygone days who thought it sounded better than Mrs Wood's original, 'See here, my child is dead, and never knew that I was his mother.' I feel, most earnestly, that you should be made aware of this outrage, in case you have to appear in *East Lynne* yourself.

In the short break I played a small part, Detective Sergeant Parsons, in an episode of *No Hiding Place* for Rediffusion TV, the only time I've ever worked with the now very popular star of *Coronation Street*, Mr Johnny Briggs. How envious I am of good actors who got the chance to start perfecting their craft when they were children and, presumably, with parental approval and encouragement. I can remember seeing Mr Briggs as a child (him, not me) in a film and enjoy his very convincing performance now as the charming, if not always scrupulous and sensitive, Mike Baldwin. And I am here to state that, off screen, Johnny Briggs is the opposite of Mike in character.

A fellow 'small-parter' in this episode – 'It Isn't Just the Money' – was Dallas Cavell, a character actor I'd known for quite a while. One day, during rehearsal, we decided to follow up an advert we'd seen in *The Stage*, offering actors work 'in the more secure commercial world of business'. I think my extolling of the Frigidaire tour helped us decide to go the reception at a Central London hotel, timed for well after our rehearsals in the Rediffusion rehearsal rooms had finished.

A couple of pints in the Salisbury to broach the meeting with an open and hopeful mind. I do not know how many others in that large gathering had also approached it with open and hopeful mind, but after sitting through some long spiel about 'structure and presentation', which went so fast we could hardly understand what was said, we started on 'meeting people who'd made it' – not the product being sold, a liquid cleaner called 'Swash' or 'Sweep' or something – but eager young men like 'Sid of Sidcup' and 'Ken of Croydon'. They were wearing huge smiles and company logo badges and leapt energetically onto the stage to 'press the flesh' and 'pump the arm' of the main speaker and declare proudly, 'Yes, I made it, folks. Wife, two point five kids, good house in Sidcup...' Dallas and I looked at each other simultaneously and said, not quietly either, 'Pyramid' and with as much noisy scraping back of chairs as we could manage, headed back round the corner to the comforts of Theatreland, St Martin's Lane and the Salisbury. Phew! A near do.

RED Riding Hood

COLIN BEAN
LYCEUM
(above),
AND
MOLLY
VENESS
EMPIRE

Chapter Nineteen

June 1966 and it's 'Scots wha hae' again, north of the border to the lovely west coast of Scotland and the 'bonny auld toon o' Ayr' and the first play of a season which would keep us busy until mid-October, Ivor Novello's *Fresh Fields*. Playing the first week as a main attraction at centenary celebrations in the nearby town of Cummock gave us a much better organising and 'settling in' period. There was expansion to The Graham Players in that, having acquired a Playhouse Theatre in addition to the Variety and Revue Theatre during out of season alterations, Butlin's Holiday Camp this year would have its own company of The Graham Players. The extremely able Suzanne Jefferies had joined Victor and myself as a play director and actor. This lightened the burden on the directorial front and the set repertoire of four plays for the Butlin's Company could be rehearsed satisfactorily.

At Ayr's delightful Civic Theatre we opened the company's ninth summer season of weekly rep with Derek Benfield's *Out of Thin Air*. Former stage manager, Anne Lee, having been in the US of A amongst other dates, returned to the Royal Burgh as a now very experienced and creative character actor. Katherine Scott and Christopher Robinson were our new juveniles, both on their first visit to Scotland. London-born Chris learned, upon his arrival in Ayr after a long journey from London, to be careful what one said in a bar in this part of the world. Feeling thirsty after all that time on a train with no buffet car he popped into the Station Hotel to slake his thirst with a glass of beer. Asking merely for, 'A half, please,' he had a bit of a shock when he asked the price. A smallish glass containing a large Scottish measure of whisky was placed before him. He'd yet to learn that a 'hauf' was a measure of this Scottish nectar of the gods and that the full 'a half-pint' or 'a glass' was the local code for beer. 'Light' and 'Heavy', as opposed to mild and bitter, confused him even further. Oh, I did it myself when I first arrived in Ayr. I knew how he felt.

One of the many things I liked about Victor Graham seasons in Ayr was that the programme of successive plays, week by week, was well balanced. Even taking into account that Ayr is a popular holiday resort the 'coming attractions' leaflet was not a string of 'Magill-type' seaside farces, alternating with the eternal Agatha Christie. Here were thrillers, including Mel Dinelli's *The Man* with leading roles spine-chillingly played by Chris Robinson and Anne Lee. There was also the crackling comedy of Neil Simon's *Come Blow Your Horn* (allowing me to be outrageous as the somewhat OTT father, Mr Baker, with Anne as the equally outrageously fussy Mrs Baker). And there was a 'family' play which I had told Victor I'd enjoyed so much when I saw it on tour with Clifford Mollison as the tramp, Tim – Leo Marks's *The Girl Who Couldn't Quite*. 'Tim' is a wonderful role and Victor and Suzanne were kind enough to ask me to play it. Katherine Scott was excellent as the very sad girl who couldn't quite and Robin Edwards' as always excellent setting made it an enjoyable week, playing to very good houses.

For versatility, how about Suzanne Jefferies? Hilarious as Mrs Piper in Jack Popplewell's *Busybody* and stunningly beautiful in such a brilliantly controlled performance as Nora in *The Doll's House* three weeks later. Victor and I both enjoyed ourselves in *Captain Carvallo* and *Come on Jeeves*. *The Reluctant Peer* was well received, as was Du

Maurier's *Rebecca*, Suzanne and Katherine outstanding as Mrs Danvers and Mrs De Winter. For Anne Lee and myself it was almost a holiday-time week as we capered through the parts of Ben and Giles Lacy – both managing to look incongruous in our Eastern fancy dress outfits (I ask you, an Arab chief with a cavalry moustache and a briar pipe!). *Fools Rush In* was given brisk direction and I directed the final play of the season – chosen by popular request from an audience vote earlier in the season – Coward's *Blithe Spirit*.

At this period of my life it seemed as if Scotland didn't want me to go home. A much reduced company moved on to present a three-week autumn season at Kilmarnock's Palace Theatre, according to the *Kilmarnock Standard* the first visit by a professional theatre company for seven years. Anne, Victor, Suzanne, Jane Jenner who proved herself as a good young assistant stage manager and juvenile player in Ayr, plus yours truly were the actors. Keith Watson and newcomer Penelope Barton provided the stage management. Victor directed the first play *Private Lives* and I took charge of the other two productions, *The Glass Menagerie* and *Rattle of a Simple Man*. With 'Amanda Prynne', 'Laura Wingfield' and 'Cyranne' all in three weeks I'm sure anyone who knows the roles will agree that Suzanne had quite enough on her plate without having to direct as well. I had played the gentleman caller in '*Menagerie*' on a previous occasion and Ricard in '*Rattle of*' was what we call a 'spit and a cough' part.

Victor with his invariable suavity was totally effective as Elyot Chase and Tom Wingfield and deliciously gullible in *Rattle* as Percy. Reviewer J.W.R.C. concluded her piece on *Rattle* as follows, 'In the past three weeks The Graham Players have brought much needed waves of freshness to the mostly stagnant pool of Kilmarnock culture.'

As the scenery we had used – what there was of it – was owned by the Palace there was no reason to go back to Ayr after the last performance with Anne, Suzanne and Victor so, as the Stranraer–London boat train stopped at Kilmarnock just after midnight, I went mad and treated myself to a sleeper compartment back to town. (It cost me all of one pound on top of my fare! Heavens above! Where will this inflation stop?)

Before leaving Scotland I must tell you briefly that in Ayr the great secret about the Gaiety Theatre's 1966/67 pantomime had just been released to the press. Directed by my dear Max Norris *Babes in the Wood* would feature Victor Graham as the Sheriff of Nottingham and guess who as Nurse Biddy Boddy. The names I get called – really!

Before that, however, my British Rail sleeper (with early morning tea and biscuits) was conveying me back to another three-week stay with the Intimate Theatre, Palmers Green, where for starters Douglas Emery invited me to repeat my performance as The Common Man in *A Man For All Seasons*. Friends Michael and Linda were there again, plus ex-Court Player, Roy Hepworth, and excellent as the Spanish Ambassador was former theatre school colleague, Richard Jacques. Besides being a stage and radio actor and an excellent pianist, Richard was now beginning to make a name as a director of musicals. Another experienced actor from Tynemouth days was fellow Northerner, Bernard Severn, as a disturbing and somewhat sinister Thomas Cromwell. A mystery by Janet Allen, *The Man Outside*, and a lightweight piece by W. Douglas-Home, *A Friend Indeed*, prefaced my return to 'the land o' the heather an' the kilt'. Please don't ask me what those last two plays were about – they were that memorable.

A couple of weeks spent sorting out my dame wardrobe, wigs and so forth, and brushing up on 'How Are You Keeping – All right?' soon saw me complete with a mountain of luggage (own wardrobe, will travel – as the old advert has it) at Euston for the Stranraer boat train. Yes, I'd decided to treat myself again to a sleeper. I was to be met in the early hours of the next morning by the redoubtable and reliable 'auld' friend, Tommy Faulds, at Kilmarnock with a small van. The prospect of the journey was clouded only by the fact that (horror!) the sleeper had shot up in price to twenty-five shillings. I think there must be some Scot as well as Scotch in my blood!

All went according to plan (by the grace of God) and I got settled into what was to be my home for some time with Nessie and Tommy Faulds – God bless 'em – in my own room in Somerset Road, Ayr, ready to start a week of intensive rehearsals on 12th December. The official title of the show, written as well as directed by Max, was *Robin Hood and the Babes in the Wood*.

Let us now proceed into the field to meet my fellow labourers. For Victor and myself this was of course terra nova and just a bit terror-making – for we were to work with a number of already established and well-known variety artistes. Handsome singer Jonathan Swift swashed his buckle as an energetic Robin, partnered by the lovely Sally Logan as his equally melodic Maid Marian. The music in this show was good. I was hesitant about introducing my humble effort 'How Are You Keeping?' but they were also an extremely tolerant crowd. If you ever saw that grand Scottish TV show *The White Heather Club* or listened to the great sound of the Joe Gordon Folk Four then you'll realise we had exactly the right person in Joe Gordon to play 'the guitar-strumming Alan-a-Dale'.

The noted Scottish summer show choreographer, Bill Cameron, carried out that job very effectively as well as playing Will Scarlett, and the babes were two very talented young ladies, the Allman twins. But what about the baddies? Well, I can assure you that these were far from being baddies when it came to comedy for they were two young 'old hands', comedian Lou Grant and actor, dancer, singer Jackie Farrell – later to be in *Take the High Road* alongside former Graham Player, Gwyneth Guthrie (the *chapeau*-conscious 'Mrs Mack'). Top of the bill was Ulster comedian Sammy Shortt ('No missis, oi spell it wit' two t's to make it longer!') who, being so popular in Scotland, had taken up residence there.

You may remember my earlier references to 'book' pantomimes; Max was a traditionalist, an expert on the subject. However, when the main roles are being played by variety artistes leeway must be given for them to show their skills 'as known' (a contract term). Skilfully Max would weave a 'speciality spot' into the action of the play without any horrible breaches of credibility and character. Most of these artistes had to have their spot. Victor and I were both a bit diffident about this as neither of us did a 'spot' per se. Much to our relief – and I'm sure this made for more amicable relations in the company because we'd be together for six whole weeks – there was a feeling of genuine happiness and bonhomie all round when we declined Max's invitation to submit how long our 'spots' would be. As Max confided to me later, 'You've no idea how grateful I am, Colin. I'm fighting the running time of the show even before we start and most dames want at least fifteen minutes.'

One of the fascinating aspects of playing the dame, for me, is the various ways in which the role can be played. In pantomime it is always interesting to judge by who is top of the bill which characters are going to be predominant. I have played 'star of the show' type dame and a 'down amongst the wine and spirits' dame. Apart from 'How Are You Keeping?' and my breakneck speed rendition of that old, old favourite 'The Coffee Pot Song' (with shortened verse), my role in this production was mainly as a feed dame. Sammy and I worked well together, especially in crosstalk comedy scenes, and he reckoned this was because,

'You're a proper actor, Colin. You know about timing.' (Yes, I know the old joke, 'What's the secret of... timing?') This was to lead to my doing a whole spring season with Sammy in the next year – but more of that anon.

The show was spectacular, packed with comedy, music and dance, and it was twice nightly. With nine complete changes of costumes and wigs you can imagine I was fairly exhausted by the time we finished (if we weren't over-running) at 10.30 p.m.

Chapter Twenty

After a hectic Christmas and very Scottish Hogmanay (I doubt if any of us remember much about the performance on Ne'erday) we were well into our stride. Sammy and I even had the opportunity to do a few daytime hospital and orphanage visits as 'Nursey' and 'Simple Sammy'. Some very good friends of the resident staff and of artistes who were regular performers at the Gaiety ran a very nice hostelry outside the town. On Friday nights after the second performance (the ghost walked on a Friday), it became the pleasurable practice of the cast and staff to pile into cars and go to this country inn for a good slap-up meal and, as guests of our hosts, enjoy a few late drinks and party-piece entertainment amongst ourselves. A very happy company and a very happy pantomime; that's how I like it. I say this because of firstly the *Goldilocks* experience of the past and secondly a pantomime production yet to come.

Two weeks back at the Intimate, Palmers Green, first as Mr Chairman of the Intimate Theatre music hall and then as Henry in *The Anniversary*. Linda, Michael and Richard were there to keep me company again and, in early March, to wave me off back to Ayr once more. With Sammy Shortt heading the bill and panto 'baddie' Jackie Farrell showing his skills as an actor in sketches and as a wonderful Scottish dancer, we were set for a season of one of those revues for which the Gaiety Theatre is renowned.

The Popplewells certainly knew how to present this mixture of colourful song, dance and comedy. Their famous summer show *Gaiety Whirl*, directed by Max Norris, appeared each year as regular as clockwork, packing the theatre twice nightly for the whole of the summer. Most of the big names in Scottish variety made appearances in the *Whirl*. Our show was a three-week spring revue called *Easter Parade*, same opening, same Part One closing formula, 'Cabaret Time at Sammy's' (sort of pocket show within a show) and the same 'Goodnight' finale. The material of items two to six and eight to thirteen, however, changed each week; good practice for the weekly programme changes to come later on in the long G.B. Bowie summer season – *Big Night Out* at the Barrfields Pavilion, Largs.

A versatile and 'dynamic' sister and brother act, 'Val and the Vs' proved to be a very popular attraction, as did the marital 'battles' of 'Mr and Mrs Comedy', Billy Denison and Diane. Without Billy and Diane who had another commitment the show, still under the direction of chief dancer Irene Campbell, moved on to spend three weeks at the Pavilion Theatre, Glasgow. Now headlined by the comedy duo, Hope and Keen, and featuring Sammy as host, the show *Spring '67* had the company enriched by the famous Scottish entertainer, 'Mr Music Himself' Nicky Kidd and his spectacular keyboard pyrotechnics. (Liberace? Nae chance, pal. 'Bye bye Blackbird')

In the panto we'd had a lovely song, given by the baddies and the sheriff, called 'There's Dirty Work Afoot' (plus all the gags like 'Hey, what's afoot?' Answer: 'About twelve inches.'). Well, although far from being dirty there was something afoot. One day Sammy asked me to meet someone who'd seen the show with his wife and family and 'has had an idea'. He explained to me that Mr Kennedy, besides being a noted Highland Gaelic singer (gold medal at the Mod no less!) he was also an entrepreneur and show presenter.

'The Mod'? Oh, please enquire of your Scottish friends. I haven't time or space to go into it all here.

How often I've caused eyebrows to be raised ever so slightly when I boast, 'Oh yes, I've played the Palladium.'

'What, in Argyll Street?' someone may ask.

'No, Fountainbridge, Edinburgh,' I must truthfully reply. A small auditorium, certainly not like its Argyll Street namesake, in a back street which, if it's still there, I'd last heard of as a garage and car repair shop.

Truly, 1967 was my Scottish year. I wasn't to go back to England until November and then only for flying visits to Wigan and Islington. The excitement of showbiz! By now Sammy and I were working well together with, he confided to me, an on-stage rapport he hadn't experienced before. Director Irene, who had worked with Sammy in shows before, remarked that my expressions and reactions seemed to make Sammy's jokes even funnier. Take that for what it's worth.

Guitarist Mal Hollander and the 'lovely to look at and listen to' singer, Sheena Andrew, joined us at the Palladium for *Calum's Ceilidh* (for us ignorant Sassenachs that's 'ceilidh' pronounced 'kay-ly'). There were three weekly changes of programme (the now well-rehearsed comedy safe in the hands of Sammy Shortt and yours truly) and the high spot each week was the big game, 'Beat The Highland Ceilidh Clock!' (I kid you not in this instance – that's what this pin-the-tail-on-the-donkey, audience participation game was.) In this version the tail had to be pinned by a blindfolded person onto a picture of a collie, 'Calum's Collie', against thirty seconds on a huge Smiths dial-timer. Yes, folks, this was the biggy with the fantastic prizes! I was not particularly happy to be appointed i/c these 'wonderful prizes' and I hated having to go to that wholesale cheap-jack warehouse in Glasgow to collect fresh supplies of these 'beautiful' coffee tables, clocks, table lamps, works of art

(*Sea Horses* and *The Green Girl* – honestly!) and boxed tea sets, made in China, all of which became a feature of my nightmares.

During the early part of the year, following the success of the Gaiety panto, and during *Easter Parade* I was in contact with the Ayr Council's entertainment officer, Phil King, like myself another North of England man but he being of the White Rose county. He had suggested that Ayr might be more attractive to visitors next Christmas if it could offer two professional pantomimes in the town instead of only the Gaiety. The outcome of this was my being invited to write, direct and play the dame in a pantomime of my own subject choice at the Civic Theatre.

The move from the Palladium, Edinburgh, to the Barrfields in Largs gave me just two days free which I spent with Mr and Mrs Faulds in Ayr whilst we got down to the nitty-gritty of putting on the panto. The original invitation or commission, because I had agreed to do it, sounded great. Write, direct, own choice of subject and playing the dame. Anyone who knows me will tell you that I am no businessman. I couldn't take fourpence-ha'penny from half-a-crown and get the correct change! When Phil and I sat down to analyse what 'the treasury', i.e. the Parks and Entertainments Dept. and the Finance Dept. proposed as our 'outside budget' even I could see from what was on offer that it would be an almost impossible struggle. Grovel and cajole as we might, nothing more was to be forthcoming.

Right then, we hard-headed (or is it thick-headed?) north-countrymen thought, 'We're not going to be defeated by the Scots. We'll invade them for a change.'

I had plenty to think of during any free time available in the Largs summer season which would run from mid-June until the second of September. The favourite summer show format, a standard 'meet the company' opening, a song scene to close Part One – *Calum's Ceilidh*, a company song and dance to open and Calum's own spot to close Part Two before a company 'Goodnight' finale. They were regular anchor points in each of the twelve weekly programmes. The opening to Part Two, the company song and dance item, would have a different theme each week. Sometimes it was just the dancers, other weeks it involved some or all of the principals. For instance, the week when the theme was the 'Old Variety Stars', Billy Denison and Diane being back with us, the scene was a stage door with Billy as a 'Will Fyffe' stage door keeper reminiscing about some of the stars of the past he had known. I got my chance for a 'dame' try-out by giving my Florrie Forde singing 'Has Anyone Seen My Pom?' impression.

I shall never forget the look on Calum's face when, at the dress rehearsal, he saw me in the 'full gear' – eyelashes and all. 'Ye Gods!' was about the mildest of his remarks but he made the first mention then of his 'Highlands and Islands Tour' in October/November and asked if I'd be interested. I had time to consider (and from other sources advised to consider carefully) for, as one friend who'd been on one before said, 'There's some pros and cons wi' it ye ken.' That was amongst things to come in this eventful year.

During the 'Glasgow Fair' holiday fortnight I was 'mugged'. Having been with the rest of the company for a drink and a bite to eat, after a second-house performance, at the very friendly Queen's Hotel next door to the theatre, I was walking back to my digs when I spied two rather unsteady gents approaching me, weaving their way along the pavement. In an effort not to impede their progress I moved to cross the road, at which point they decided on similar action. Whether or not these two gents had seen *Big Night Out* and been either disappointed or offended I do not know but, with the damning accusation of my being 'that bloody sassenach frae yon show' they promptly assisted me to lie on the pavement with two broken front teeth, a bloody nose and a strangely coloured eye. Obviously this was their 'big night out' as they went on their way in what sounded like hysterics.

On the next morning a dentist was able to fix me up with temporary dental fittings whilst he prepared some proper crowns for me. Make-up disguised the strangely coloured eye but, oh boy, didn't those 'Satchmolike' sore lids make singing and playing in the many sketches in which I appeared extremely painful!

Still, time heals and we got through a successful summer season. Sammy, Mal or Billy always took me to my digs in a car after the après-show drink and snack. I now had a few weeks free, having finally agreed to go with the 'Highlands and Islands Tour' of *Calum's Ceilidh*. Before that, however, there were calls to make, en route to London, in Ayr and Wigan. In Ayr we got down to the task of dealing with the minuscule budget and our practical resources. The scenery for the show would have to be that used by The Graham Players. It must not be altered in any way apart from being appropriately painted. There were no back drops and costuming would obviously have to be kept to a minimum. Now came the all-important matter of the actors and paying them. As writer, director and dame I would get a staggering twenty-five pounds per week. Phil, I think, probably had to include his performance as part of his duties as Entertainments Officer. I had enough (Equity minimum salaries) for four other professionals!

Chapter Twenty-One

So the problem to cogitate upon was how to write, produce and direct a 'family pantomime' with only six principal artistes, seven dancers from the Ayr School of Dancing, three teenage dancers and one young acting unpaid 'helper' who was 'dead keen' to help. For the outcome you'll have to wait until December because, as it was now October, with script written and my own costumes and gear packed I was heading northwards again for Aberdeen via Ayr (dropping off said costumes and script) to join the touring version mainly one-night or two-night dates – of *Calum's Ceilidh*.

No Sammy this time (he'd done it before!) and much more for me to do ('all good experience' as has been said to actors since the days of Aristophanes). Billy Denison and Diane, Sheena Andrew *et moi* plus the Heather Isle Band – pianist, Sandra Adams, accordionist Bill Marshall, and drummer, Jimmy Miller (affectionately known as 'oor wee Jum'). Besides being the 'band' they also had to play in the comedy scenes, such as they were. With Calum as top of the bill we were the 'all-star cast'. Who the et ceteras at the bottom of the list were I never did find out.

That ruddy collie (and its tail and a box of drawing pins because some of the places we played, I'm sure, had heard only of nails) became the bane of my life. The 'fabulous prizes', the same chipboard coffee tables, some with only three legs, the 'works of art' (how could one live with that green girl looking on?), the elegant standard lamps and shades (bulb and plug not supplied) were also part of the nightmare. The six-place tea sets which, with all the rough travel in a not very well sprung coach, ended the tour in November as what I suppose nowadays we'd call 'mix and match' six-piece tea sets. All had to be unpacked, set up on display and repacked at each venue.

Do you like lists? 13th and 14th October, Inverness; 15th, Elgin; 16th, Brora; 17th, Thurso; 18th and 19th, Kirkwall, Orkney; 20th and 21st, Lerwick, Shetland (and a day off!); 23rd, Wick; 24th, Tain; 25th, Dornoch; 26th, Dingwall; 27th, Fort William; 28th, Largs (at last some-where I could locate Woolworths and Boots the Chemists first go); 29th, Dunoon; 30th, Oban; 31st, Perth; 1st November, Blairgowrie; 2nd, Montrose; 3rd, Frazerburgh; 4th, Inverness; then a final three-week stay (again) at the Edinburgh Palladium, after restocking the 'fabulous prizes' at that Glasgow wholesale warehouse.

The day off in Shetland came about because there were no flights to the mainland on a Sunday. Sumburgh Airport (two Nissen huts and a windsock) was an hour's drive from Lerwick and the last flying 'twelve-seater saloon' on Saturdays left during daylight. Playing the show twice nightly meant that our supper and party at the hotel (owned by a very jovial and accommodating Yorkshire couple) saw dawn well and truly broken before we hit the sack on Sunday. We even had shepherds from the surrounding meadows dropping in at about 3 a.m. with their fiddles and pipes – to give an unbelievable concert of spontaneous Celtic music.

First plane out Monday morning landed at Wick by 11 a.m. where a BEA (British European Airways) official asked me if I was 'all right'. He confessed that when he saw this weird assortment of haggard, bleary-eyed zombies getting off their little craft he was worried about the airline's reputation. He seemed happier when we assured him that it was not that kind of turbulence but a Lerwick/Yorkshire weekend which was at the root of the matter.

The show was, of necessity, very basic in props, furnishings and costumes. Sitting in a rickety bus and/or small plane with a large folding-board picture of a collie dog (tail and pins in my bag) and nursing a large box of assorted 'made in China' china is not the ideal way to tour the Highlands and islands. The large dial timer would, thank goodness, not fit through the door of the plane so it was left at Wick and, for Kirkwall and Lerwick, 'the crazy bit of family fun with super prizes' had to rely on my Timex watch for limiting the time a contestant took to pin the tail on Calum's collie. What price your National Theatre and Old Vic now, eh? I've played Brora, Wick and Thurso with 'pinning the tail on'!

The hectic preparation for the pantomime (one week's rehearsal and preparation) was almost a relief. The posters were out, courtesy of Phil King's department, advertising the first royal burgh civic pantomime, *Robin, Son of Crusoe*. Honestly! I have beside me the Lord Chamberlain's office licence – must have been one of the last ever issued – giving permission for a new stage play, a pantomime in two acts entitled *Robin, Son of Crusoe* to be performed 'without any further alteration whatsoever' and 'given under his hand' no less, 20th day of November, 1967. (Pause for subsidence of hysterical sniggering.)

Why? You may well ask. With only six actors I could not think of any panto subject I could reasonably curtail to a cast of six. As it was, two actors had different roles in Act One and Act Two. Man Friday was out even if I'd tried to do the traditional 'Crusoe' storyline. So Robin, a likely young lad of the village and younger son of Widow Crusoe, found a battered old diary and a map in an old chest in the attic. (It gets worse, dear reader, please bear with me.) This revealed the travels of one Robinson Crusoe, now deceased.

'That was your father,' said I as the proud widow. Phil King was Phil Crusoe, the 'Simple Simon' element, and the (thank heavens) talented Lisa Young was Robin. She also did the choreography and arranged most of the music. As I had my work cut out as dame, director, scene-painter and prop-maker, Lisa and Margo also took charge of rehearsing the chorus and supervising the dancers' wardrobe.

Time to introduce three former Graham Players, fortunately all resident in Ayr. Margo Milroy had the thankless job of breathing life into the principal girl role, Lady Mary. Margo, daughter of the gentleman who came to our aid some years previously at short notice to play the Frenchman in *Dry Rot*, had, at that time, been a younger acting assistant stage manager with the company and had, in subsequent seasons, become a good stage manager and had played both character and juvenile roles very well. She and Lisa worked well together so my principal boy and my principal girl were able to give out a very welcome feeling of confidence in both rehearsal and performance. Poor Phil as the Parks and Recreation Department's manager had so many multifarious duties, it being the festive season, that his brief acquaintance with his given lines might not have been in line with the Lord Chamberlain's dire strictures but it certainly added an element of spontaneity and surprise to the comedy scenes.

I said three former Graham Players. Keith Watson had also been an acting assistant stage manager of good account and, like Margo, was on Christmas vacation from New College of Speech and Drama, London. Besides playing the 'heavier' roles he and Michael Owen were also such a great help with the scenery and properties preparation. Michael, although an Englishman, had been in Scotland for some time. For Victor Graham he'd been a stalwart and mainstay of The Graham Players Butlin's Holiday Camp company and was now 'into' singing in Glasgow recording studios – so at least we had one male 'proper singer'.

Frank Small, a protégé of the officer i/c of the Civic, Tommy Faulds, was my stage manager/lights operator with Billy and Tommy Steven as his stage crew assisted by our 'young helper' Michael Blaikie. It was not long before this Michael found himself dressed in items from my rep wardrobe as the ship's captain to swell the numbers for the quayside Part One finale. This, and working on the scene changes, was 'all good experience'. Having very little headroom and no flies, the Civic could not accommodate cloths which were lowered in and flown out; in any case we had only the rep company/Civic Theatre scenery 'which mustn't be altered, apart from re-painting'. We did manage to scrounge another tab rail so that we could have a second set of tabs in front of which to play the 'frontcloth' scenes.

Being Scotland, the first performance was at 7.30 p.m. on the 25th December and we played with matinées on Saturdays, Boxing Day and New Year's Day at 2.30 p.m. until the 13th January, 1968. In addition to our Ayr School of Dancing girls we had teenage dancers, Jackie Leeson, Monica Keane and Beverly Richards for variety. Michael Owen, after his 'Baron Hardup' type in Act One became 'King Woolomboomba' of 'the island' in Act Two. You didn't know that that was the eventual dignity reached by 'Man Friday', did you? This fact, when revealed, made extra plot material. You may accept more easily that the crafty 'Uriah Heep' type tax collector of Act One became a very wild witch doctor on the same island. (He also painted the wonderfully colourful tropical plants which would never be recognised at Kew Gardens.) Well, someone had to do the 'ghost' gag with Phil and me!

Near to the Civic Theatre was the town's fire station. Occasionally a production would be intruded upon by the sound of fire bells and engines. Not too much of a hazard in, say, pantomime or uproarious farce but a bit of a bind if one was in the middle of a tense dramatic scene or a tender love scene. During one rep season it had been known to evoke an uncontrollable, unrehearsed hilarity among actors and audience. During a coffee break in earlier rehearsals this subject was being discussed by those of us who know and loved the Civic (it is a most delightful little theatre) and the newcomers. Perhaps it was stage manager Frank Small (wicked sense of humour that he has) who joked that perhaps next time, Colin should write a pantomime about a fire station then the bells wouldn't matter. 'If there is a next time,' I added uncertainly. How logical can you get? It made me think.

Before the end of the run Phil King confided in me that his boss, the director of Parks and Recreation was, in Phil's tyke language 'right chuffed' with the show. A motion was even then being put to the Parks and Recreation committee that I was to be invited to return with a pantomime at the end of 1968. The moment I mentioned 'budget and actor' Phil chimed in, 'Not to worry.' He had already taken the points up and had made it clear that both essential factors would need noticeable enhancement. Don't you just love all this council/committee language? By the end of *Robin, Son of Crusoe* I'd been told that I'd receive an official commission to write, direct and appear in the next Civic panto and could I give some clue as to what it would be? The commission arrived.

Aladdin has always been one of my favourite subjects. I liked the range of characters, enjoyed playing a classic Widow Twankey and it has scope for colour and comedy. But this nagging thought of fire engines kept intruding. Phil and I put our heads together, metaphorically, and at the end of the season we were able to announce that next year would be another 'specially written for the Civic

Theatre' pantomime called *A Lad an' His Lamp*, subtitled 'A New Twist to an Old Tale'. Oh dear! Be brave, read on, please.

The show *Robin, Son of Crusoe* was extremely hard work and this gallant team all worked very hard. It was a 'first' and we were in competition (though hardly on the same scale) with the Gaiety's twice nightly Scottish Star panto. Considering all this the council was moved to express publicly their complete satisfaction with the production, the players, the audience and the returns from the box office.

The only people I did upset were my dear old friends the famous theatre historians/researchers, Mander and Mitchenson. As always on a panto first night, I got a card from Raymond and Joe. This year it said, 'Very best wishes. May God and Daniel Defoe forgive you!'

Chapter Twenty-Two

The next two months after the end of *Robin, Son of Crusoe* were, apart from a day on a filmset (the subject of which I cannot remember; my logbook merely notes '22nd February: Gateway Films: £10.10'), a 'resting' period. I put the word into quotation marks because it was in fact a very busy period behind the scenes, as 'twere. The rest of 1968 was fully planned, a great feeling as any actor will tell you, particularly when the projects in view all had such pleasing and hopeful prospects.

George Alfred Black Ltd had sent for me, interviewed and engaged me for a summer season in Torquay, to run from the beginning of June until the end of September. Before this, however, came another 'Perry-inspired' change of direction, as momentous for me as being given the opportunity to play a pantomime dame in my own right. It was also to give the story its title.

'Don't panic!' All will be revealed. For some time there had been talk of a new BBC series about the Home Guard. Jimmy Perry had talked to me and other people fortunate enough to be counted among his friends about this idea for some time. The full story of 'how it came about' is all told, in exciting detail, in Bill Pertwee's book, *Dad's Army: The Making of a TV Legend*. The how, why and when are all fully explained. Suffice it to say here that after visiting 'the concrete doughnut', i.e. BBC TV Centre, Wood Lane, to meet Jimmy and be introduced to David Croft, I was engaged to be a member of the Walmington-on-Sea Home

Guard for all six episodes. As Bill explains, behind the front-line stars of the show would be people whose faces would become known, because Home Guard units didn't change personnel week by week. In the 'platoon on parade' format I was invariably standing behind that doyen of 'character old men', Clive Dunn.

February and March also saw the completion of the script for *A Lad n' His Lamp*. Phil and I were far more organised this time. At least we had some idea of what we were doing and what problems, if any, we'd have to face.

The script was approved by 'them upstairs' and most of last year's cast were re-engaged, firstly because they all worked well individually and as a team, and secondly because as with most casting, although one is looking out for new talent, when rehearsal time is short (one week again) – 'better the devil you know'. Lisa Young, alas, was not available to play principal boy. She had not surprisingly gone onto bigger things so another talented all-rounder (seen in performance by Phil and Margo), Tricia Ingram, had been engaged to play Aladdin. With a slightly better budget we were able to engage another former Graham Player, Barton Sullivan, to play a forceful Abanazer. From New College for her Christmas vacation (and, I believe, first visit to Scotland) would be Larry Minor. With nine main characters at least the storyline had a bit more scope and all the comedy work didn't fall upon just Phil and me. Some of us had had a preliminary meeting in London, at Margo and Larry's College digs, and we were all happy with the script and saying, 'Roll on *Aladdin*'.

First however I had to get my small contribution to a piece of television history 'in the can', so to speak. In the platoon, apart from the famous principal stars, were those who constituted 'the second line of the chorus' as we called ourselves were some old friends: Hugh Hastings, pianist/author/cabaret entertainer (I'm still sure 'Teddy

Bears' Picnic' was his idea but, being a gentleman, Hugh won't tell); former Palace Theatre manager, also an Equity member, Frank Godfrey; opera singer, George Hancock, retired from leading roles; musician, actor and director Richard Jacques and others.

With excitement and anticipation we boarded the coach at 'the Doughnut' for the start of what I invariably described as 'our paid holiday'. Of course at that time we did not know it was the first of many such visits to Thetford. The formula became that before each series was recorded week by week episodically in the studio, all the outdoor location work, covering all the six ensuing episodes, had to be filmed ready to be slotted into its appropriate place in each week's episode. In other words, we had six days of rather disjointed (which often caused it to be rather amusing) little scenes being filmed.

Some days we lesser mortals, who had no actual lines to say, would speculate as we marched along a tarmacadam road 'out in the middle of nowhere' (in Norfolk actually) just which episode it was we were filming for and what it might all be about.

At this time an 'I'm Backing Britain' campaign had been up and running for a while. The country seemed to be swimming in a sea of bags, wrapping paper and badges, all featuring the Union flag, either seriously or whimsically. Consequently the very first episode of *Dad's Army* and our first day's location filming was a post-wartime 'I'm Backing Britain' dinner held in Walmington-on-Sea. By this time, twenty years or more after World War Two, the characters were all much older. Indeed some had already passed away. The scene – the function room as it was then of the Anchor Hotel in Thetford. Opening shot – a 'top table' at a luncheon, chaired by Mr A. Wilson and to be addressed by that other leading citizen of Walmington, Mr G. Mainwaring. Look to the left of your screen before the camera pans along the table and there you will find the profile which, in a later series, would become the minor but fairly regular character, Pte Sponge. ('Man of the Hour' is the episode's title, recorded for TV on my forty-second birthday!)

Once the location work was done *Dad's Army* was a bit like weekly rep (but for us 'small-part actors' not so taxing). In sequence, week by week, each episode was rehearsed and, at the end of the week, recorded in front of a live audience. The relevant pieces of location film were slotted into the programme at the appropriate times and watched by the studio audience on monitor sets. That allows me to refute a remark I hear made so often – 'Well of course it's all canned laughter, otherwise how about when they're outside!' There was no canned laughter on *Dad's Army* I can assure you, nothing but the genuine article. When, as happens during a recording, a 're-take' was required one of the stars of the show might step forward and say to the audience, 'Sorry about that. We've made a bit of a muck of it. David [Croft] says we must do it again. Laugh twice as loud this time otherwise we'll be kept in after school!'

On another occasion someone might say, 'We're getting too old for this lark. Bear with us – and please laugh again!' That usually got its own laugh, which helped, and possibly made the audience feel that they were 'part of it' which, of course, they were. I mean to say, without them, well, 'Who Do You Think You Are Kidding?'

Bill Pertwee's book, which I call the *Dad's Army* encyclopaedia, gives full and detailed lists of every episode of the show. The whole book is a fascinating slice of television history. We of the 'second line' were not always required for more than one brief appearance. In some episodes we don't appear at all, and I was not to become Pte Sponge until later on.

Now it was 'Wagons Westward Ho!' to, for me, pastures new. After rehearsals in London under the direction of ex-

Court Player Dennis Spencer, *Wedding Fever* hit Torquay for a summer season, from 2nd June to 28th September. That amiable and genial gentleman, Sidney James, headed the cast with Beryl Mason as the long-suffering wife. Kathleen Worth and I were Emily and Willie Beattie who, according to the *Western Morning News*, 'were gloriously funny as the neighbours, they being the sort of neighbours who spend more time in the Jones's home (Sid and Beryl as Sidney and Peggy Jones) than they did in their own.' The charming Veronica Page played the beautiful bride to be, Jones's daughter, Sally. Robert Blacklock was the 'football fanatic' son and another ex-Court Player friend, Nicholas Brent, had a whale of a time as a loud, big-hatted American glorying in the name of Hiram P. Hingleheiffer. The bridegroom's parents were a glorious combination of the grim 'stately as a galleon' mother and a harassed 'wilting petal' of a father as played by two great artistes, Dorothy Dampier and C. Denier Warren.

And the hapless son of such parents, the bridegroom? You may well ask. He and Sidney James were magic in their scenes together – belly laughs came thick and fast. And, if you ever want a demonstration of how to lay out and fold up a pair of trousers, ask John Inman. Since it was our first work together since that *Goldilocks*, at coffee break we would regale the rest with horrendous tales which one day, I remember, had both Beryl and Sid in tears of laughter.

Tuesdays, Wednesdays and Thursdays we played at 6 and 8.30 p.m., the other nights at 8 p.m. with no matinées. With some good weather that year it was indeed a grand season. Trips out and picnics were organised. Because of different performance times we were able to see *Show Time* at the Princess Theatre just across the greensward from the

Pavilion Theatre, and one Sunday we enjoyed a party given by Sidney and his wife at the house they'd rented in the countryside just outside Torquay where we met members of *Show Time* including the legendary Arthur Askey (and his sister who could well have been his identical twin if she'd been a lad!). Because he was doing a Sunday night concert at the Princess, a charming young man with a famous singing voice was also there. His name was Tom Jones and it was a pleasure to talk to him. He'd seen our show the previous evening and was avid for information about (in his lilting Welsh accent) 'this here acting lark'. It was a lovely 'windows wide open' and hilarious afternoon.

Kathleen and I were also understudies to Beryl and Sidney, so on Friday mornings before the ghost walked, we'd get together with stage manager, Unity Dennis, and her deputy, Graham Edwards, to run through the Jones's lines and moves. Mercifully our 'cover' services were never called upon. Imagine having to go on in front of a full house audience who has just learned that 'Unfortunately Mr Sidney James... and the part of Sid Jones will be played by...'

It had been agreed with Dennis Spencer and G. & A. Black Ltd that, should Sidney (God forbid!) ever be 'off' I would not attempt to imitate his unique personality. Let's face it, like Arthur Lowe, 'There's only one.'

On the Friday before we closed – after the ghost-walking – was a company lunch at the Livermead Hotel which was more or less a farewell party. This is often the practice in seasonal companies, particularly when you've all got on so well together, because on the last night you are 'packing as the play proceeds' and most of us are ready to get away. I was getting a car lift back to London and so checked out of my digs on Saturday morning. Lovely place that it is – palm trees included – the only drawback from which Torquay suffers, in my humble opinion, is all those hills. Except for the promenade one seems to climb mountains to get anywhere. The taxi firms did well out of *Wedding Fever*.

"WORMS' EYE VIEW"

COLIN BEAN Playhouse 1953

Chapter Twenty-Three

Back to London for some more episodes of *Dad's Army* and then the beginning of December found me heading north once more for a few days in Wigan. Father's condition was obviously deteriorating but, in his own obstinate manner, 'he could manage'. This was, perhaps, the first real inkling I had that fairly soon he would not be able to 'manage', but as he would not contemplate nor discuss the prospect there wasn't much I could do but get on my way, by coach this time (my panto wardrobe and so forth all being in storage in Ayr), to start work on the 'Festive Season's Family Show', the second Civic pantomime – *A Lad an' His Lamp*.

Briefly, the local panjandrum, the mandarin Abanazer, owned most of the buildings in 'Old Chuckling', a small town roughly in China a long time ago (or was it only yesterday?) in the province of Peekin, near the city of 'Ping Pong'. (So programme synopsis of scenes noted.)

Again we had dancers from the Ayr School of Dancing and the principal, Audrey Montgomery, worked with the principal boy, Tricia Ingram, upon some very inventive and effective choreography. The scenery (rep company scenery. Mustn't be altered!) was a parade of very colourful story-book-like backgrounds painted by Keith Watson, Michael Owen and myself. The finale (I like to have a colour-themed finale) was in blue and white/silver. Suspended behind the step – it's only a small stage – for the walk-down was Keith's glittering blue and white, with silvery highlights in glitter, willow-pattern plate. The only difference made to the original design of this classic piece of pottery was that the little bridge was actually on stage to serve as the walk-down entrance. From my Japanese gardens book I got the outlines of an elegant stone garden lantern which I painted in white and light grey highlighted with silver glitter on two blue flats as wings. (Well, Japanese, Chinese, it was Eastern, so what!) Tricia and I both supplied our own costumes – the budget wasn't that much improved – but Margaret Martin made lovely blue/white and/or silver finale costumes and some colourful mainstream costumes for the rest of the cast.

The addition of Barton Sullivan and Larry Minor to our little pantomime company made a great difference to the overall effect of the show because nobody had to 'double' roles. In pantomime the principal girl has, in my view, a difficult task. Compared with the other characters there's very little into which she can get her teeth as it were. Mainly overshadowed by the principal boy and all the strangely delineated 'Funnies, Goodies and Baddies', Margo Milroy did a wonderful job of making Char Ming Mimosa, daughter of the Mayor of Chuckling, Keekabo, as lively and as interesting as possible. Her duets with Tricia went very well with all audiences. Originally I'd named the mayor 'Peekaboo' but in Scotland, having a quick, sly look at something can be known as 'haein a wee keek', so he became 'Keekabo'.

The tall Keith Watson and petite Larry Minor made excellently funny Chinese Policemen. Sergeant So Hi Hup (chief of the Chuckling police force) and Constable So Lo Doon, making a whirlwind first entrance with whistles, flashing lights and on roller skates to the theme from TV's *Z Cars*, were a very popular pair.

So Lo Doon merely echoed the last two words of anything So Hi Hup said, sometimes with a most unexpected and hilarious effect. Michael Owen brought his usual dignity, quiet sense of fun and pleasing singing voice to the role of the mayor and Barton appeared to be thoroughly enjoying himself as an Abanazer to outwit all Abanazers. Aladdin's job was as leader of the town fire brigade with Wishee Wazir (Phil King) as his second in command. ('Whenever that rascal is needed he's never about and you wish he was here!') Oh, we were not short of 'corn' in this show!

The *raison d'être* of this story was that, unable to squeeze any more money out of the good people of Chuckling, wicked old 'Ave a Banana' thought that burning down a few buildings to collect the insurance might replenish his purse. Alas, he'd reckoned without the magical properties of the environmentally friendly fire engine 'Ting Ting'. (Well, it had a bell in its little pagoda-shaped top which rang as it ran along). Not to bore you with the complicated story of how it was acquired, I'll merely tell you that Ting Ting had a lamp on its front which had magical properties, i.e. it 'sensed' fire anywhere in the town and would set off of its own accord to find the fire and sound the alarm to alert all good fire fighters. Crafty Abanazer clocks onto this after a while so – well you've probably guessed the rest by now.

We still managed to get down to 'a deep, deep cavern' and into 'the haunted pagoda' plus, instead of a comedy kitchen we had a comedy fire station including Phil and me with an old hosepipe lent by the Ayr Fire Services to perform the ancient 'endless rope' gag. All great fun – chases round the auditorium and all the traditional panto elements, but no 'ghost gag' as we did that last year.

'Ah, but what about the genie of the lamp?' the purists will ask and may well enquire further into how 'Ting Ting' ran about by itself. Well, we hadn't reached the West-End technology of radio remote control; it was Michael Blaikie inside, propelling this cute little Chinese fire engine and 'directing' the ornate, traditional 'Aladdin's lamp' which sat on a pivot at the front. In the cavern, where Abanazer had hidden the lamp, Michael then appeared as a spirit creature, 'The Brownie In The Light Blue Jeans', who communicated, very expressively, only in mime. By the finale, 'The Hall of the Honoured Willow', of course all had been resolved. Abanazer had mended his ways when 'persuaded' to confess by the now *Inspector* So Hi Hup and *Sgt* So Lo Doon (they still had nobody else in the police force but what the heck!).

Ken Dawkins gave us some great accompaniment from the Hammond organ and Charlie Gunn provided enthusiastic support and myriad sound effects from the 'pots and pans' department. Stage manager Frank Small again lit and ran the show, effectively assisted by Billy Steven and Tony Mancini.

The last night went through reasonably smoothly. It had been a heavy season and perhaps we were all a bit tired but Charlie kept us on our toes with one or two unrehearsed sound effects – oh, and the real fire engines obliged outside for the first time during an actual performance.

And for next year? 'Weel, would you consider *Sleep In, Beauty*?' Alas, due to circumstances beyond my control and, I believe, some internal politics in Ayr, this was not to be. Having packed my wardrobe, I travelled back to London on 14th January, 1969 to start on almost a year of TV and film work. I do hope that 'Ting Ting' found a good, fireproof retirement home. Later bulletins told me that there had been 'romance' in Ayr – Larry and Barton got married. Tragically, only a few years later Barton Sullivan, a highly talented young actor in his late twenties and with all prospects of a good career, died. RIP George Barton Sullivan, LLCM, ALCM.

Chapter Twenty-Four

Jimmy Perry had been engaged upon writing another TV series called *The Gnomes of Dulwich*, to be directed by Sydney Lotterby and starring Terry Scott and Hugh Lloyd. Messrs Scott and Lloyd and any other gnome-sized characters were the only people seen full-size. Humans were mainly feet and voices; in the first episode I believe I was the feet and voice of a policeman. The second one I did was a very weird experience. Jimmy and Gilda were in my scene also as ornaments on a bric-a-brac stall at a garden party at the rear of 10, Downing Street. Frank Williams, the *Dad's Army* vicar, and Nigel Hawthorne were among the assorted humans (feet and voices) as were Barry Cryer and Mvyanwy Jenn in brilliant vocal and choreographic portrayals of Harold and Mary Wilson. Gilda was a porcelain shepherdess figurine. Jimmy was a plaster bust of Napoleon and I was a matching bust, on a named base, of Beethoven. As our make-up had to appear solid our few lines had to be 'one-off' takes. The scary part was being made up in the studio make-up rooms with a quickly setting mixture covering face, ears, wig and clothes, with two small holes under our nostrils so that we could breathe. Last to get 'plastered' were our eyes, then, when the plaster was all set, we were led into the studio behind a curtain, so that the audience wouldn't be deprived of the surprise element when we spoke, and positioned on our statuette bases. With only very small holes in the ear plaster one had to listen very carefully for one's cue over the audience's laughter. My few lines played on Beethoven's deafness (Da da da *dah*!) after Napoleon had made some cutting remark, the joke being that at the end of the garden party the only items left on the bric-a-brac stall were the two garden gnomes. (Ahhh!)

For London Weekend Television I played a prison inmate in an episode of *The Gold Robbers*. On my bathroom wall I have a London Weekend cheque for three pence, payment for a 'repeat showing' of this one-line contribution to the art of television. Back to the BBC for episodes of *Broaden Your Mind* (Graeme Garden and Tim Brooke-Taylor with Bill Oddie and Jo Kendall), *Liver Birds* (Nerys Hughes and Polly James), and a call from former Northern Theatre School graduate, David Giles, the TV, film and theatre director who was about to embark on a major episodic production of *The First Churchills*.

A very distinguished cast (I really felt that I was getting somewhere) had John Neville as John Churchill, Susan Hampshire as Sarah Churchill, James Villiers looking remarkably like pictures of the character he was playing, King Charles II, John Standing as Godolphin and noted film veteran, Austin Trevor, as Lord Halifax. I appeared in just two of the episodes (silly man had to fall out with the king and get himself banished from court) as Lord Russell. Arthur Pentelow, ex-Northern Theatre School and later of *Emmerdale Farm*, Margaret Tyzack, Daphne Heard, Lisa Daniely and John Westbrook are all names that catch my eye as I scan the cast lists.

One and two-line 'bits' were the order of the day until it was panto time again. As I said, *Sleep In, Beauty* was not to be so I was 'available' and was engaged by a company called Divek Ltd to play King Wolf in *Red Riding Hood* at the famous Theatre Royal, Stratford East, E15. With regret I must tell you that it was not a happy experience. The one good factor was a fortuitous meeting with an amazingly versatile actor/writer/director, then in his early days, called Roger Tolliday. I'm happy to say that Roger remains a friend to the present day. Eventually we shall come to the version of *Sweeney Todd, the Fiendish Barber of Fleet Street* which he wrote for 'Uncle' Colin and in which we were to tour, but that's in the future. Roger was to play the Witch to my King Wolf and, being a master of make-up and costume design, he was one of the few good things in this otherwise sad festive season fiasco.

After two days of rehearsal the dame sent in laryngitis sick-notes (two of them just to make sure his message got home!). I was asked to play the dame using my own wardrobe and wigs for the same salary as I was to get for King Wolf in a very tattered, ill-fitting costume as supplied by the management. 'Not likely!' The scenery and costumes had obviously been acquired as a job lot. The backcloths had been folded up for so long that even at the end of this awful three weeks one could still see all the cracks in the painted canvas. There were half a dozen kilts and three rather mangy sporrans (poor things should have been peacefully 'put down') and one dark scene which, when it was hung and lit, appeared to be some sort of castle. Before this was a frontcloth ad lib scene, i.e. no written script, which was given to Roger and myself.

Now come on folks, anyone who knows about panto, an ad lib scene between the two supposedly frightening baddies? 'What the hell!' we said as we plotted what we'd do. Our only 'direction' was that we make it long enough to cover the main scene change going on behind us. We worked hard – young Roger proved to be an excellent pupil, eager to learn – so that after some 'evil-type' verbal swordplay we launched into a breakneck speed version of that oldie gag 'The Man With the Power'.

For the uninitiated, it starts off and can go on, with variations, for years.

1. 'You remind me of the man.'
2. 'What man?'
1. 'The man with the power.'
2. 'What power?'
1. 'The power of voodoo.'
2. 'Who do?'
1. 'You do.'
2. 'I do what?'
1. 'Not *what*, *who*!'
2. 'Doctor Who?'

and on and on and on, through what, which, who, where and so on until one arrives back at:

1. 'You remind me of that man.'
2. 'Who do?'
1. 'You do.'
2. 'Help! Let me out!'

We climaxed with, when we got a thumbs up from the stage management:

Me (as King Wolf): I have got a lot o' land'
Roger and me: So off we go to Scot-a-land!

Even our musical director, Graham Bond, groaned very audibly each time we said it but we had to get from one tatty scene to the other somehow. Things became so bad in the company that we decided a cast meeting would be in order. We'd already hit the *Stratford Express* with a headline, 'Narrow Escape for Red Riding Hood' and I was asked if I would agree to be Equity deputy for the company. The management became even more obtuse. The cast having already agreed, reluctantly, to take a cut in salaries to keep the show open, I had to approach Equity to insist that

Divek Ltd paid us all in cash each week as most of the last week's cheques had 'bounced'. A meeting with the management was arranged – for on stage – with Priscilla Meredith of Equity HQ in attendance. Denzil Ellis, who played the Lord Chancellor, Roger and I had to protest most strongly – and made sure it was 'noted' by Equity HQ – when the director not only became professionally but personally abusive and insulting to Priscilla and Equity members.

Divek had, apparently, rented the theatre en bloc. After the final performance I had to follow the Divek management rep into the bar to collect money as he took it over the counter in order to pay our troupe of dancers. Deservedly certain names duly appeared on Equity's 'Inform Head Office Before Signing Contracts With...' black list in *The Stage*.

Roger Tolliday was interested in playing the dame in pantomime and he had seen me as a dame as well as appearing briefly in *Dad's Army* so we had long discussions on the subject. In years to come I was to see Roger as a very funny and most ingeniously dressed dame in some number one panto productions, and I am very proud of his claim that, in that field, he is 'one of 'Uncle' Colin's protégés'. It's been an honour and a pleasure to be professionally associated with 'a real professional'.

It was also a pleasure to 'celebrate' the end of that panto, even with the prospects of, 'See you in Orchard Street next week.' (Orchard Street, the labour exchange in Victoria seemed to cater mainly for actors!)

INTERVAL

Chapter Twenty-Five

From mid-January until mid-April was quite a long 'rest' which, in turn, particularly because of the disastrous pantomime, led to one or two acrimonious exchanges between the bank manager and me. I can't remember now whether or not bank managers had started on their penchant for living in cupboards but mine most certainly had a hot typewriter. Both he and I were glad when up popped another episode of *Liver Birds* (as a factory gate strike agitator).

In May the Walmington-on-Sea Home Guard was called to the colours again, this time for the great experience of the 'Royal Television Gala' in the presence of HM the Queen and HRH the Duke of Edinburgh. This was held at the Television Theatre, Shepherd's Bush (the former Shepherd's Bush Empire), even though the majority of 'small-part' players had to dress in and perambulate from a nearby hall. Although converted into a TV studio there were still never enough dressing rooms at this old theatre, as I was to find out in future TV shows.

It was naturally a star-studded bill, timed to the second, with such luminaries as Morecambe and Wise and Frankie Howard who, with our stellar front line, was presented to Her Majesty after the show. We, the 'second line', formed a sort of guard of honour through which the guests could proceed onto the stage.

Again I was, as I am still, in total admiration of the inventiveness of Messrs Croft and Perry. The Walmington

Mr Chairman

Caius Lucius

Mr Churchill

Widow Twankey

Pte Sponge

platoon had, in an emergency, been sent to London to help out the Buckingham Palace detachment of the Home Guard. The noble captain, as you may well imagine, was totally in his element there! Even Sgt Wilson, for once, had to fasten his tunic's top button. The Coldstream Guards were to be shown how the guarding of the royal family should be done. 'No sloppiness here! Stupid boy!'

Poor old Fraser, Jones and Godfrey especially, it was felt, might not enhance the synchronisation of drill movements and were detailed off, under the command of Lance Corporal Jones, to form the rearguard, i.e. guard the rear of the Palace, just under the kitchen windows, by the dustbins. The last shot of our contribution to this Gala occasion was of these three lovely old boys bemoaning missing out on all the pomp and circumstance of us doing guard duty on that famous forecourt, even though it was now night-time. As they stood by the dustbins the viewer saw the backs of two little girls approach the trio, from camera, carrying three mugs of cocoa. It brought the house down for the two little girls, judging by their dress and hairstyles, looked remarkably like the young Princess Elizabeth and the young Princess Margaret Rose. Jimmy Perry told me later that it had met with something even warmer than royal approval. 'That Was A Night, That Was', to misquote the title of another show.

An appearance in a BBC TV production *Where Was Spring?* led up to seven continuous months of work on *Dad's Army*; seven episodes, prefaced by outdoor location work in June and July and seven more in October/November. In-between these we made *Dad's Army – The Film* for Columbia Pictures. Bill Pertwee has dealt with it quite fully in his 'encyclopaedia' book and so I'm not going to dwell at length upon what, for many, were not the happiest weeks of this otherwise momentous year of *Dad's Army*. Suffice to say that until the intervention of Arthur

Lowe, Clive Dunn and other principals, we of the 'second line' tended to be regarded as daily employed crowd extras. Being a film there were well over one hundred extras in Home Guard uniform, some of whom were possibly employed – as film studios are wont to do – on a daily basis, particularly those engaged only in long-shot scenes. To one rather officious crowd marshal (according to his very prominent armband) Arthur introduced us as 'an essential part of this team which enables this show to retain its popularity.' He asked this man, in authoritative tones, if he'd be so kind as to remember this in future and when it came to catering and 'break' times we were part of the artists' cast. The said gentleman was, if no longer so officious, even less cordial towards us than before. He'd issue shouted orders to 'You extras!' and then equally loudly remember – 'Except, of course, these stars.'

A number of old pals turned up as supplementary platoon members and small-part players, including David Fennel who had only recently finished being a popular young member of the cast of the television show *Crossroads*. You'll find out why I single out this particular actor in due course.

Another of the year's developments did not concern *Dad's Army* but the Palace Theatre, Watford. It would seem that, having had somewhat less than a success with their last effort at a pantomime and the previous year's non-pantomime children's play production, the cry had gone up, 'Bring back the Perrys!' Alas, Jimmy and Gilda were both heavily engaged otherwise and regretted that they couldn't come to the rescue. I had a phone call from the theatre director, the renowned and highly respected Kay Gardner, inviting me to go over to see her. As Giles Havergal and Peter Elrington had moved on there were few people on the staff I knew. It would seem that the last panto, *Cinderella*, on a modernistic three-dimensional silver setting on a revolve stage (against black surrounding drapes) had not met with any great approval by cast or audience, despite them being assured that it would spring to life in a blaze of colour and movement with costumes.

The general verdict seemed to be that it was lifeless, colourless and more like *The Trojan Women* with silver glitter. Upon my visit I was greeted almost royally, Miss Gardner pointing out to me that the council of management had given her strict instructions to 'get a proper panto, a Perry panto!' The result of her contact with the Perrys was her phone call to me. Believe me, it was an honour to learn that Jimmy and Gilda had suggested that if the Palace wanted a traditional pantomime I was the person to approach. After a long talk and 'fields of activity and authority' defined, a salary to direct and to play the dame was settled upon. Thus, when I went back for the final week of shooting of the film at Shepperton Studios, David Fennell came into the pantomime ambience.

First, however, back to wartime (the period and the atmosphere on the sound stage) with 'The End' in sight and the prospect of another TV series coming up. It is not for me to analyse the ins and outs of what went on during the making of the film. On the grapevine one gathered that, as time progressed, the relationship between those involved at Columbia and those who had created the show at the BBC grew less cordial. As we marched along one day in Chalfont St Giles, the film's location for Walmington (can't think what Thetford had done to upset them), Desmond Callum-Jones, another original and long-serving member of the 'second line' as Pte Desmond, and I spotted some of our BBC technical crew and our studio floor manager among a crowd of 'out of camera shot' onlookers. We couldn't resist it. As it was a rehearsal march, together we cried, 'Come back, BBC. All is forgiven!' Such, dear reader, was the depth of the platoon's depression. Bernard Severn

(Intimate, Palmers Green) and Bernard Archard (Sheffield Playhouse) were among the old friends who were also involved.

The autumn episodes of the television show are noted, as far as I am concerned, because during this Pte Sponge arrived in name. During rehearsal of one of the later episodes Captain Mainwaring had to instruct someone to carry out a duty or action but this time, 'Yes Captain Mainwaring,' had not been assigned to anyone in particular. It was, I think, a fairly important duty – probably a message to be conveyed – and so it couldn't be ignored. Director David asked co-writer Jimmy to whom the captain's request was directed.

One principal replied, 'Well it can't be me because I've just left the hall.' Another said, 'And I'm not in this scene.' So it was given to Colin, and it was established that for identity and continuity I'd need a name. This was 'directed action with set lines by a definite character' category work.

From the contractual point of view these circumstances make a difference. This, it was agreed, would be 'sorted out in the office' and a name for this minor character would be invented before the episode was recorded. Jimmy Perry had a remarkable memory as well as sense of humour. Earlier in the year, as they had driven around Norfolk seeking some suitable outdoor locations, Jimmy had pointed out a butcher's shop with the name 'Sponge, Butcher' over the window – one of those little snippets he was likely to store away in his memory for possible future use. Thus I became Pte Sponge. The other chaps of the 'second line' congratu-lated me. I think I was the first of our supporting group to achieve a character name, and as dear George Hancock (later to be Pte Hancock) pointed out, at least it confirmed that the name had nothing to do with Bean's known capacity for pints of ale!

During the final week of work on the film version, conversation at a break period had veered onto the subject of what one would be doing for Christmas. Ian Lavender and David Fennell seemed to become intrigued with my projected pantomime, both saying that they'd never done one. Well of course to me if you haven't done panto you haven't lived, you're not a 'real actor'. Much light-hearted and good-natured banter resulted in my enquiring if they would be interested in the possibility of playing the broker's men at Watford in *Mother Goose*. I was to direct and appear in the eponymous role.

That evening I phoned Kay Gardner to discuss such a possibility. Ian Lavender of *Dad's Army* and David Fennell of *Crossroads* as Biff and Boff would be a great added attraction to the show. Kay agreed and the next morning I approached the two gentlemen and asked if they were still serious about it. They were. Their agents made contact with the Palace Theatre and it was 'all on' for a start to pantomime rehearsals early in December. The TV series finished just before rehearsals in Watford commenced, with rumours of 'the next series being the last'. Well, we'll just have to wait and see.

Ferdy Fox, the crafty villain of the piece, was played by prominent radio actor, Christian Rodska. In many ways it was unfortunate that the version of *Mother Goose* chosen, and to which we were committed, was a new-look and not very traditional pantomime version with, brilliant as they were, music and lyrics already set in by Malcolm Sircom. There had been quite a few weeks' hard work put in by me to rearrange the script into traditional pantomime form which was the commission I had been given.

For a start, it was far too long. Musical director Peter Murray and I had decided that other pieces of music would need to be introduced including somewhere at least a reference to 'Who Do You Think You Are Kidding, Mr

Hitler', my own 'How Are You Keeping, All right?' and a number which Peter and I had written in place of a song in the eviction from the cottage scene which neither of us liked. Our own 'Out Into the Cold', although still appropriate to the situation, was far less dirge-like and minor key. Felicity Harrison and Wendy Pollock were respectively principal boy and girl, Jack and Jill, and friends Bernard Severn and Derek Tobias fulfilled a number of roles in this very colourful production. With scenery and costumes designed by Hans Christian and skilfully lit by Ian Callender, this sixteen-member cast show in its toy theatre setting was, I'm happy to say, successful.

Derrick Gilbert was an excellent Baron Bluster with whom I enjoyed playing a number of dialogue scenes, one of which included a delightfully hilarious song and dance number 'For the Want of Anything Better'. The traditional dame's undressing scene in this version was far funnier than the usual (which I find boring) cod-stripper scene. The baron and the broker's men all got involved in it and there's a lovely picture of Biff and Boff and Mother Goose all inside one extra-large lady's foundation garment.

'We'll do the corset tango,' said I.

'Why the corset tango?' chimed Ian and David.

Wait for it! Wait for it!

'Corset's the only dance I know!'

Lines like that will never die while there is panto alive and kicking. A pre-finale, frontcloth, song-sheet scene had to be included and, at the start of the show, even without a line of dancers and chorus, one couldn't start a Perry-type traditional pantomime with the dame merely walking on to open with a speech. Rearranging it was a big job. The choreographer and my assistant director was the highly inventive Virginia Mason and we all worked under the eagle eye for detail (and stopwatch) of Kay Gardner for six weeks.

During these last two years I had also fitted in appearances in an episode of *Up Pompeii* and of *The Harry Worth Show* plus three episodes of *The Eric Sykes Show*. Working with Frankie Howard was to work with a meticulous expert in comedy timing. The wonderfully 'laid-back' casual approach, every 'Ooh' and Ahh' was counted and timed, which could make rehearsals rather long but as fellow northerner, Elizabeth Larner, and comedy/revue actor Max Adrian both said, the finished result was well worth it. Mrs Siddy-bow-tome, Jeanne Mockford of my Scarborough summer season, was giving forth with glorious, 'Woe! Woe! Woe!' cries as Senna, which all added to the fun.

1971 got under way with some one and two-day small roles in ATV's *The Prize*, BBC's *Idle At Work*, Thames TV's *Armchair Theatre* and *Hine* for ATV. *Two Tramps* was the working title for a projected BBC series which didn't seem to run into many episodes. This one involved an eventually riotous 'pie-throwing' uproar in a rather posh London hotel (filmed on location!).

May found me in episodes of *Budgie* (LWT) and *Bird on the Wing* (BBC) before my involvement in 'The World Premiere. An outstanding event in the theatre. Dame Agatha's first new play for years.' You've guessed it, Agatha Christie again. 'Successful? It should be. Look who wrote it,' said one paper. 'Queen of suspense plays for laughs,' said another. '*The Mousetrap* this is not,' opined a third.

Yes, I'm afraid it was something of a curate's egg entitled *Fiddlers Five*. Barry Howard, doubling as a Sikh doctor (with the unlikely name of Doctor Nolan) and an undertaker, Mr Moss – a prelude to his much later performances as Mr Sowerberry in *Oliver* perhaps – was the only genuinely funny element in the play. Most other laughs, I fear, were probably nervous giggles of embarrassed hysteria.

Despite one and a half pounds of nose putty, wig and moustache there was not a lot I could do in a large role with a name like Mr Bogusian.

Chapter Twenty-Six

The production of *Fiddlers Five* was put on by veteran actor/manager (one of very few of the 'old school' still active then), J. Grant Anderson. Directed by John Downing, Jimmy himself played the lawyer Mr Truscott. My character seemed to be a 'joking, Jewish, shady dealer', the plot of the play highly improbable, and the whole thing coming under the banner of 'a comedy thriller'. Quite a number indicated that 'thrills' were few and far between, a lot of the comedy was probably unintentional and the 'scripted' jokes certainly needed to be worked on to raise genuine smiles. But it was after all, 'Dame Agatha's first play for years' and that was its selling point.

The tour started in Southsea, opening (with Dame Agatha in the audience) on 7th June, 1971, after which it was a pleasure to revisit Bristol for a week. Some of the *My Fair Lady* friends were still around and an extraordinary meeting of the Doolittle Club was held in the bar of the Grapes opposite the stage door. Many happy memories were revived, incidents and cricket matches recalled and photos brought in. All too soon it was time to move on for a week's stay in Nottingham, Manchester, Birmingham and Wimbledon.

The stay in Wimbledon was to be for four weeks which, at first, I thought a little strange. *Fiddlers Five*, with all due respect to the 'Queen of Crime', was in my opinion not strong enough or good enough to run in the large and prestigious Wimbledon Theatre for such a long time. The discovery that I was right produced very mixed feelings. When the tour got to Wimbledon, J.G.A. announced that we weren't going to do *Fiddlers Five* for four weeks. We were to present a short summer theatre season.

'Ello, 'ello, what's this?' I thought. Upon enquiry my worst fears were realised. *Fiddlers Five* would be the play for the first week only, followed by three other plays. Back to weekly rep! And here was me thinking that I was progressing up the theatrical ladder. 'What fools we mortals be!'

The programme announced was *The Ringer*, *Uproar in the House* and *A Murder Has Been Arranged*. The *Surrey Comet* and the *Wimbledon News* had quite a time at the expense of the summer theatre season. 'March of Time makes even Edgar Wallace Creak' and 'The Ringer strikes a flat note' were headlines for our first effort. My efforts as 'an intelligent police doctor... shone like a beacon among a rather concrete cast', said the *Comet*. Barry Howard was the only person to impress the *News* as 'the star of the show' in *Uproar in the House* with the verdict by the *Comet* being the headline 'Noisy and Futile. This play is an utter disaster.' All encouraging stuff!

The reasons for selecting the final play, even though it is by Emlyn Williams, eludes me still. When I first saw it in rep, many years ago, I thought *A Murder Has Been Arranged* was a very contrived and somewhat incredible affair. Even as the subject of the arranged murder I could not raise much enthusiasm for Sir Charles Jasper, despite a rather splendid nose putty job and a distinguished looking hairpiece. 'Murder in More Ways Than One' was, I think, a justifiable newspaper headline.

Although *Fiddlers Five* was due to resume its tour after this there would be cast chances. Valerie Dane, Johnny Barrs and I had other commitments coming up. For me, a few more TV small parts and a visit to Wigan to be fitted in before my return (by request) to pantomime at the Palace, Watford.

Crisis, however, is never far away. Valerie and I received calls asking us to go to the Arts Theatre, Cambridge, for one more week of *Fiddlers Five* because our replacements were not quite ready to take over.

The BBC's *Take My Wife* starring Sheila Hancock and Donald Houston saw me playing the man in a rainmac in an art gallery. No lines for this. A couple of audible reactions to an overheard conversation between the stars – and indications of that for which 'men in drab raincoats in art galleries' are noted – got a lovely exit laugh which prompted Miss Hancock, in a most genial and friendly way, to point this out to our live audience as a perfect example of how to steal a scene without saying anything.

Two episodes of *The Goodies* were both great fun to do and in October came another 'first' for me. The pantomime at the Palace this year was to be *Jack and the Beanstalk* with myself as Dame Durden. As I'd had quite a busy year and as I've never really liked both directing and playing in the same production, it was arranged that Virginia Mason would direct the panto as well as continue as choreographer. Dame Durden proved to be an extra long role for a dame so I was quite relieved by this arrangement.

Before the panto, however, another 'first', an orchestral concert with the North London Sinfonia on 16th October. Under the direction of twenty-two year old Royal Academy of Music prize winner Adrian Brown, the NLS consisting of young musicians, many studying for a professional career, was based in Bushey Heath. As the *Watford Observer* had already announced that I would be 'back home at the Palace', and the event at St Peter's, Bushey Heath, was aimed at attracting young people to orchestral concerts, the players had decided that *Peter and the Wolf* with the narration by someone known locally might be a good idea. An afternoon performance for local schools was given before the 'black tie' concert in the evening. I was very happy to read later that the review was headlined, 'NLS concert best yet'.

In the meantime, as 'tis said in all the best convoluted plots, I had had a visitor from Wigan. A new arts and entertainments magazine called *The Wigan Scene* had been started by one John D. Slater. A request came for me to be interviewed for Issue Number Six in a monthly feature called 'Wigan Profile' which, it appeared, dealt with us Wiganers who had 'emigrated' into the world of drama, music and literature. Little did I know then that this was to lead to a theatrical business association which, from 1973, was going to last on and off for over twenty years. John D. Slater, not the film star, is another name you'll be coming across quite a few times before we get to our destination.

So, 22nd December to 22nd January was panto time once more! This time we had a fairly traditional script by John Crocker, with music by Eric Gilder and our own musical director Peter Murray. Christian Rodska joined our company as the eponymous climber of the beanstalk and my old pal, Derek Tobias, as what may sound very unglamorous – one part of Daisy the cow. Angela Easterling was the heroine Joan, and Clive Cable was the Duke and one head of our very effective two-headed giant Blunderbore paired, literally, with David Jennings as the other head. The children loved that, especially when the two 'fell out' with each other. With Christian as a hero with a sense of fun came Bernie Smith and Jack Galloway as Bubble and Squeak.

Derek Tobias in the forward position with Robert Philips aft made Daisy the cow very affectionate and 'alive'. The former's operation of eyes and mouth and the latter's tail operating were a joy to behold. After that crucial decision to send Daisy to market (to pay the dastardly

Duke's dues) I had the job of telling her what was to happen and to take a sad farewell of her with the song 'Can I Forget You?' – for which Virginia brought us to the front, downstage right, to the run-out steps. As I sang and Daisy acted, the lights lowered except for a spotlight on us which as I finished on a very quiet few notes reduced to a pin point and, on the last note, blacked out. Not a dry eye in the house! Clever Virginia, because this gave equal poignancy to the next bit as the lights came up again, when I told Jack to take her to the market because 'I couldn't face it'. Reprise of music as they exited down stage left and I did my 'tragic muse' exit stage right.

One particularly clever scene among the excellent series of sets prepared by Bob Ringwood and Anushia Nieradzik was the interior of Dame Durden's cottage. Built on two 'trucks', when the tabs opened it looked like a small inset scene with a practical door in the centre of the back wall and a practical window through which to throw the despised bag of beans. After my entrance and initial chat, including 'My sister Nelly, just had all her teeth out and a new gas oven in', Jack entered, told of his disposal of our beloved Daisy, suffered my severe reprimands and, as I disposed of said beans, exited by the door. I sat on a convenient chair to weep and ponder and, very quickly indeed, nod off to sleep. To music our inset cottage room suddenly split down the middle, door and door frame included. Each half, with me still on the left half, glided silently offstage to reveal a storybook garden. The last sighting of Jack, as we came to the interval, was of him climbing up towards the theatre flies, finding footholds between the leaves of this very practical plant which had grown up 'before your very eyes' on cleverly disguised piano wires. What a great round of applause that got.

Press features of the day included a very honourable paragraph and photograph in *The Stage & TV Today* on 30th

December and a picture of the 'Dame of Watford' in the *Watford Observer* of 16th December with statistics to show that, at the Palace Theatre, I had appeared in forty-eight plays, five pantomimes and an Old Time Music Hall since I first went there for Jimmy and Gilda in 1962.

A lot of the success of *Jack and the Beanstalk* came from the sheer exuberance and enthusiasm of a fairly young and very active cast. Chris, for example, not only being a swimmer, fencer, ice-skater and an equestrian, had only recently finished whizzing around the countryside on a motorbike in twenty-six episodes of *Follyfoot*. I was the 'oldie' in the company! Thank heavens I was never asked to ride a motorbike in *Dad's Army*. As we shall see, in time, I had enough trouble with a horse.

As we opened before Christmas I had arranged to go to Wigan after the matinée on 24th December (no evening performance) about 6 p.m. The London–Glasgow train included stops at Watford Junction, Crewe, Warrington and Wigan. A further arrangement was that I'd bring Father back with me for a few days to stay at the Station Hotel, almost opposite the entrance to Watford Junction station and a short distance from the Palace Theatre. By applying in advance I was able to ensure that he would be looked after by British Rail staff on his return journey. His physical condition was now deteriorating more quickly. He might not be able to get away on many more long-distance pleasure breaks. Watford was, after all, not unknown because of the number of holiday stays we'd had there with our old family friends – 'Aunty Nan' and 'Uncle Joe' Johnson and their two children, 'adopted cousins', Win and Ken. They of course were no longer there but a trip round the town, the park and High Street by taxi brought back some memories as he recognised places not visited by him since before World War Two. 'Uncle Joe' had been a close pal of Father's in World War One and was also a 'Geordie'.

Pa was not overly impressed with the pantomime though he liked Chris and Angela. I got into trouble when in front of most of the company over a post-show drink in the bar, he said in a very loud voice (he was also suffering from a severe loss of hearing) that I'd made him look like a fool. That certainly caught the general attention. Apparently when I'd said my farewell to Daisy the Cow ('Can I Forget You?') Harry Bean had been seen shedding tears in public and couldn't I have chosen another song? I should have known that that song was one of my dear, late stepmother's favourites. The fact that the song was required by the script and director mattered not one jot to Father. We should all 'have known better'.

Mercifully Derek, I think it was, got him a large Scotch, came and sat with us and happily changed the subject. Derek is still an old chum for whom I have a very high regard and is now an excellent panto dame in his own right. I like to think he learned a little from his mentor in dame technique, and in recent years he's paid me the compliment of featuring one of my dame songs and some of my material in his panto performances – so Pa didn't put him off his Beans in 1971.

At least, over Christmas, he'd had episodes of *Dad's Army*, *The Goodies* and *Liver Birds* on TV, so perhaps it wasn't too bad a festive season for him. His comment on the phone on the first Sunday after his return to Wigan – 'It was all right, I suppose, but the milk's gone off. You didn't put it in the fridge before we left' – must, I suppose, suffice as approval.

Chapter Twenty-Seven

Mid-April, 1972, was taken up by three days' work on a programme for ATV whose name I've forgotten (*Man From... Somewhere*) and on the 29th I was back on to the coach at BBC TV Centre for another stint of *Dad's Army* location shooting in Norfolk. Pte Sponge now seemed to be popping up a little more frequently; since 'The Battle of Godfrey's Cottage' in series two he'd appeared twice in series three and five, once in series six and a 'grand special' called 'The Battle of the Giants'. In the majority of all the other episodes, and the Columbia film, I'd been 'a member of the platoon'. The programmes from 1972 until 1977 were what one might call 'Sponge's heydays', over twenty episodes involving this rather solidly built and not, perhaps, the brightest of sheep farmers. Series seven and eight, of seven and six episodes respectively, took up quite a lot of 1972 and Sponge was beginning, occasionally, to say a little more than 'Yes, Captain Mainwaring or 'Right, sir'. He even had the odd funny line which, in a half-hour comedy show with stars of the calibre of our 'Magnificent Seven' plus Bill Pertwee (Warden Hodges), Frank Williams (Rev. Timothy Farthing) and Edward Sinclair (Verger Yeatman), was quite a consideration by the writers. After all, Bill, Frank and Ted were 'known' names too.

However, if I was involved in a scene with any of the stars of the show I was never made to feel under pressure or, as I've experienced with some other stars, 'Oh for God's sake get on and get off – you're only a bit player.' No names, no pack drill, but in an episode of one very popular show in which I had a small role I experienced the show's top name calling to the director, as if I was not even present, 'Look, do we need that odd line from whatever his name is? It interrupts my flow.' This never happened with Arthur, Clive, either of the Johns, Ian, Arnold or Jim. On one occasion Arthur called me over during rehearsal to say, 'Colin, that line of yours [I had only one line in this episode], if you'd "lift" it at the end and say the last word right at me, I'll pause and you'll get a good laugh on it.' That's the sort of folk the *Dad's Army* family was.

The first group for 1972 included 'Soldier's Farewell' in which Mainwaring, after a cinema visit and cheese for supper dreamt that he really fulfilled Hodges' nickname for him – Napoleon. As Marshal Ney in this dream sequence I was, with others, required to sit upon a horse to view the battle. Arthur, an experienced rider, was on the famous white horse called Whisky. I was eventually hoisted onto a strapping fine animal called Caesar, who seemed a lot taller that he looked once I was on his back – if you see what I mean.

Well there I was, dressed up to the nines, as the French marshal. To Napoleon's enquiry, 'What of the battle, Marshal?', I replied with the same line that I'd said as we left the cinema earlier – 'I couldn't see very well. I told you we should have sat in the ninepennies!'

Once clad in my very well fitted uniform, complete with plumed cocked hat, I was on the horse for ages. Stills photographers were all snapping away at us in these magnificent outfits. Arthur's portrayal of the French emperor is the only time I've seen Bonaparte wearing spectacles. At one point David Croft came over to me to ask, 'What's going on?' to which, as photographers will, cried, 'Just one more!', 'Look this way!', 'Can you turn the horse's head?'

In his quiet but meaningful way David intimated that, much as he appreciated the work they had to do, he had a recording schedule to keep to and lighting conditions to watch. 'Right, Colin,' he continued. 'I'd like you over there, to the left of Arthur, please.'

Without thinking I said, 'What, on this?'

David laughed and said 'Of course. Why else do you think you're up there?'

Caesar decided he wanted to go the other way so I called, 'Help! Where's the driver?'

Jimmy Beck rode over and said a few calming 'Whoa, Caesar, whoa boy' type phrases and helped me to get to my place.

After some hours, tight-fitting doeskin trousers do begin to have a numbing effect on one's limbs, especially if one has never worn them nor sat on horseback before. From the waist down I couldn't feel a thing so when David called, 'And – cut!' on our final take of our final shot and said, 'Thank you, everyone – nice one,' it was time to dismount.

Arthur, with experienced ease, swung over Whisky's back, left foot in stirrup; Jimmy and the others likewise. Sponge though couldn't move. I felt paralysed. One of the horse-tenders, known for some reason as a stable lad (he must have been sixty-odd and small and thin as a jockey) came over. 'Are you having trouble, Mr Bean?'

'Too true, mate,' I replied. 'I can't move.'

His advice was to pull my right foot out of its stirrup, then my left and lean over to my left so that I'd slide off the horse's back. Caesar was very patient throughout all this, probably having a quiet inner laugh at this stout idiot he'd been carrying. The idea was, according to the stable lad, that as I slid off he'd catch me. All sixteen stones of me!

I did say, 'Well, on your head be it!' and it was. The plucky man certainly broke my fall and prevented my white doeskin trousers and braided tunic from going into the muddy ground. It was a bit like a cartoon where after being pressed into the ground by a heavy weight, upon removal the poor victim leaves a perfect body impression in the ground. Thank goodness we got all those shots in one session. Had I had to dismount I'm sure I would never have got on again. Sorry, Caesar, nothing personal!

The next day most of the platoon were not required until after lunch, and weren't my posterior and I glad of the respite because in the next bit of filming, for a different episode, we were on an initiative test assault course. After running across part of a field as a team of six, carrying short telegraph poles on our shoulders, we then used the said poles to ford a stream. The 'Magnificent Seven' were with the pole nearest to camera, my section was in long shot. The efficiency of Pte Sponge's section was somewhat marred by the fact that Pte Sponge, as first across, was pulling himself along sitting astride a telegraph pole and already suffering saddle-soreness when suddenly he couldn't move any further forward. Number one section, the stars, were going great guns with all their comedy business but I don't think Mr Croft had scheduled further chaos on the pole in the background as well. One of the assistants waded into the stream in long waders to discover that, although the props department thought that they had checked everything, the seat of Sponge's trousers was caught on a nail. Fortunately this hold-up in operations was accepted with good humour, even by a sorely embarrassed Sponge – and a loud comment from one of my fellow platoon members, 'Good for you, old Bean. Can't even ride a telegraph pole, never mind a horse!'

Being Pte Sponge was having its uses to the writers now because 'Sponge' was beginning to be recognised a little. To get from a scene involving the whole platoon into one involving just the stars and/or a featured player, Captain Mainwaring could issue orders to the effect, 'Pte Sponge will maintain watch here with his section whilst we silently infiltrate' or command, 'Right, Sponge, you and number two section go round the other way'. To most of which, naturally, I had a line in reply.

In one particular episode at a party the gallant captain left Sponge in charge of the drinks department with an admonition that the booze must be kept safe. Messrs Croft and Perry gave me the lovely reply, 'Don't worry, Captain Mainwaring, not a drop shall touch our lips.' Then as we exited, I muttered to Pte Desmond, 'We'll use two straws.' Even now, twenty or more years later, people will come to me in a bar and say, 'Not using your straws?'

The last episode for series seven was 'in the can' on June 30th and in mid-July I was in Westcliff-on-Sea rehearsing for my friend, Mr Tony Clayton, at the Palace Theatre there. I had known Tony from his short stay with The Graham Players during the ill-fated South Shields season. Let me add, the season's ill fate had nothing to do with Tony who is an excellent director and designer.

For four weeks during August he was to present a music-hall-type show called *The Best of British Music Hall*. His six resident artistes, with me as chairman, rehearsed two different programmes of old-fashioned songs, mono-logues and melodramas so that anyone on holiday for two weeks could see two different shows within the same context. The novelty in this case was that for each of the four weeks we'd have a different star, top-of-the-bill artiste. Thus the unforgettable Jimmy Wheeler ('Ay, ay! That's yer lot!') preceded the 'voice of them all', Peter Cavanagh. He was followed by a man who must surely have originated the term 'laid-back', even if we weren't conscious of it at the time – the delightful Irish 'Strolling Vagabond', Cavan O'Connor. This most enjoyable short summer season was rounded off by the great entertainers Bob and Alf Pearson ('My brother and I'). And for such a beautifully designed and presented show in this lovely theatre just look at the ticket prices – sixty pence, fifty pence, forty pence and gallery twenty pence.

September brought along work in two programmes, in Terry Scott's series *Scott on...*, each programme having a different theme, and a show called *Love Story* for ATV. Then I was asked to go to see former *Dad's Army* floor manager, Harold Snoad, who had now become a TV director. Harold was about to embark on a very strange Sherlock Holmes mystery, which, I'm sure owed only the names Holmes and Watson to Conan Doyle. N.F. Simpson's witty pen was responsible for *Elementary my Dear Watson*, with John Cleese as the great detective, William Rushton as the good doctor, Norman Bird and Chic Murray as the police inspector and constable. John Wells was the prime minister and Bill Maynard played Frank Potter. Somewhere involved also were Dawn Adams, Josephine Tewson, Rosa Hill, Michael Knowles, fellow ex-Court Player, Ivor Salter, Patrick Campbell, Alan Coran, Frank Muir and Robert Robinson. Me? In the cast list I'm named Newsboy and was heavily made up to look about a hundred years old!

October and part of November, besides an episode of *Here's Harry* with quiet and amiable Harry Worth, were mainly taken up with thirteen episodes of the first TV show for children that I'd ever done. But I feel that I must tell you first a reminiscence of Mr Worth.

During some location shooting in one of the North London suburbs in a shopping centre, rain came down quite heavily, forcing us all to retire to the coach in which we'd travelled. As the rain got heavier we sought various diversions and one lady of our company started on a crossword puzzle. Well, as nobody filmed or recorded us trying to do a crossword with help from Harry Worth, one of life's greatest impromptu comedies has been lost for all time. We were in 'full flight' as it were, almost hoping the rain wouldn't stop just then. It didn't, but a member of the camera crew sitting up front became aware of a small, rather elderly lady, covering her head with a newspaper and knocking on the coach window. He went to investigate, invited her in out of the rain and asked how we could help. It emerged that her bedridden daughter was an avid Harry Worth fan. Seeing him actually filming across the road from her bedroom window viewing point had given her one of the greatest thrills of her life. Her mother had been to a nearby shop, bought a blank-pages notebook and wondered if Mr Worth would be kind enough to sign and, perhaps, send a photo if she gave him her address and a stamp.

Harry was on his feet at once, signed the book after asking the name of the young lady and got an eight-by-ten glossy out of the production assistant's briefcase. Then he looked around and said, 'Colin, you're Private Sponge. You sign too, and you Jeff and Debby.' He then asked the mother which was the house in question before turning back to say. 'All of you, with your names put the names of your latest TV show before this one, even if you were a non-speaker.' When this was done, did he hand the book back to an obviously grateful mother? No, he grabbed a BBC location staff umbrella and went off with this very happy lady, over to the house, saying to the director with a 'pointing upwards' gesture, 'Tell Him not to stop raining just yet.'

When he returned after about fifteen minutes, in a very quiet mood he asked us to wave to the upstairs window opposite because he didn't think a very brave youngster would be leaving that room very often before she was much older. The weather cleared. As we 'de-bussed' we waved and at the 'wrap' he insisted we all wave again. That was my one and only experience of working with Harry Worth.

Chapter Twenty-Eight

Thirteen episodes of a programme for children were spent also very happily – in a madcap way – with the incredible Michael Bentine. The programme was *Michael Bentine Time* and the fun was non-stop. Norman McLeod and I were engaged for what we understood to be the first episode of Michael's new show, complete with new micro-puppets, mad inventions and crazily funny children's participation contests. John Downes was director and at the first rehearsal (Latymer Mission, Western Avenue, for those who remember their rehearsal rooms location map) John asked if we'd worked with Mr Bentine. I think Norman's reaction was, as mine, 'Oh dear, does this indicate trouble, temperaments and difficulties?' We had both worked under such unpleasant circumstances with other 'name' artistes.

At our negative reply he gave a wry smile and remarked, 'Then you're in for quite an experience!'

And how! Michael Bentine was a most amazing gentleman, versatile and not just in the Thespian sense – a genius of serious as well as comic invention – very articulate and very funny. The script we had been given had all the usual first and second page information – cast, staff, director, camera, rehearsal and transmission times and so on. Apart from odd pieces such as announcer, opening credits, introducing Michael and later on 'Michael's latest invention' and 'introducing this week's guest artiste'… there were no clues as to what we, Norman and I, would actually be required to do.

Michael 'whirlwinded' into the rehearsal room with, 'Let's have a coffee. I've something to tell you.' He introduced himself to Norman and myself because we, apparently, were the only ones he didn't know. With coffee we sat down and listened, absolutely fascinated, about how a South American government had accepted his invention, the working prototype he'd made of a back-support stretcher for mountain-rescue work. He's also a ballistics expert. Stories along those lines occupied another of our five mornings of rehearsal.

Before we knew where we were it was lunchtime and, as we were scheduled to rehearse each day from 10 a.m. to 1 p.m., the last fifteen minutes of our time would be spent discussing the programme with this interesting, absorbing gentleman. He'd describe an idea for a visual gag, have us all in fits of laughter then, looking at either the director, John, or our floor manager, Bruce Millard, he'd give that well-known, high-pitched, goonish giggle and almost leading an old familiar chorus, chant, 'But the budget won't stand it.' His exit line – he invariably had to be somewhere else five minutes ago – was usually, 'Don't worry. We'll have something ready. Bound to be funny.'

Bruce would intimate also that we were not to worry but to be ready for a very long and very busy day on Friday in the Shepherd's Bush Theatre studio. Friday was transmission day and, it seemed, the day when most of the programme was 'invented' and put together. Some of the others had worked on Michael's other shows and they assured us that we would not be left with egg on our faces, that the never idle Bentine brain would be in one department working out ideas.

On the second day's rehearsal the finale, the children's participation piece, had been worked out; a guest artiste had to be found and booked and a set built. Norman and I were told, 'Just stick with Michael.' One week the set was a barn and a farm where two teams of three children, on a split set, had, as a hooter sounded to perform various tasks such as milk a model cow, collect swedes cascading down a chute, and put sacks onto a hook which came down from the roof, paused briefly and then went up again.

Another week my dear friend from Watford days, Jill Simcox, was our guest. Jill and I were passengers at a table in a very wobbly railway dining car (shaken on its spring mountings by stalwarts of the stage crew). Michael was the catering manager, Norman the head waiter. Two children were the waiters who had to serve Jill and myself from the largest pile of spaghetti I've ever seen (actually thin white plastic tubing tossed in tomato sauce). I leave the rest of the mayhem to the imagination.

Yet another of our grand finale 'set pieces' involving children featured some very weird goings-on and strange animals in a tropical hospital in the jungle. For this, and one of the other weeks, the guest artiste was dear old friend Peter Butterworth. Once again at coffee breaks a company was regaled with tales of the horrendous *Goldilocks* panto.

At the finish of transmission of the first programme John Downes came into the dressing room, which Norman and I occupied, to tell us that Michael liked us and our work. Apparently we were adaptable enough and 'fitted in' to the show's formula. Would we be prepared to do the other twelve shows? Would we? We would!

It most certainly was adventurous. Some weeks, apart from the finale and Michael's sand-tray puppetry, Norman and I might not know until we got into studio on Friday morning just what we would be doing. One week Michael told the audience that he'd often wondered how those corridor tea and coffee machines worked and 'it just so happened' there was one here in the studio and he'd found out it was due for re-servicing. At this point Mr Bean entered in long white coat with bowler hat ('Good morn-

ing, Mr Bentine!') and a large Gladstone bag. Much
fiddling with a huge ring of keys then, leaving the door just
slightly ajar. I opened the bag and took out a large metal
teapot and ditto a coffee pot. At this point Michael offered
to open the door 'as you've got your hands full' and
crouched inside was Norman, in white coat and bowler-
hat, with one teapot and one coffee pot.

'Evening, Mr McLeod!'

'Evening, Mr Bentine!'

And exit Mr Bean with Michael saying, 'So that's how
they work!'

★

Although I had reason to be very grateful for and apprecia-
tive of the spiritual help and comfort of the Actors' Church
Union – *vide* Scarborough 1960 – I began, during this year,
to become more involved with this society. Once I had
discovered and visited the beautiful church of St Paul's,
Covent Garden thanks to *Dad's Army* friends, Frank
Williams, 'The Vicar of Walmington', and Pamela Cundell,
'Mrs Fox', two ACU members of long standing. The
ecumenical nature of this organisation and its relationship
with its 'neighbour around the corner' – the Catholic Stage
Guild (CSG) at the Church of Corpus Christi – in Maiden
Lane, appealed greatly to me. Besides ACU members, quite
a number of professional friends and working colleagues
are members of the CSG.

An actor who had impressed me greatly during a production in which he'd appeared at the Palace, Watford, was
the late Alan Foss. A fine actor and one whose playing of
Winston Churchill was, I must confess, better than mine!
In time Alan and I corresponded and met and, of course,
discovered these two societies. I admired and appreciated
the joint services and occasions they organised. With Alan's

extensive knowledge of the CSG I gathered and formulated the twenty-minute talk which I still give occasionally to interested groups – 'Out of the Limelight', a brief dissertation upon the history and work of the ACU and the CSG.

When Alan died suddenly in 1989 – a blow to them and a loss to us all – a memorial service was held not at Corpus Christi but at St Paul's. Alas, because of work in the North, I was not able to accept the invitation I'd received to attend. I was asked if my Pavilion Theatre, Glasgow, story about meeting a chaplain backstage might be read out to the congregation. Alan had, it seemed, kept a copy of it among his CSG papers. The occasion was to be one of thanksgiving for his life and work. Of course I was delighted and honoured to agree. How I wish I could have been there to do it myself. I'm told it got what I would call 'a warm, audible smile' from the large congregation.

So, how did this closer contact with these organisations come about? (Taking a deep breath!) Well, during 1972 and through work on *Dad's Army*, my good friend Bill Pertwee introduced me to what I still think of as 'my London club' – the 'Concert Artistes' Association' (CAA). This is a professional social centre, probably known more by the name 'the club for actors and acts' since it has widened its horizons. The club premises in Bedford Street, WC2, are also used frequently by the CSG and the ACU. Moreover, the main entrance to St Paul's, Covent Garden, and consequently the HQ of the ACU – is virtually across the road from the entrance to the C... Ergo, involvement.

The CAA played an important part in the remainder of the time I was to live in London. Many happy lunchtimes, with reasonably priced lunches even a 'resting' actor could afford, and many very happy 'members' evenings' meant that I had a social and professional centre to life 'in town'. Taking part in a number of the shows put on in the concert room gave me great pleasure and happiness. Working to an audience of fellow and sometimes much more experienced thespians is something nobody should miss out on. To be a member one must be nominated and elected. An invitation to participate in a specific entertainment, in those days, served as a kind of audition for membership. Whether or not this is the case nowadays I don't know. Alas, the CAA doesn't have 'country membership'. It is, by its very nature, a London club. I'm happy to say however that upon visiting the club since I moved back to the North, I have always been made most welcome for the day.

Three events in particular stand out in my happy memories of those 'members' evenings'. These were when I was first asked to be a 'members' evening' host, i.e. help organise the evening and the entertainment; when Bill and Marion Pertwee included me in the cast of their uproarious evening – *The World's Worst Concert Party* – which included old friends such as Norman McLeod and Mary Moreland; and when I was invited to perform on an evening on which Pamela was one of the hosts. That one led to a pantomime engagement for the impresario Bunny Baron, which we'll come to in due course.

Meanwhile, again, back to the main plot.

Chapter Twenty-Nine

Pantomime this year – 1972 – was to be in the lovely old town of Bury St Edmunds and in the delightfully restored Georgian theatre there, the Theatre Royal. *Cinderella* is not, from a 'dame' point of view, my favourite subject. In this story the dames have to be baddies and, unless one is part of a recognised double act or well-known ugly sisters partnership, playing the roles is not easy for either actor. In partnership as 'sisters' I'd seen Max and Maisie Morris, Bartlett and Ross, Burden and Moran and, in my estimation, the best 'uglies' – John Inman and Barry Howard. I'm still of the opinion that playing the ugly sisters needs an established rapport brought about only by experience.

For this Duggie Chapman production I had two other difficulties with which to contend. *Dad's Army* was well up in the TV ratings and Mr Chapman had advertised Pte Sponge of the said programme as 'Top of the Bill'. This in itself was bound to have an unbalanced effect on how the part was to be played. Also, of course, I never did a 'solo' spot or 'act as known'.

After the first publicity material had been published the actor who had been scheduled to play the other ugly sister pulled out of the engagement quite suddenly. I had already been to his home in London to discuss what we were going to do, and how. Characters, costumes and so forth had been gone into in great detail. Just before leaving London to travel to Bury St Edmunds I was informed that this gentleman would not be playing 'Anastasia', my fellow sister. (How's that for a contradiction in terms?) My opening lines to introduce 'her' after the *Dad's Army* signature tune, 'Well it makes a change from boots and battledress', usually got a recognising round of applause. 'I'm Gert-rude – the one who gets about a bit – and this is (enter other sister) my sister who doesn't – Anna-stays-here.'

Our very talented director, Tom Howard, who had been cast to play Baron Hardup found himself with the much more complicated job of playing Anastasia. A noted cabaret performer, he had also written some very tuneful and singable musical numbers for the show. By putting our heads together we concocted a frontcloth 'progression' comedy number for all the principals to perform. 'If I Were Not Upon the Stage' needed a rest and brings everyone out of character as far as the pantomime audience is concerned. So I wrote the words and Tom the music for our well-received 'The Town Brass Band', the premise being that being hard up the Baron had to raise money somehow and ordered everyone to join in with their instruments.

All of us mimed these instruments as we set about playing them, each in turn and then together, except for little Frankie Parker as Buttons. Poor ol' Buttons got it wrong again! He arrives carrying the largest (and lightest) bass drum we could borrow, from Long Milford Prize Silver Band. The drum was more than half as tall as Frank himself and, of course, he had to be the last one to join the band. I needn't go into all the gags possible with such a set-up but both children and parents howled with delight.

All in all it was an enjoyable season with very pleasant company. The script had all the traditional awful jokes – which Tom insisted, quite rightly, we played seriously which of course makes them even funnier.

Anna: Oh Gert, the prince is in the vicinity.

Gert: Funny, he's usually in the Rose and Crown!
          Bu-boom!
Buttons: The Crystal Slipper! You couldn't get your foot in
          the Crystal Palace!

Even though it burned down in 1936 the line still got a good laugh.

Apart from one unruly performance, due I'm sorry to say to an audience composed mainly of Boy Scouts and Cubs, things went well. As ex-Scouts ourselves both Frankie and I were very upset by this and even more so by someone purposefully 'leaking' the news to a sensation-seeking Sunday paper. By the and of the season, however, all that was over and done with. I have many happy memories of my stay in Bury St Edmunds; over Christmas/New Year it is a particularly pleasant place to spend the festive season.

After the return to London in February, unpacking and so forth, it was time to head for Wigan again. Ostensibly the object of the trip was to be a guest speaker on 22nd March at the Wigan Little Theatre (of which I am a very early and a life member) under a general title of 'To Play As Cast'. A talk about experience in showbiz and trying to answer questions and such like. In the main I'd come to observe more closely life at home and how Father was coping. The more personal side of all that has no place here. Suffice it to say that 12th September, 1973, found me giving up my home in Islington to move back to Wigan.

April brought me a brief re-association with John Inman and Mollie Sugden (whom I'd first met at a party given by Bill and Marion Pertwee) for an episode of *Are You Being Served?* And for director Sidney Lotterby, yet another episode of *Liver Birds* as a factory gate strike speaker. 25th April to 5th May also saw me playing on what (not, alas, for much longer) was home ground. A company called

'Forestage' engaged me and a young actor from the then currently running West-End show *Godspell* – Miles Fothergill, like me a Northerner – to premiere a short play by Bolton-born Melville Lovatt called *The Grave*.

The Grave is a strange play about a seemingly studious young man meeting a scrounging tramp in a cemetery. We all enjoyed the outdoor photo call for this because our director, Kendall Johns, had got permission for us to have it in the renowned Highgate Cemetery. Although still in its early days as a theatre venue, The King's Head, Islington, had already become well-known for its lunchtime productions. *The Grave* opened at 1.15 p.m. on 25th April and ran, except for Sundays and Mondays, until 5th May. Admission was twenty-five pence. Bring one's lunch and/or drink through from the bar. Although the play didn't grab the theatrical headlines it did create some interest.

Agents and managers always say, 'Let me know when you are in something in town. I may come to see you.' Whereas many would not consider travelling into the 'provinces', i.e. Watford, the King's Head was considered an 'in' place! At one performance I was delighted to meet again former theatre school colleague Tom Bell and at others a number of agents made themselves known. As we were followed at 2.15 p.m. by another production, some days could be quite hectic.

Another member of one of the last of our audiences was the friend from Wigan, John D. Slater of the *Wigan Scene* magazine. As it had now been settled that I was to return to Wigan and approximately when I would move, John and I were making possible future theatre plans for later in the year. The big move was to be in September so in May the first steps of 'arrangements' were started in order that everything wouldn't – we hoped – be left until the last moment. Well, we all know what happens to the best-laid plans, but more of that later.

Mid-June to mid-July was the period of the ninth series of *Dad's Army*. In the eighth series, made late in 1972, had been one of my miniature 'moments of glory' as Pte Sponge in the episode 'All Is Safely Gathered In'. Earlier that year I had mentioned to Jimmy Perry that in autumn, during the war, I remembered our local Home Guard helping the farmers gather in the all-essential harvest. The scene in the wheat field was my very prominent moment. Nobody seemed to know how to work the threshing machine including, as Sgt Wilson called them, 'Those very charming young ladies', the Women's Land Army. The ever resourceful captain had the solution one so often heard him say, 'Ah, I wondered who would be the first to spot that.' Addressing me with absolute confidence he said, 'Sponge, you're a farmer.'

'Yes, Captain Mainwaring,' I replied.

'Right, show us how this thing works!'

'I don't know how it works!'

To which, with that wonderful Arthur Lowe 'inner explosion', he said, 'You don't know how it works? But you're a farmer!'

'Yes,' said I, 'a sheep farmer!'

This remark was beautifully underlined by a pause and the expression on Arthur's face.

The ninth series in 1973 – after we'd enjoyed our usual 'ten-day working holiday' on location in and around Thetford – was to end on a note of great sadness. Just before the studio recording of the penultimate episode, 'Things That Go Bump in The Night', we learned that Jimmy Beck, loved by millions as the archetypal 'spiv' Pte Walker, had collapsed and was seriously ill in hospital. Sadly, he died a short while after.

So whenever you watch the episode of *Dad's Army* called 'Things That Go Bump in The Night' you will notice that although Jimmy plays a prominent part in the outdoor scenes, once the platoon are inside the old house Pte Walker is not present. Pte Sponge seems to be more involved in the general action than usual – for me, certainly, a sad way for my character to progress. Even today Pte Walker is one of our best-remembered characters of the show. The 'essential supplies' was kept alive in the stage version of the show by John Bardon and in the radio adaptations by Jimmy's friend and neighbour, Larry Martin.

At this point I must record that I cannot write much of either of these versions of *Dad's Army* because I was not involved in them. The stage show because, in my purely personal opinion, it was not a good idea at all. It upset me somewhat to have to say that to Jimmy Parry and David Croft because they had, I believe, certain cameo roles lined up for me to play. Seeing the stage show during its national tour after a West End run, alas, convinced me that I was right. I would not have been happy. The production, for my taste, was too 'hyped up', glamorised and far from the spirit of the TV show, except for a few interpolated scenes in the parish hall based on one or two TV episodes of *Dad's Army*, the programme.

The brilliant adaptations for radio by Harold Snoad and Michael Knowles require only the main characters and the occasional guest artiste. The 'second line of the chorus' would serve no useful purpose in a radio production – too many voices lead only to confusion for the listener. Background murmuring and 'rhubarb-rhubarb' noises can, as is said in radio parlance, be performed by 'members of the cast'. I did, however, have the pleasure of being introduced to the audience on the two occasions I visited Paris Theatre Studio to hear recording sessions. As with the television version, the audience reaction is the real thing. I can assure everyone there is no 'canned laughter' in dear old *Dad's Army*.

The last episode of series nine was recorded on the 22nd July by which time plans were being laid for my move back to Wigan. This was to coincide with Festival '73 in my home town and the setting-up by John D. Slater and myself of our own professional theatre, company, Bridgeman Productions. The office was in Astral House (appropriate?), Bridgeman Terrace, Wigan.

However, there were things still to be done in London.

COLIN BEAN & J W TERRY AS THE TWINS .. in Out of. The frying Pan 1956 LYCEUM

Chapter Thirty

It was around this time, during periods of 'resting' and thinking about what I would do after the move north, that I started on the idea of giving reading recitals. One of my favourite authors had done it himself with great success, one Mr C. Dickens, and other actors were now adopting this format of entertainment. Indeed one actor I'd always admired, Emlyn Williams, was giving a brilliant reconstruction of such a recital as Charles Dickens himself.

Now I have formed a 'menu' of short, half-hour reading recitals, one of which is based on this author, *The Voice of His Age*. Others include *How do!* (a miscellany of 'old ones, new ones, loved ones and neglected ones'); *The Great Magonagal* (self-explanatory); and *A Christmas Stocking*. This latter is, as the name implies, 'a festive season entertainment of a somewhat quieter nature'. By itself sixty minutes long, parts of it can be integrated into Yuletide concerts and carol services. All this was to eventually lead up to a two-hour reading recital which was later to prove quite popular in a number of North Country venues. This is now the well-established Lancashire reading recital called *A Gradely Neet*. More to come on that subject.

After 'Things That Go Bump In the Night' came the last episode of series nine of *Dad's Army*, 'The Recruit', recorded on 22nd July, 1973. Series ten would not get under way until April of 1974. David Croft and Jimmy Perry would, obviously, have to consider carefully the sad loss of one of the most popular characters. In the meantime yours truly had a very full and varied period in view. Also in July 1973, Marion McLeod (Mrs Bill Partwee) and I had been host and hostess, at CAA's concert evening on the 16th. Besides entertaining with songs and monologues ourselves, we opened membership to an artiste who was exactly as *The Stage* described him when it said, 'Don Gordon, not only debonair and handsome but musical and versatile.' Marion and I had 'persuaded' a number of friends with good, strong acts to be on the bill – champagne-like singer Jenny Wren and the indefatigable Mr B. Pertwee himself – and we closed the programme with another introductory act, 'The Gladstones', a harmonious and hilarious quartet of Edwardian gentlemen singers. A happy reunion was the fact that one of the four was Marion's brother, and my ex-Bentine colleague, Norman McLeod.

In August there was another, for us, momentous occasion. I had heard rumours that someone had converted the old Woolwich tram-shed into a theatre. Sounds like shades of Harry Hanson! However the go-ahead director of this new venture was the talented actress, Maggie Ollerenshaw, later to become a 'name' on TV. I was invited to take the role of Mr Chairman in the opening programme which was a music-hall show in the old style. Again it was a pleasure to have ex-Watford Palace colleagues on the team with me in the persons of that very polished performer, Michael Lomax, and a gentleman who never fails to make me laugh – intentionally I hasten to add – the one and only Peter John. His 'Little Boy Coming Home From a Party' always reduces me to uncontrollable tears of laughter. The delightful songstress, Corinne Marlowe, and comedy lady, Stella Courtney, also formed part of this opening show.

Programme two a fortnight later was to bring old friend Rex Jameson, the unique Mrs Shufflewick, back into my ambience. I can still hear Rex's 'wide-eyed innocence' delivery of, 'I've had a letter from my son [pause]. He's in the Navy [pause] on *our* side!'

12th September, the day arranged for the move back to my native North Country, was fast approaching. There was time, however, for one more dramatic development before I left 3 Horsell Road, London N5 (just off Holloway Road, next to Islington Library). Dear friends Pamela Cundell (Mrs Fox of *Dad's Army*) and Rowena Vincent were due as joint hostesses to open the CAA's concert season after a summer recess. I was honoured to be asked if I would be on their bill of artistes. Well, one doesn't decline an invitation from such charming and delightful talented ladies to be part of a prestigious company playing to a 'full house' of prestigious fellow artistes and their friends. Of the various items I had performed at CAA evenings, always being aware of performing in front of my peers, I had so far not inflicted my pantomime dame on them. After all, a number of the members were far more experienced in that art than me. Tentatively I suggested I might indulge in 'damehood' adding that, if I was no good, I was due to leave town in five days' time!

On the night, as I completed my painstaking make-up in the dressing room, who should breeze in but friend Bill Partwee. 'Oh, my God, Bean! What do you think you're at?' was his immediate reaction. Bill hadn't seen me in panto so I can well understand his shocked surprise; my eyelashes virtually swept him out of the room again.

A great and more important consequence of the evening was that in the audience were Miss Lisa Gaye, production supervisor, and Mr Gordon Holdom, general manager for Bunny Baron Productions Ltd. Two days later I had an invitation to visit Mr Baron himself for an interview. Result? An engagement to play the dame (second top of bill) in *Puss in Boots* at the Playhouse, Weston-super-Mare, where B.J.B. Productions summer shows and pantomimes were both extremely popular. Quite a responsibility!

Top of the bill, playing Simon, was a young gentleman who was in the process of building a great reputation as an official Al Jolson impersonator, comedian Steve King. Also in support of Steve was veteran comedy man, Sonny Farrar. I played Queen Wilhelmina to Sonny's King Ron, complete with his hilarious solo violin act 'The Flight of the Bumble Bee'. No, dear reader, not a variation of the old 'busy Bee' gag which I always decline to do, but a real violin solo. Ever since I once saw a child spit in another's face with the excuse, 'Well, they did it in the pantomime,' I have refused to perform 'busy bee'. I still refuse to do it.

The full story of my move back to Wigan really deserves a book in its own right. Here I'll simply acknowledge, with gratitude, the sterling and virtually solo assistance of friend and fellow artiste, John D. Slater. This story is about my professional life so let's stay on that track.

Now back in the North plans made by John D. Slater and myself began to unfold and take on practical form. We set up Bridgeman Productions as a professionally registered theatrical production company. The premises in which John's *Scene* magazine was produced and printed and where Scene Print and Design operated also had one spare first-floor office which was cleared to become Bridgeman Productions company office. The address? 28 Bridgeman Terrace, the very aptly named 'Astral House'. Intrepidly we referred to it as 'The home of the stars: Wigan's [then] only professional theatre company.'

For starters the furnishings were what had been brought from my flat in London. Corridor racks and shelves for all my pantomime and considerable rep wardrobe, in addition to John's not inconsiderable 'Hawkley Players' costumes, comprised our wardrobe department. The office itself was decorated with my quite multitudinous collection of theatre posters and theatrical reference books and directories. We even had curtains on the windows and carpeting underfoot and a phone so we felt that we truly were a theatrical management! An added advantage of this change in my life was that, being at the back of the building, the office window looked out onto the back garden of my home in Dicconson Street which enabled me to 'keep an eye on' and be in communication with Father. Not just once did I have occasion to leave for home in a hurry because he, insisting that he could manage, had taken a tumble while overdoing the gardening. 'Well, I can't see why you're not interested in gardening. Your grandfather was a professional gardener,' was a constant cry of Father's in those days. The rejoinder that I was a professional in my own field cut no ice with him – it was still 'not a proper job'.

Life became both hectic and exciting. Our artistes, if not at this point all Equity members, were all paid artistes. Those who stayed with us did eventually become members of the Association and we used Equity contracts.

Our first major project was to be our participation in 'Festival 73', scheduled to be one of the first major gatherings of all the arts in Wigan and district or (as we were then still known) 'The Ancient and Loyal' County Borough of Wigan.

This was to run from the end of September until the end of October with a full programme of events covering theatre, music and visual arts. To promote this, John and I, by virtually 'blockbusting' our way in, had secured a small unprogrammed site in a corner of the marquee at the earlier 'Late Summer Show' in Mesnes Park where, with a miniature stage setting and some posters and photographs, we were able to introduce ourselves to the unsuspecting public of Wigan.

To go forward at this point, to explain our acquisition of five prestigious patrons for our Bridgeman Productions letterheads and posters I must, perforce, take you back for a while to 1961.

In that year my good friends, the theatrical historians/researchers/experts Ray Mander and Joe Mitchenson, published their then latest book *The Theatres of London*. This was the first complete historical and biographical book on actual theatre buildings since 1889. Knowing of and having received examples of my abiding hobby of calligraphy, Ray and Joe had invited me to take part in the launch of the book at the famous Foyle's bookshop, Charing Cross Road. The truly delightful line illustrations for each theatre had been executed by a very talented artist, Timothy Birdsall, who – a sad loss to arts and theatre – was to die far too tragically young. My job was to letter the captions to be placed under the some thirty or more famous originals of Timothy's illustrations of the prominent London theatres. Truly an honour accorded to me was the wholehearted approval given to my small contribution because the pictures would be the centre piece of a display at the highly esteemed Foyle's literary luncheon which was to launch the book officially.

Guests of honour were to be Dame Sybil Thorndike and Sir Lewis Casson. A terrific thrill for me was to be told by Ray and Joe – over a drink in the Salisbury actually – that 'Of course you'll be there. Semi-formal, lounge suit, one for one thirty next Wednesday.'

So I met, was introduced to and talked with Dame Sybil and Sir Lewis, both of whom had commented on the pictures and their captions before Joe introduced me to them. A truly glittering affair, with Christina Foyle herself in attendance as well as many theatrical management luminaries. During the next two or three years I was to be greeted by Dame Sybil with, 'Hello Colin Bean who does lovely writing', on four different occasions of a theatrical nature. One of these was when I volunteered to help at a theatrical charities garden party being opened by her.

Okay so far? Right, back to 1973. John and I agreed that if we were going to get 'names' for our list of patrons why not aim high? We did, and now dear reader you'll see how things fit into place. Our patrons who each supplied a ten by eight photo (with permission to reproduce) were Dame Sybil Thorndike, Miss Thora Hird, Miss Glenda Jackson, Mr Arthur Lowe and Mr John Le Mesurier. When *Dad's Army* returned in 1974 both Arthur and John expressed a keen interest in what we were doing in what John laughingly called 'the frozen north'.

One innovation was the introduction into Wigan of lunchtime pub theatre. This was made possible firstly because of a deal negotiated by John D. Slater with Messrs Greenall Whitley Ltd and secondly because we were included in the official festival programme. Already we had plans for a small-scale touring pantomime which would be taken to different venues for one-performance dates early in 1974.

Now we had to concentrate upon our first two productions. For the lunchtime theatre Phyllis Hart and I played John D. Slater's half-hour comedy *Foreign Air*. In the evenings we presented 'An Evening at the Music Hall'. Phyllis and I were joined in performance by J.D.S. plus Miss Evelyn Brown, Miss Lesley Holmes and Mr Graham Jones. Five artistes for a two-hour, full-length show, accompanied at the pianoforte by our hard-working musical director, Liz Jones (no relation to Graham). As will be seen, in the not too distant future Liz was to come to my rescue in a somewhat musically dramatic manner.

Chapter Thirty-One

The period 1973–75 was a hectic time, so much so that I will not even attempt a chronological account of what John Slater and I got up to, attempted and achieved with our newly set up Bridgeman Productions. Certainly we took some headlines in the local press when we introduced lunchtime pub theatre to Wigan.

As John so succinctly expressed it in one of our press releases, 'Asking people in a pub to take their food and their drinks into another room to watch a play was a bit like asking them to travel to Mars.' But we did it! Not always successfully but at least we were consistent. Visions of playing to an audience of three spring to mind – one of whom was the author of *Foreign Air*.

So here I must introduce a lovely friend of mine, the actress Phyllis Hart. Yes, a friend with a capital 'F' and an actress with definitely a capital 'A'. For those who never worked with Phyllis all I can say is, 'Hard cheese! You don't know what you've missed.' A lady to whom even a revue sketch requires the utmost concentration and full use of her long and wide dramatic experience. To work with Phyllis is a joy – especially when she approaches you in the wings as you are about to make an entrance and says, 'Now, Colin darling, have I got everything on?'

Dear Phyllis! Together we did John's Play *Foreign Air* as part of the Wigan Festival and in other places, sponsored by Greenall Whitley, in pubs all over the local area. We were both involved also with the evening *Old Time Music Hall* show, complete with twelve-inch high stage, proscenium arch, curtains, lights and music which we were touring in the evenings.

Phyllis was a stalwart in both shows. I have memories of us driving down the M6 in Phyllis' car to fulfil a lunchtime date at The Good Companions in Warrington. As we drove along so absorbed were we in going through our lines – I told you she was a perfectionist – that we missed the turn-off for Warrington and had to drive on until we could find a slip road which got us back to Warrington in time to set up just three minutes before we were due to start the play, with an audience waiting for us.

In Bolton we were due to do four lunchtimes in the upstairs lounge of the Wheatsheaf (also Greenall Whitley). Despite our best efforts at advertising, the first day's audience consisted of the very jovial female cleaner who said that she had hung on 'to see what it was all about'. What's more, she went downstairs into the lounge bar and told everyone how good it was. Day two we thought we had an audience of two (a fifty per cent increase on audience figures!) gentlemen in very smart raincoats who turned out to be detectives from Bolton police station to tell us that, although licensed for music and singing this room was not licensed for dramatic performances!

The music hall programme also enjoyed a tour over a wide area of Lancashire, including a huge concert room at the Mersey Hotel with an audience of about six people. In the opening number 'Smile Please', the members of the cast stepped off the twelve-inch high stage to go out into the auditorium to shake hands with people. I was chairman of the show and Phyllis came back, singing her heart out and in passing saying, 'Darling, I couldn't find anyone with whom to shake hands.'

One of our best dates was when John negotiated a deal with the prestigious Grand Hotel in Wigan town centre where on each Monday for the month of April, in collaboration with the manager John Nixon, we presented *Those Were The Days* including hotpot supper in the basement bar – all for one pound. From scratch we set up our own stage and ambience, musicians as well. The dressing rooms were part of the kitchen but so what? At one performance – almost a royal command – we were graced with the presence of the Mayor and Mayoress of Wigan. On top of the one pound ticket fee we managed to raise some money for the mayor's charity, and a pound was still quite a considerable sum of money in those days.

We did plays, pantomimes, recitals – you name it, we tried it. Out of all this came what eventually became quite a strong characteristic of the theatrical life of Wigan, 'The Bijou Theatre', the little jewel which in one form or another still produces shows, and Theatre In Education workshops and seminars in many different places.

Visions of the initial season 1973–1974 included the first ever pantomime to be staged at the newly converted Linacre Hall in Wigan then part of a high school, a successor to the ancient and honourable Wigan Grammar School, founded 1597 eventually to become a so-called comprehensive and now completely disappeared as a school. Why this conversion was ever carried out is a mystery to me! A perfectly good school hall with stage facilities, excellent auditorium and acoustics was transformed at great expense into a badly planned, ill-lit, multipurpose assembly area. It had a ridiculously wide stage made up of what were supposed to be moveable units, electronically controlled heavy velvet curtains which took an age to open and close, side seating from which only a third of the stage was visible, bleacher-type auditorium seating, no stage–auditorium pass door, an inadequate number of dressing rooms like the proverbial broom cupboard and a very scholastic and untheatrical approach and foyer.

For our first production of *Aladdin* in 1974 the electric curtain machine broke down so we had to use a very inadequate hand winch which promptly came free of its moorings. The backstage to auditorium control room communication system constantly broke down and a first performance was almost postponed because it was discovered that the centre section seating was not adequately secured and had to be inspected and repaired.

I hated playing the Linacre theatre then and I still do.

This auditorium has still to decide whether it is to be a theatre/concert hall or a school general-purpose facility. With a noble past history in theatrical life how sad that Wigan's only 'proper' theatre is the prestigious and wholly delightful Wigan Little Theatre, the home of a very high standard amateur theatre, of which I am proud to have been a very early member in 1944 and to be a life member still.

By its very nature the Bijou Theatre Co. and its productions were on a small scale. We were, by intent and declaration, a touring theatre and whatever the production might be it all had to fit into a transit van. Touring consisted invariably of two, three, or four-night 'dates' (a week at some places with pantomimes) at venues such as Oswaldtwistle, Hyndburn, Haslingden, Ashton, Hindley, Kirkby and other places which, until we started to visit, had seen little or no professional theatre for years.

Eventually around 1975 John and I, after discussion, felt that he had theatrical interests in other directions and so did I. We were to work together very successfully in a few years' time but, for the present, it was felt that we'd done all we could.

Chapter Thirty-Two

During this time *Dad's Army* was still very much 'on the go'. No longer resident in London I was very fortunate in having friends in East London with whom I could stay for the weeks I was required at Television Centre – invariably Studio 8.

For the location shooting I made my own way to Thetford courtesy of National Express Coaches. In Bill Pertwee's book on *Dad's Army* there are accounts of activity during our stay in Norfolk and, of course, reminiscences appear in copies of 'The Dad's Army Appreciation Society' newsletter.

One morning the few people concerned with an early 'shoot' were walking down a lane to the location when someone spouted up, 'Anyone seen the papers this morning? The birthday honours list?'

To which Arthur Lowe replied, 'No, I didn't get the chance. Too busy having a difference of opinion with an uncomprehending waiter about the undercooking of my sausages.' Arthur didn't accommodate fools gladly!

'Oh,' said the original speaker, naming an actor well known to us all, 'so-and-so's got the OBE.'

'Oh, very good,' said Arthur. 'That'll be for all that marvellous charity work over the years.' Then, turning to me, he concluded, *sotto voce*, 'Can't be for the acting!' Mr Lowe could have his 'cutting edge' when he wished.

On another occasion, when a famous cricketer was boring us all to death on the coach with an endless stream of club stories, Arthur was heard to mutter, 'Oh God! Couldn't someone bowl him out?'

At home I began tentatively on my ideas of doing one-man reading recitals and began a major occupation for the next five years – my association with hospital broadcasting in the form of 'Radio Wrightington'. Wrightington Hospital was the studio base of a land line network which in those days covered Wrightington, Wigan Infirmary, Billinge, Whelley and Astley hospitals.

An acquaintance, John Mather, 'spun the discs' on Sunday mornings from 10 a.m. to midday. Being associated with *Dad's Army* was the reason for my being invited along as a guest one Sunday morning. This seemed to raise enough interest to warrant a further invitation to discuss with John other aspects of my career, theatre and music in general. The programme producer, the late Charles Fishwick, suggested that I might like to consider being a regular co-presenter, dealing with non-musical aspects of a real 'Sunday morning magazine' type programme. My field of activity included finding amusing 'filler' items and, from local newspapers, horoscopes, readers' letters, weather reports, news of forthcoming hospital radio sports commentaries and the like. After a time I was invited to bring 'an interesting guest' to the studio.

Showbiz personalities are not exactly thick on the ground in Wigan. After interviewing people from local drama societies I widened the field to include a serving police constable, a local councillor, a store detective (a fascinating morning), a deep-sea diver, a railway engine driver, a Wigan rugby player and my one failure, a wrestler.

This not-so-young gentleman, whom I had met occasionally, always conducted most verbose accounts of his days in 'the square ring'. Eventually I persuaded him to come to Radio Wrightington one Sunday morning to 'reveal all' on air. On the morning in question, transported by his wrestler son, he turned up at the studio, in almost pristine condition. He was dressed in an obviously uncomfortable suit, collar and tie, face shining, hair plastered to head. On arrival I was mid-item so I indicated that they should take a seat. When a break occurred I ushered my guest up to the microphone – noticing that he seemed somewhat reticent. As I joked, 'Surely after the wrestling ring a mere microphone shouldn't hold any terrors for you,' he merely gave a sickly smile. John gave us a big 'build-up' and switched my microphones on with 'Over to Colin.'

Well, the list of questions I had prepared to reveal all the secrets of wrestling, which revelation and 'the full works' had been promised, soon ground to a halt as the only replies I seemed to elicit were 'Yep' and 'Nope'. After some three desperate minutes I looked at John and Charles through the studio control window. They must have seen panic in my face because the next record was hastily brought into the show. Once off-air I tried again to put my guest at his ease, asking him to talk about wrestling as he had done to me in the past. Forget the questions I had planned. His son joined in at this point to explain that it wasn't the questions which had upset the old boy but in his efforts to get all dressed up and look his best for the interview his dad had forgotten to put his teeth in! The rest of this hastily curtailed interview had to be restructured – more or less off the cuff – to evoke answers of 'Yep' and 'Nope'. Needless to say, as soon as we decently could, in order not to upset him, we found we had a lot more music requests than usual to get through.

The 1975 *Dad's Army* episodes included 'My Brother and I' which was quite an education to watch in the shooting process. Arthur Lowe was playing two roles. Besides the staid and authoritative Captain Mainwaring he appeared also as his own somewhat dissipated and often unsober brother. To see Arthur create and differentiate between these two men was fascinating, especially when the brothers played a scene together.

In the meantime things were developing in Wigan where I had been recruited by the Wigan Metro Council to write, direct and play the dame in a festive seasonal family pantomime. The idea, basically, was that instead of hiring another company to produce and present the show the Metro itself should go into theatrical management.

I don't think they quite realised just what they were taking on! With the best will in the world a theatre company can't run as a department of local government, like 'Cleaning' or 'Finance'. For instance, one day I was 'pulled up' for not being at my desk at eight forty-five, as per engagement. The fact that I was at home actually creating and writing *Babes in the Wood* (for that was the subject) was unacceptable. How I was expected to do this in my office with other typewriters clattering away, phones which had to be answered and queries and visitors not remotely connected to the matter in hand, I'm not quite sure. After much tribulation though a script finally came out and casting started.

Again, the budget became a problem ('twas ever thus) and subject to many a confrontation with 'them upstairs'. In addition I was undertaking other department of leisure work, such as compering concerts, talent shows and the park summer show. Fitting in dashing to London to do *Dad's Army* episodes added to the complications of life.

Babes in the Wood was to be one of the biggest headaches I've ever had. How fortunate the outcome was such a success. This was mainly due, I hasten to add, to the stalwart teamwork of the cast. My old friend, Derek Tobias, joined us to play one of the baddies in partnership with an experienced actor from Manchester University drama group, Clive Hopwood. Ann Daniels and Bobby Bright were equally no newcomers to showbiz and the value of all these professionals became clear as the one week of rehearsal allowed (the Metro wouldn't pay for more than one) unfolded. Besides proving to be an admirable Maid Marian, Ann also supplied costumes for the character far superior to anything our meagre means could have provided. Bobby Bright, besides being a very hissable and booable Sheriff of Nottingham, was also a tower of strength in rehearsal when I was dealing with the problems arising in other directions all around me.

Having written what I considered to be quite an heroic role for Robin Hood the part had to be cut down to the bare bones. The Metro, in their wisdom, decided to cast the winner of a local talent contest who had also appeared in the finals of *New Faces* on TV in the role. The gentleman was undoubtedly a fine microphone concert or club singer but learning a 'book production' show was completely outside his experience. Naturally enough, his main concern was getting the sound system right for his songs.

Which brings me on to a another disaster area, the musicians. The department booked as accompanist musicians an organ drums duo who, apparently, had played at other Metro functions. I was assured that they were 'very good'. A meeting arranged so that I could hear them play seemed to consist mainly of them telling me of all the famous names for whom they had played. One small problem was that because of their 'real work' they could rehearse only in the evenings which, for the rest of us, after a full day of rehearsal, was very tiring and disorientating. We couldn't rehearse numbers as they occurred in the show. Added to this, the duo had also never taken part in a 'book production' show and had absolutely no idea of following a script or picking up cues. The saying of a cue line by a character prompted them to start a search for the appropriate piece of music. Thankfully Derek and Clive were coaching and rehearsing with the two youngsters who were to play the babes while Ann helped Robin by working out moves for him and helping him to learn what bit of dialogue was required of him.

By Wednesday I was in despair and could see disaster staring us in the face. Going by the old adage 'in crisis shoot for the top', I by-passed my immediate departmental superiors and marched dramatically into the 'inner sanctum', the office of the director of leisure. ('Shock, horror, scandalous, unheard of, that's not the way it works!') and laid out my mountain of grievances and fears.

His department and the name of the Metro were at stake unless action was taken. Four days, including Sunday, working for twenty-four hours a day might save things! As far as music was concerned, I insisted that someone I knew I could trust was brought in immediately as musical director and thus Liz Jones, our former Bijou Theatre pianist, joined us next day to take over at the piano. Liz could rehearse with the company during the day and then do battle with the lethargic duo each evening. Liz could be relied on to come in on cue. In fact, with any show, after a couple of rehearsals Liz could often prompt the actors as well as the other musicians. She was able to put our 'talent show winning' Robin more at ease with his songs and give a quiet word prompt if and when he needed it. At last we principals began to have a little confidence, knowing that when music cues came up at least the piano would be there to take us into the number. Well into our three-week run the duo began to get the idea of what a 'production' on stage was all about. There simply wasn't time to stand on stage like lemons waiting for one of the duo to put his pipe down and try to find the sheet music required.

It was fortunate that I had my own fairly extensive wardrobe of stage clothes. Besides supplying myself with nine changes of costume for Nurse Daisy Dogood I was also able to help out other members of our cast.

This pantomime was a little different from the normal panto in that it didn't have a chorus of dancers. The concept had been decided upon early in the initial planning stages, mainly because of the legal and educational difficulties of engaging a team of school-going children from a dancing academy and the added expense of a team of adult professional dancers. To complement the principals I had written in three minor characters who not only helped to make up members in the musical parts but gave us extra speakers of storyline. Kathy Carver as Marjorie Daw, Angela Curran as Polly Flinders and Peter Small as Jack Horner served also to help the stage manager as assistant stage managers. With a fairly small cast the pace of the show was pretty hectic – one almost seemed to 'exit stage left and enter stage right' at the same time! Bobby, Derek and Clive worked like Trojans in the very many comedy and knockabout scenes I'd written in. With so many problems on my mind they often helped the dame out with prompts, even though I'd written the script.

One night during the run Peter had a moment of mental aberration. His offstage job, when not helping in scene changes, was to act as my dresser. As I said, I had nine complete changes of costume and some of them had to be quick so they were as well rehearsed as my actions on stage. On the night in question I came dashing down to the dressing room (almost as big as the cupboards at Linacre Hall) where Peter had a costume for me to dive into just as soon as I had discarded the one I was already half out of as I approached.

As we put on and fastened up the nightdress we were horrified to hear, over the stage sound system, 'Fearless Frank and Evil Ernest are planning to capture the babes in Daisy Dogood's schoolroom.' And there was I fully dressed in a nightdress. Without being aware of it Peter and I had skipped a whole scene! Too late to do anything else now as Peter grabbed my academic gown and mortarboard and managed to get them onto me as we dashed back onto the stage, literally just in time for me to ring the bell for the traditional panto schoolroom scene. Quite a few 'gag' comments ensued from the other members of the cast, I got hopelessly lost in the dialogue and the audience cottoned on to what had happened. Thank goodness everyone thought it was funny, except poor Peter who was also in the scene. From past experience I know that being a dresser is no sinecure.

By now it was 1976 and by the end of the run the 'powers that be' were already talking about next year's panto. I suggested that before making any decisions we had a department meeting to have a long hard look at the Metro's efforts at theatrical management.

Chapter Thirty-Three

1976 was the year when only one episode of *Dad's Army* was made for television, a special called 'The Love of Three Oranges'. This was mainly due to the stage version of the show. This had been first discussed in 1975 and, I'm afraid, my own opinion was that in the form it had been described to me it was not a good idea. I gather it did have a certain amount of success but my own personal opinion was confirmed when I saw the show on tour at Manchester Opera House. John Laurie, I discovered, had also decided not to do this hyped-up musical revue interspersed with a few 'parish hall' scenes which were similar to some of the TV episodes. The sight of the 'vicar' and the 'verger' (still in flat cap) rumbaing away in a full-blown 'Carmen Miranda' style South American scene amid a bevy of clamorous dancers was not my idea of what *Dad's Army* was all about.

In the meantime I had my hands full in Wigan and Edinburgh. For the weeks of the 5th and 12th July I was booked by my old friend, Duggie Chapman, to be Mr Chairman for his old-time music-hall programme *The Good Olde Days* to be staged at the King's Theatre, Edinburgh. An ambition was achieved in that at long last I appeared on the same bill as a couple I'd admired and whose work I'd always enjoyed in Scotland. –'Your own, your very own Clark and Murray'. Grace Clark and Colin Murray (Mr and Mrs Glasgow) were two of Scotland's most popular comedy personalities. Also in the show we had 'The World's Famous Singing Blackbird', Adelaide Hall, and

'The Voice of Them All', Peter Cavanagh. The great pantomime dame, George Lacy, and 'The Immaculate Male', Joan Pendleton. As the show didn't have the usual dancers each half of the show got under way with accordion virtuosity from Terry Doogan.

Second 'top of the bill' to Clark and Murray was that delightful star of over twenty musicals, Bruce Trent. My job was to integrate all these separate acts into some semblance of an ensemble rather than a straight variety show. Being individual artistes, each performing their 'act as known', I also had to keep a strict eye upon (and issue a couple of warnings about) timing of acts. Not an easy job when the people one has to warn have already been famous names in their own right for many years. I hope I was diplomatic. Anyway, the concerted finale which I arranged and directed seemed to go well and our two weeks ended with everyone in harmonious relationship. Clark and Murray became Christmas card-exchange friends for many years after that.

Also crowded into the summer of 1976 was another show for Wigan Metro, a small-scale revue called *The End of the Pier Show* which toured, with a very simple self-standing setting and a piano, to various Metro community centres, some of which didn't have a stage or directional lighting. We were trying to prove that conditions need be no deterrent to entertainment. With the same small company we also ran a daytime 'play-schemes' production based upon my adaptation of an old mediaeval script of *St George and the Dragon*.

1976 also held two other important 'happenings': my debut in North of England television and BBC Radio. Some time previously I had auditioned for that doyen of the old north region, Alfred Bradley. The call came from Trevor Hill of BBC Drama, now firmly ensconced in the New Broadcasting House, Manchester.

I was engaged for a nine-part production of J.B. Priestley's *Festival at Farbridge*. The cast included many luminaries of radio drama. Anna Cropper and Jack Watson headed a large cast and, amongst others, I was able to renew acquaintance with David Mahlowe (of Sheffield Playhouse days), and a gentleman who in 1978 was going to be responsible for another major move in my life.

The television engagement came via a gentleman I'd known for some years, the prolific television writer Brian Finch. Brian lives in Wigan and we are both members of Wigan Little Theatre (in fact as I write Brian is now president of WLT). He and his wife Margaret had been stalwarts of the prestigious Little Theatre for many years and we were all acquainted with each other's work.

Brian had written a new children's TV serial called *Potter's Picture Palace*, a comedy show about an old cinema. Another local actor, fellow Equity member and friend Colin Hurst, and I were both engaged to play small roles in a couple of the episodes. I was the vicar and Colin was a pie delivery man. I can tell you that when we came to it the slapstick pie-throwing contest was quite a humdinger!

In-between filming *Potter's Picture Palace* (starring Melvin Hayes, Angela Crow and the late John Comer) and my commitments in Wigan, *Festival at Farbridge* was still being recorded. Playing Captain Mobbs was the tall, distinguished director of the Octagon Theatre, Bolton, Mr Wilfred Harrison to whom I had written on a number of occasions. We got on well together and, in the not too distant future, Wilfred was to invite me to join the resident company at that famous theatre-in-the-round.

Before that came about I still had some months of fairly hectic activity before me. By now the script for *Dick Whittington and his Wonderful Cat* had been completed and was in the hands of the department of leisure of Wigan Metro. Casting and other essential details were being sorted out by films and theatre officer Bob Jones who was again to fulfil the roles of company and stage manager for the production. Again I was to direct and play dame. Fortunately, thanks mainly to Bob's efforts, things were much better organised. We'd all learned a lot from *Babes in the Wood*.

In advance of the panto I was instrumental in the organisation of what the *Wigan Observer* (3rd December, 1976) described as 'possibly the biggest carol service in Wigan'. The Wigan youth services organiser approached me about doing a festive season concert with young people in aid of the Mayor of Wigan's charity. This was to take place in Wigan Parish Church (All Saints) on Sunday, 12th December. Everyone, including His Worship, agreed that it was a great success and an enjoyable and moving experience. Another old friend, Lancashire poet and writer Cliff Gerrard, even produced a brand new dialect Christmas poem for me to read in the concert. 'The Telly' was not exactly 'snow-flecked shawls' and 'clogs crunching in the snow' – it was a fairly hard-hitting comment on Christmas and the contemporary effect that television has had on this religious festival. It went down well with the audience and now forms part of my solo Christmas reading recital *A Christmas Stocking*.

Now it was time to settle down to getting Dick Whittington to that thrice mayoralty of London. The 'powers that be' decided that instead of the traditional principal boy, this production should be played by a male actor. My heart would have sunk had we not been fortunate enough to be able to engage the multi-talented Bobby Bright again. Actor, singer, instrumentalist – Bobby was an acceptable choice for the eponymous hero.

As I've mentioned before, in panto the role of principal girl can be a pale, frustrating and uninteresting part to play. Having tried to write Alice Fitzwarren into as much of the action as possible we were fortunate enough to be able to engage an experienced and charming young actress, Kay Adshead. Colin Hurst forsook his normal role as the dame with WLT to play Alderman Fitzwarren. He and Kay – heavily disguised – doubled as the Sultan and the Princess during 'Dick's adventures overseas.

Having played the Sultan in serious and ponderous manner throughout the run of the pantomime, in the final performance he managed to 'corpse' us all by appearing in sunglasses and playing the lines in an accent strongly resembling Frank Carson. Having a Sultan say, 'It's the way I tell 'em!' certainly finished me completely. Being an established panto artist Colin knew that a 'last-night gag' had to be something that the audience could appreciate as well as his fellow actors.

Chapter Thirty-Four

Rejoining us for his second Wigan panto was a friend of long standing, Derek Tobias, to give an admirable epitome of admiralty, 'Captain Horatio Cuttle' of the *Saucy Sal*. Alas, his erstwhile 'oppo', Chris Hopwood, was not available this time but we were fortunate in recruiting a versatile young actor called Steve Dixon to play bosun Eustace Fish.

As we've reached the fish course let me mention some of the terrible jokes which, to me at any rate, are an essential part of a good old-fashioned English pantomime. The name Eustace Fish gives scope for a pun by Dick Whittington. Referring to his wonderful cat Tommy (played with feline excellence and feeling by Angela Curran), Dick said, 'Oh, I can see Tommy likes you, Bosun. Well, he's used to his fish!'

Even Tommy hid his head over that one.

When stocking up in Fitzwarren's shop for the coming sea voyage, before they falsely planted the money on Dick, the captain and bosun enquired of Sarah the cook (yours truly) about various goods on offer, 'These cakes are very hard.'

'Well, what d'you expect. They're rock buns.'

'The matches in this box won't light.'

'Well, they're safety matches.'

And of the sandwiches on offer, 'We've got lettuce and ham, lettuce and spam, lettuce and jam, lettuce and lamb or honeymoon salad.'

'What's honeymoon salad?'

'Lettuce alone!' (Boom! Boom!)

The very effective villain was a portrayal of the king of all rats by David Calladine. David managed to get the children booing and hissing him on his very first entrance in the prologue.

This time 'them upstairs' had listened to me and consequently we had the traditional chorus, a charming group of dancers who, for the pantomime, we called 'The Peal o' Belles'. Under the guidance of choreographer/dancer/teacher, Betty Buckley, they proved to be a popular part of the show. The musical side of the show was in the hands of the expert and widely experienced hands of keyboard virtuoso, Maurice Houghton. Alternating between organ and piano – and at one point playing organ with the left hand and piano with the right – Maurice had percussionist Ken Prescott to accompany him. Ken was also an experienced musician with a seemingly endless supply of 'funny effects noises' amongst his equipment and never missing an atmospheric drum roll or cymbal clash.

By not being so stressful, *Dick Whittington* was a much happier and more enjoyable experience than *Babes* had been. I think the Metro were beginning to realise that I did know something about the job after all! It pleased everyone that we evoked almost unqualified praise from the local press.

By the end of the pantomime most minds had already begun to concentrate on preparations for HM the Queen's Silver Jubilee. *The Evening Post and Chronicle* (were newspapers really only seven pence in those days?) announced the leisure department's contributions. In addition to running an open 'jubilee poem contest' (with prizes supplied by the Greater Lancastrian Co-operative Society) there was to be a jubilee week tribute. I conceived and submitted for the approval of 'them upstairs' my ideas for a celebration in music and verse to be called *In Jubilation*.

Having researched, collected and written material for the spoken parts of the programme I was fortunate in being able to recruit two prominent members of the Wigan Little Theatre, June Whittaker and the (now late) Norman Kinley. The musical side was executed by the Hindley Prize Band and the James Hedley Singers, both having been winners of radio band and choir contests. Two performances of this 'journey round the British Isles in words and music' were arranged for the start and finish of the actual jubilee week. On 4th June it was performed at Wigan Parish Church and on 11th June at Leigh Parish Church. Inspiration by the rectors of Wigan and Leigh led to each concert (at 7.30 p.m.) being preceded by celebration peal changes by the respective church bell-ringers.

Unfortunately I had to miss the second performance because I was once again off to London for the final series of *Dad's Army*. Yes, after a number of previous 'probably the last series' this one, taking up the month of July, was definitely to be the twelfth and final group of six episodes, in five of which I appeared as Pte Sponge again. The end came, not without a few tearful eyes, with 'Never Too Old', recorded in Studio 8 at TV Centre in front of a live audience as usual on the 29th July, 1977.

In-between all these activities I managed to fit in appearances at various charity events, Pte Sponge being called upon to crown a couple of May Queens and conduct a charity auction (another contribution to the Mayor's charity).

In June there had been a royal visit to Wigan. As the Queen and Duke of Edinburgh had spent time in Wigan town on a previous visit it was decided that although the royal train would arrive in Wigan there would be a ceremonial procession to the other centre of Metropolitan Wigan, the former borough of Leigh, where the main part of the visit would take place.

To entertain the great waiting crowd in the Leigh town square a continuous programme of entertainment had been arranged from 2 p.m., with a commentary on the progress of the royal procession being given to everyone over loudspeakers by yours truly. This was achieved by my being ensconced at a good vantage point in Leigh's Turnpike Gallery and constant headphone communication with the police escort. Besides introducing the various entertainments taking place before them I was able to keep the crowd informed of exactly where the procession was at any given moment. Happily there was no need to inform everyone when the Queen was approaching the town square as one could hear the cheering from adjoining streets. After viewing an exhibition of children's work inside the gallery and watching part of the entertainment in the square, Her Majesty and the Duke then embarked on another long car journey to Longford Hall, Trafford.

As part of the jubilee entertainments Wigan Little Theatre staged a production of Royce Ryton's *Crown Matrimonial*. Although I had been a member of WLT since its earliest days, *Crown Matrimonial* was another 'first' for me. The play was directed by Colin Hurst who invited me to undertake the role of Walter Monckton KC who played an important part in this royal family drama. A strong cast did full justice to this intriguing play with Norman Kinley making Edward VIII's abdication speech the most moving moment of the evening.

By this time I'd also accepted the position of Hon. Vice-President of the Comet Youth Club which involved me in their annual carnival and various charity concerts, including a performance of a sort of two-hander play called *Can We Come In?* I wrote this for Phyllis Hart and myself, based upon the characters the Hardcastles which we had played in John Slater's *Foreign Air*.

The concept is somewhat unusual in that the audience play an integral part in the play. Previous to the entry of the Hardcastles a compere addresses the audience, 'Ladies and gentlemen, imagine if you will that you are sitting in your front room on a Sunday afternoon. The teacups are set out, as you see, and you are expecting two visitors to pop in. Unfortunately the couple who turn up are probably not the couple you expect when you hear…'

Marjorie Hardcastle offstage, 'Yoo-hoo! Can we come in?'

The idea seemed to work but I think we both found it a very difficult play to commit to memory. We haven't done it since although other brave souls have given it performances.

During the summer preparations also got under way for another Metro pantomime. This year's subject – *Jack the Giant Killer* – came from my pen rather like a version of *Jack and the Beanstalk* without the difficulty of a beanstalk and Daisy the cow. This was due to open on 4th January, 1978, before which I had undertaken to arrange and take part in a Christmas concert at my own church, St Michael's and All Angels. This was 'The Christmas Story in Carols and Verse', held in aid of the Church of England Children's Society, on 18th December. Happily we had a 'good house' for our 3 p.m. performance. The subtitle 'Let's Make the Rafters Ring' certainly encouraged everyone to join in.

For *Jack the Giant Killer* the tables were turned; this time my old pal, Derek Tobias, wasn't available but Clive Hopwood (our *Babes* baddy) returned to play a main comedy role this time as Simon, son of Widow Penelope Stamp (the village postmistress) known to all of course as 'Penny Stamp'. Bobby Bright returned for his third Wigan panto as our hero of the story, Jack Horner the village baker. Colin Hurst again brought considerable strength and experience to the show as the giant's factotum and henchman, the very dislikeable Oliver Grabbe. Gwenda Hughes, Janet Tolan, Jacqueline Maxwell and Wendy Wilkinson were Fairy Goodheart, Gillian (Simon's sister), Jenny (Jack's sister) and milkmaid Molly Muffet respectively.

Lord Blunderboss (the giant lord of the manor) was played by newcomer, Chris Beazley, who had the pleasure of reading in the *Wigan Observer* that 'Lord Blunderboss was handled with style by Chris Beazley. Chris isn't pencil-slim by any means but he does the niftiest tap dance in the business.' In fact we managed to arrange a couple of 'dance surprises' for our audience. As the Buckley Belles (Betty's dance troupe again) launched into the 'Parade of the Wooden Soldiers' routine they were joined by the large-sized but nimble-footed Chris, much to the delight of all concerned.

In the finale to Act One we 'pulled a gag' which, because everyone played it seriously as I'd insisted, worked well. For the ballet prior to the 'magic' opening of the formidable gates to the giant's castle, a slight 'accident' was arranged. Bobby Bright, as Jack, announced to the audience that unfortunately one of the Buckley Belles had twisted her ankle. So as not to spoil the enjoyment of this moment the ballet would be started again with her understudy completing the line. The 'understudy' was of course 'Penny Stamp', who according to the *Post and Chronicle* 'actually joins the Buckley belles and succeeds in giving one a fairly good idea of how a suitably attired elephant might look in Tchaikovsky's *Swan Lake*.' All in all, another happy and enjoyable pantomime season with Maurice Houghton and Ken Prescott in charge of the musical side once more.

During the early months of 1978 I was recalled to New Broadcasting House in Manchester for a series of radio productions which included both dramas and documentaries including *Incident at Agadir*, one of the 'Best-seller' series about the book *Robinson Crusoe*, two episodes in the *Shipwreck* series, *Patmore* and other characters in *Heaven and Charing Cross*, plus a number of characters in *Fame is the Spur*. Trevor Hill, Stanley Williamson and Herbert Smith were the producers for whom I undertook these roles, all veterans of BBC Radio drama from the north.

I have always found work in radio to be interesting and absorbing and I still do. The extent to which one can try out and use the human voice has intrigued me since my studies at theatre school with the late Charles Gordon. Having this spell of radio drama and documentary work increased my interest to the extent of starting to read and experiment further and to my first research for what, eventually, would lead to me being granted a degree for my dissertation 'Speech and Projection: The Music of Words and the Words of Music' by Somerset University, an independent, European-based distance education institution. Concentration on the voice and the delivery of the material in hand is increased by the fact that, although thoroughly rehearsed, one is usually spared the pressure of having to remember the words as well.

May 1978 also found me making another appearance in a WLT presentation. This was an excellent production by the late Norman Kinley of G.B. Shaw's *Saint Joan*. Headed by a terrific performance as the saint by Joan Lathom, a cast described by the press as 'talented' including many of WLT's most experienced players, this long work was played in full.

'I don't think I've seen such concentrated talent at WLT at one time,' said another seasoned press reviewer, Geoffrey Shryhane. 'This play deserved it; without doubt a wonderfully stimulating experience.' We of the cast also felt that there was something special about this production. The very simple settings and costumes concentrated both players and audience onto the drama taking place each evening.

A significant 'early indication' occurred during this play. As the inquisitor I had for the trial scene a chair mounted on a dais. The two steps up to my chair were quite steep and, for the first time, I began to notice a slight ache and uncomfortable feeling in my left hip after climbing up there. Dismissing it as part of the ageing process, I merely tended to start moves up and down steps on my right foot.

WLT had a flourishing junior group under the leadership and guidance of the very experienced Paul Buer. Membership of the group, however, had an upper age limit of eighteen. Some of the members who had reached that age during the last two years and who had not yet been cast for major roles in 'senior' productions were keen theatre helpers backstage and in the front-of-house activities. Once one has the 'acting bug', however, mere association with activity does not suffice. These young people had learned a lot in the junior group and now clamoured for a chance to show people (and the play selection and casting committee) what they could do. I was approached by them for ideas and, after committee meetings and discussions, it was decided to form an intermediate group which, like the junior group, would have a public two-night performance each year to 'show their paces'. By choice of the young people themselves I was asked to be the first chairman and director of what became known as the 'Midway Group'.

They didn't want to do a 'play for kids' or an 'entertainment' which, in discussion, was thought to be an easy option. 'Proper plays' were to be considered. Having about ten group members, at my suggestion we settled on Robert Bolt's fine domestic drama *Flowering Cherry* which gave seven of the group worthwhile parts with the others understudying and taking on duties such as prompter, props and so on. Being only a two-night production, resources for a setting were naturally somewhat limited. Friend Phil Harris, another senior WLT member, joined me as designer and evolved what an enthusiastic press called 'a 1950s set which was as imaginative as it was workable and sound and lighting added atmosphere'.

For young people between eighteen and twenty to play much older roles is not easy if the parts are not to be 'guyed' or exaggerated. After two nights the opinions of the general public and the WLT committee were that Jackie Littler, Tony Fleming, Paul James, David Reeves, Susan Riding, Malcolm Hughes and Sara Boardman acquitted themselves exceptionally well and that some fears of it being a substandard production were unfounded. I enjoyed directing the play and working with this dedicated group. I'd like to direct it again sometime. Alas, occurrences in the summer of 1978 took my work out of Wigan again and, with reluctance, I had to relinquish my chairmanship of the Midway Group.

After opening the Wigan Infirmary annual garden party on a brilliantly sunny August afternoon my next port of call was the Octagon Theatre in Bolton. Recalling our meeting in *Festival at Farbridge*, theatre director Wilfred Harrison invited me to visit Bolton to meet his assistant director, Felicity Taylor. After giving a couple of 'pieces' for them the outcome of our chat was that I was to join the Octagon Company at the start of the Shakespeare season in September, 1978. Thus, on the twelfth of that month, I made my first appearance at this prestigious post-war theatre as Gratiano in *The Merchant of Venice*, a play I was to meet again towards the and of my time at the Octagon in 1983.

Again I did not feel like a complete stranger. Ex-theatre school colleague, John Pickles, was already an established member of the company. Nona Williams playing Nerissa was a friend from Tynemouth Repertory Company days and I had met Anthony Wingate, who played Shylock, in the BBC Manchester radio studios.

Playing an 'in the round' theatre is an amazing experience for anyone who has been used to working with a proscenium arch for most of his career. Theatre Outlook in Liverpool, many years previously, had been my limited experience of an open stage. *Merchant* was played in the form the Octagon termed 'thrust stage', i.e. very much like a stage in Shakespeare's day with audience on three sides.

By the time we came to *Julius Caesar* in the Shakespeare season, I was getting used to the forty-minute journey to and from Bolton. Little did I know then that I'd be undertaking it daily for the next five years. Later, during periods when Father was in hospital, I made the journey four times a day in order to visit him between morning rehearsals and evening performances with, of course, the exception of matinée days.

The journey became 'study time' for learning my lines for the next play. After years in weekly repertory having three and a half weeks in which to learn and rehearse a role was almost a luxury! Spread over that time rehearsals were, of course, much more intensive than when with Harry Hanson and Victor Graham. The Octagon had high standards of production to maintain; costume fittings and parades plus 'as per performance' dress rehearsals were also a new departure. No trying to complete Act Three with the first house already moving into their seats on the other side of the curtain here!

This was the seventh Octagon Shakespeare Season. Wilfred Harrison had started them when he became director of the theatre. After the summer break each year the three months of autumn were taken up with three Shakespearean productions. The second play was *Julius Caesar*. With large casts a number of these plays require actors to 'double' i.e. play more than one role. Mine for

Caesar were Casca and Titinius, the latter complete with uncomfortable full Roman armour and helmet. Directed by Felicity Taylor with Wilfred as Caesar, the company were getting to know each other better and old friends Nona and John were playing Calpurnia and Brutus. For the end of the run of this play two of our younger members arranged a teatime event for the break between Saturday matinée and evening performances in the form of a mock awards ceremony, complete with music, razzmatazz and 'people who couldn't be here today' – a wicked send-up of the Oscar and Bafta awards. The awards themselves were cleverly designed using wire coat hangers mounted on wooden bases by show designer, Bill Cort. The nature of the awards is reflected by the one I won for the 'Actor Coping With the Silliest Prop'.

The stage management props department designed and made small plastic sachets to contain 'blood' for the murder of Caesar. These were to be concealed about one's person until the appropriate moment. As Casca it was my job to strike the first stabbing blow. What a good job we had time for practice rehearsals of this as I think most of the actors concerned had difficulty in locating these sachets within the generous folds of the togas! The idea was that as I took up my sword to commit the act I would conceal the little bag in my sword hand, squeezing it as I drove the sword in. Thus as I withdrew the sword, 'Kensington Gore' would be gruesomely running down the blade. At our first go with this operation I must have held my sachet incorrectly; instead of running down the blade my 'blood' shot up in the air generously spattering itself over the surrounding white togas.

The ensuing silence was aptly broken by the comment of one of the senators who merely commented, 'Bloody hell!' I think the only person who didn't join in the laughter was the wardrobe mistress when she saw what had been pristine garments when we started the rehearsal.

The next production was *The Winter's Tale*, in which I had played a part in the opening dialogue at Bradford Civic Playhouse. Many people find 'the statue Hermione' hard to accept (and 'Exit pursued by a bear') but it remains one of my favourite Shakespeare plays. I played Archidamus, a Bohemian Lord, at the start of the play, and 'doubled' as the Old Shepherd, a role I'd wanted to play for many years.

David Plimmer proved to be a delightfully roguish Autolycus and Peter Walmsley had to make the famous 'exit chased by a bear'. At one performance the actor in the bear costume, with limited vision, missed his footing on the edge of the 'thrust' stage as he gave chase and finished up across the laps of some very surprised front-row patrons.

Chapter Thirty-Five

The Christmas attraction at the Octagon was Wilfred Harrison's adaptation of *Beauty and the Beast*. Being a theatre-in-the-round production the scenic department had the wider scope of using the whole of the auditorium as the setting. Entrances by characters through the audience and musical numbers strung out all around them were an integral part of the show. The theatre was transformed, whichever way one looked, into a magical forest.

My role was that of a nosey, verbose, interfering neighbour. In deference to my somewhat portly appearance, Wilfred named the man 'Frederick, Alphonse, Thomas, Terence, Ignatius'. Which, if one took the initials, became 'FATTI'.

From the Shakespeare season we had Nona Williams, John Pickles, the two Peters – Chandler and Walmsley, and David Plimmer as principals. We were joined by an actress with whom we were to work very amicably for quite a while, Lesley E. Bennett, an excellent artiste with the sort of sense of humour which 'twinkled'. In a number of the plays which followed there were some scenes in which I simply dared not catch Lesley's eye or I'd have cracked up, but an enjoyable person with whom to work.

At the end of the exhausting six weeks of *Sleeping Beauty*, with lots of extra matinées, we had a short interval in which to allow Bolton Operatic Society to present *South Pacific* while Nona, Lesley, John, the two Peters and myself got stuck into rehearsals for *Mrs Warren's Profession* (directed by

Felicity Taylor), the G.B. Shaw play which caused scandal and outcry when written. 'Shaw's Prostitute Emerges Triumphant' was typical of the press headlines on first-night newspaper reports, although I'm not quite sure how to take one reviewer who commented, 'Colin Bean, professional as ever, is eminently believable as the boorish buffoon!'

Whilst indulging in my boorishness each evening I had, during the day, an enormously difficult task. (Well, I didn't find it easy.) The play in rehearsal was Tom Stoppard's *Enter a Free Man*. As the 'impossible inventor' called George Riley I think I had about ten minutes off stage in the whole show. Director John Pickles, very wisely, started rehearsals initially at the long transition speech in which George has to move the action between time zones. *The Stage* commented that my performance 'makes Riley, the middle-aged, hopelessly failed inventor, and his fantasies his own kind of pathetic, swaggering, vulnerable, maddening and loveable loser, gloriously triumphant even in complete defeat'.

Even in 1979 a number of the reviews referred to the play as being 'a bit dated', the entertainment's main value being, apparently, in the excellence of the performances. During the run of the play I also managed to fit in a contribution to Wigan Little Theatre's hosting of the one hundred and first conference of the Little Theatre Guild of Great Britain. On the Sunday morning I delivered the script to accompany Jaz Whittaker's slides and photos at one of the 'Theatre in Action' seminars which was the theme of the two-day event.

To follow the Stoppard play we really became 'dated', back to Lancashire in the 1820s in fact, and a real old-fashioned 'trouble at t'mill' work by Harold Brighouse called *The Northerners*.

Marion Shakespeare and David Williams, who had appeared at the Octagon before, rejoined the company for the play, as did David Acton who was to stay longer. Notices on this production seemed to be merely contrasting it with *Hobson's Choice*. Many thought it too 'heavy-handed'.

In complete contrast of appearance, mood and pace was Sheridan's *The Rivals*. By now I felt that my limp was becoming too noticeable and started to wear a 'lift' in my left shoe. Much later I was to be told by specialists that this was the worst thing I could have done, but then I didn't realise that it was an arthritic hip. As Sir Lucius O'Trigger I began to find entrances up and down the Octagon's long audience staircases a bit of a trial, even with a stick. Our director, Jolyon Coombs, rearranged a couple of them so that I could enter and exit down the vomitories on stage level. Beautifully costumed and with a good old blustering Sir Anthony Absolute by Wilfred Harrison, *The Rivals* was an enjoyable show.

In complete contrast the next play in the season was Alan Bennett's *The Old Country*. Not all the reviewers thought it was Bennett at his best but, to my mind, it remains a fascinating play. This particular production, directed by John Pickles, was of great interest in that it allowed me to study two very different actors tackling the same very long part. Audrey Barr, who had been our Mrs Malaprop, played Bron, the patient and tolerant wife of Hilary. The man in exile in this remote, forest-surrounded dacha, Hilary, was played by Wilfred Harrison. Lesley E. Bennett played his sister, wife of the stuffy establishment figure, Duff, whom I played. Peter Walmsley was the rather 'lost', enigmatic Eric, with Elaine White as a fur-clad Olga. Wilfred played Hilary from the 5th to the 14th June, at which point he flew to Poland on a mission to theatre in Poznan. John himself played Hilary from the 14th until the play finished on the 30th. Both performances were equally valid and sincere, but the contrast in playing was compelling for their fellow cast members. One critic wrote, 'One day, one feels, Alan Bennett will write a great play. This isn't it but it comes pretty near.' For me it will always be remembered with more than a little interest. In 1979, of course, we hadn't encountered the brilliant *Talking Heads*.

To end the season the play chosen was P.G. Wodehouse's adaptation of the Ladislas Fodor comedy called in English *Good Morning, Bill*. Wilfred approached me in his often quiet and understated manner and said, 'Have you ever directed in the round?' Upon my negative reply he put the script of *Good Morning, Bill* into my hands, continuing, 'Now's your chance!'

Regular members Lesley E. Bennett and Elaine White, with John Pickles, Peter Walmsley and David Acton, were joined by a delightful young actress who had played in *The Rivals* and was destined to make a later career in television – Amanda Burton. As adapted the characters were, of course, pure Wodehouse from Lord Tidmouth (Squiffy) to the dizzy maid.

I have to confess that I approached this 'first' with some trepidation until I started to discuss an 'in-the-round' production with designer Bill Cort, lighting chief Stephen Henbest and stage manager Jolyon Coombs. Having spent a long part of my past career in proscenium-arch theatres and a relatively short time here at the Octagon, plotting the moves, the entrances and exits was an adventure indeed. One suddenly became aware of the freedom of movement that this form of theatre presented. Masking and upstaging have completely different meanings and, of course, lighting is more naturalistic. Bill's two sets – 'The Esplanade Hotel', all light, bright and tubular steel furniture and 'Paradine's Country House' – couldn't have been more highly contrasted. All this achieved by changing furniture, floor coverings and low set-piece panels around the acting area.

One day I had a couple of visitors who had not visited the Octagon before. I got permission to take them on a short tour of the place. On stage was the setting for Act One ready for the evening performance, but of course without the set lighting. As we came into the auditorium one of the guests commented, 'Oh another lounge, but where's the stage?'

My direction was reviewed as 'rapid', 'cracking' and 'lively'. We certainly all had great fun in rehearsing the show and I think the actors enjoyed playing it. *The Evening Post and Chronicle* headlined their review, 'Rather Spiffing Play, Old Bean' – rather Wodehousean perhaps. Being the last play of the present season we all felt it was another 'let your hair down' production so we ended with a rather lively 1920s dance number arranged by Peter. Naughty perhaps but it certainly sent the audience out smiling!

TAP (Theatre Appreciation Project) was a smaller Octagon company based at a centre outside the town, which produced programmes and projects mainly for schools and individual young people, which invariably were complementary to whatever was being presented at the theatre itself. Therefore, in 'end of term' mood during the run of *Good Morning, Bill* I was involved also in leading the TAP company in a programme about comedy in the theatre (we didn't touch TV or films in this) called 'Come on. Give Us All a Laugh.' which ranged from *The Taming of the Shrew*, via Sheridan, Bennett, Stoppard and Brecht to *Good Morning, Bill*.

During the summer break I was able to do more radio work and some 'charity' events. Father was also requiring more time spent on his welfare and, as his disabilities increased, more attention physically and medically. In mid-August rehearsals started for the next Shakespeare season which opened with *Henry V*. My interpretation of Pistol did not, apparently, meet with universal approval. One reviewer described me as appearing to be 'A TV wrestler with a desperately fading career.' Happily I met with the approval of guest director, Helena Kaut-Howson, even if we did all vanish in a cloud of 'thick fog' on the first night due to a rather over-enthusiastic mortar discharge at Harfleur. Again, the company had to be enlarged to cope with works by the Bard. Friends David Williams, Terence Skelton and Marion Shakespeare rejoined us. An actor I had not met before impressed me as the Constable of France. This was a happy return for Ken Binge with whom I was to appear in the regular company for some time to come.

Next in the season came that mighty drama *King Lear*, with Wilfred as the King and Marion, Lesley and Amanda as Goneril, Regan and Cordelia respectively. Ken and I were the Dukes of Albany and Cornwall and David Williams gave an excellent performance as Fool. Directed by Felicity Taylor the production was stark in setting, costume and interpretation.

The final Shakespeare for this year was a lively production, directed by Jolyon Coombs, of *Much Ado About Nothing*. The 'rude mechanicals' certainly made the most of their appearances a bit like a Shakespearean 'Crazy Gang' with yours truly playing 'Dogberry' in the manner in which the late Robb Wilton might have played the role. Purists were aghast but everyone else found it to be great fun and the language very appropriate for this official.

Chapter Thirty-Six

Whilst enjoying *Much Ado* we were rehearsing Wilfred's adaptation of *Jack and the Beanstalk*. As he knew his company, the parts he wrote ideally suited the actors playing them. To Rita Lester's Queen Eleanora I was King Harold, parents of a delightful Princess Penelope, played by Amanda Burton. 'Fun and action by the minute,' said one of the review headlines, which included friend David Williams' town crier's confrontation with the pantomime cow.

Magically, the giant varied in size according to the kind of tantrum he was in and, thanks to the wizardry of Keith Kay, we were at one point all involved in a display of plate spinning! As *Jack and the Beanstalk* concluded, David, Penny McDonald and I were also involved in the TAP programme on the plays of D.H. Lawrence for in the coming season the main house theatre would be presenting *The Merry-Go-Round*.

Before that, however, the TAP Company had also presented 'Two Thousand Years Mystery and Nativity' which had included a very comical and inspired production (directed by John Pickles) of my own *St George and the Dragon*. During January the Wigan Little Theatre gave an excellent presentation of my pantomime *Babes in The Wood*. My old mate Colin Hurst certainly gave Nurse Daisy Dogood a new, vigorous and hilarious interpretation, proving that even within the confines of playing a dame great variation is possible. Directed by Colin himself and

Margaret Finch, this was a much bigger production than mine had been at the Linacre, with no limitations on number in the cast and a full musical chorus. I'm the first to admit it was a better production than mine had been.

After recovering from our antics in-the-round with *Jack and the Beanstalk* there couldn't have been a bigger contrast than when, on 4th March the Octagon Company opened the stark essay in persecution and revolution, Ugo Betti's *The Queen and the Rebels*, with a great performance by Lesley E. Bennett as the mysterious Argie. I was a very shaggy, bearded Biante, the general, and a particularly effective David Acton was Raim. *Tempus* did indeed *fugit*. Before we knew where we were it was 1st April and the opening night of the D.H. Lawrence somewhat unusual (for him) comedy, complete with sets on a revolving stage. Well, it is called *The Merry-Go-Round*. At one performance our enthusiastic assistant stage managers must have had a mental aberration. We, on the set, had braced ourselves to revolve into position to play a scene. Our assistant stage managers for some reason spun the revolve in the other direction. Thus Lesley, David Acton and I appeared before the audience in anything but tableau position!

In Shaw's *Major Barbara* I was but briefly engaged, as Bilton in Act Two, and so had time to work on J.B. Priestley's *The Linden Tree* which was to be my second stab at directing an Octagon production. I've always loved J.B.P.'s books and plays. (*The Good Companions* was almost considered to be Bridgeman Productions' Bible!) From my point of view it was a wholly enjoyable experience from first rehearsal to final performance. Going against the prevalent opinion I suggested to Wilfred and Felicity that David Williams be cast in the Lewis Casson role of Professor Linden. David is a wonderful comedy actor but I had seen depths in his work (especially as the fool in *Lear*) which urged me to suggest him for the role. In the end they agreed and with Elizabeth Kelly as Mrs Linden, Ken Binge as the student, Fawcett, and Marion Shakespeare playing the voluble Mrs Cotton, Peter Chandler as Rex and Penny McDonald as young Dinah, I had a great cast. David in particular was so eager and enthusiastic – this was a new departure for him that he infused keenness into us all. Happily the play had a great reception from very well-attended houses and creditable reviews, including the *Daily Telegraph*'s Stella Flint summing it up as 'a well-paced performance; a charming production against an authentic setting by Peter Fairchild'.

A number of us were involved in another TAP production which overlapped *The Linden Tree* and the next play. David had devised 'A Night at the Music Hall' for which he asked me to write a brief history piece as a prologue to be delivered by Ken. Ken, Penny and I augmented the TAP company to present a more extensive than usual project upon the British music hall. I managed to get my contribution as dame in at the point where music-hall artistes started to play pantomime.

And so, once again, it was 'end-of-term' time. From 24th June to 19th July we, and the audiences, had a rollicking time with Terence Rattigan's *While The Sun Shines*. John Pickles as the imperturbable Horton, Ken as able seaman the Earl of Harpenden, Lesley as the flighty blonde Mabel Crum, Penny, Peter Chandler and I were all joined by David Bauckham as 'Lootenant Mulvaney – US Army'.

During 1980 I managed also to do two small television roles. Mr Robinson in *Cousin Phyllis* for the BBC and a police sergeant in an episode of Granada's series *Cribb*. This was possible by virtue of them both being 'one-day shoots'. Cribb was on a Sunday when Manchester town hall was reasonably quiet and unoccupied. The centre courtyard of Manchester town hall, which I'm sure many Northerners never knew existed, doubled admirably for a misty

Victorian London location. *Cousin Phyllis* was made possible by virtue of a hectic car ride to Bolton from an old farm-house in the wilds of Cheshire to get me there in time for an evening performance.

September 1980 saw the start of our next Shakespeare season with guest director, the delightful Helena Kaut Howson, paying a return visit to lead another augmented Octagon company through *Henry IV (Part 1)*. This was to be a Shakespeare season of very mixed reviews and reactions. The Octagon policy of straightforward, non-gimmicky presentation of the Bard's works had become very familiar over the years, and one knows what is said about familiarity. Even a novel and almost story-book-like production of *The Taming of the Shrew* raised little more than mild praise. This was a bright, colourful presentation with strong performances by Lesley E. Bennett as Katherine and Robert Duncan as Petruchio. The sudden transformation of the dull, dark opening set into a riot of colour by the company approaching with pieces of scenery from all parts of the theatre to make a picturesque Padua, got applause from the audience present but little mention in the press.

The third production of this season of Will's works, *Cymbeline*, again managed to arouse little general enthusiasm. As this play opened on 5th November, *The Post and Chronicle* could not resist a headline next day which read, 'A Damp Squib at the Octagon.' *Cymbeline* is a very long and, I think, complicated play, not one I would choose for entertainment value. Apart from being one of two gentlemen in the opening of the play, my main role, with the aid of a Roman nose job and uncomfortable armour again, was as Caius Lucius. I have to confess that during the final scene of the play, as we all stood on that cruelly raked set awaiting the denouement, there were moments when, unforgivably, my mind wandered somewhat from the play to wonder whether or not I was going to catch the last bus back to Wigan!

Early December saw the first performance of Wilfred Harrison's adaptation of the famous Grimm story *The Golden Goose* which he and I co-directed. In a fairly straightforward role as King Fulbert I didn't appear until Act Two and so had time to help Wilfred with setting and rehearsing a lengthy Act One. Ken Binge gave a spirited and enchanting lead as Simon, the boy who finds the golden goose to which a whole string of comically bizarre characters manage to get themselves stuck, including in the end the King himself crying, 'Am I stuck to this thing as well? What a way for a king to behave!'

At each performance our young audiences almost raised the roof with a rendition of 'I Went to the Animal Fair'. Penelope McDonald was the princess whom Simon finally caused to laugh. As in previous years the production made full use of the whole auditorium thus giving plenty of scope for movement and chases. One person missing from such excursions was yours truly. My hip was now beginning to hurt even more and stairs were becoming more of a problem.

By 24th January we'd all been stuck to our golden goose for the last time and were about to embark on an international play season, starting in the North of England. From then until June we would perform plays from America, Hungary, Poland and Belgium.

To start the ball rolling was a robust presentation of Walter Greenwood's *The Cure For Love* in which, as Harry Lancaster the pub landlord, I got a good helping of delicious Lancashire hotpot at each performance. The odour of this, I was told later by friends who came to see it, had members of the audience craving for a plateful! The press were approbatory and audiences obviously enjoyed a play which by 1981, with its wartime associations, was already becoming something of a Greenwood classic and a period piece. 'The company is shot through with excellence. There is not one stereotype to blur the picture,' said the *Guardian*'s reviewer.

After enjoying a month of nightly hotpot I was again offstage for our American contribution to this international season. I had the job of directing Wilfred Harrison and the very strong company in a very strong drama, Arthur Miller's *A View From The Bridge*.

"A VIEW ON THE STREETS"
COLIN BEAN
LYCEUM 1956

Chapter Thirty-Seven

A View From The Bridge is not, in my opinion, an easy play to direct or to play in, especially for non-Americans. One or two of the reviewers 'had a go' at the accents employed by some of the actors but comments such as 'fine all-round acting' and 'director Colin Bean gets good results' made it a worthwhile project. Wilfred Harrison gave us a very strong Eddie Carbone and Ken Binge an impressive Rodolpho. The trial of strength engendered between the two evoked some very tense situations; one could virtually 'feel the atmosphere'. Peter Fairchild gave us an effective all-purpose setting which admirably set the mood of the play.

From 7th April to 2nd May we were all involved in a Ruritanian-like ambience with Ferenc Molnar's *The Wolf*. This tale of marital jealousy is, to say the least, a very 'wordy' comedy. One critic appeared to sympathise, 'Colin Bean seems to get the bulk of the long, difficult speeches', but qualified that by saying that I 'brought my experience to bear in the role of the long-suspicious husband.'

Lindsay Blackwell had the equally difficult role as my wife, Vilma. The part of our son Janil was played, at alternate performances, by Ken Binge's son, five year old Leo, and his school chum, Matthew Leigh.

Both gave excellent performances and, according to the *Evening News*, spoke 'their few lines so well that they're in danger of stealing the show'. Master Leo Binge found only one aspect of playing Janil distasteful, which was having to wear a long nightshirt while sitting on my knee to be told a bedtime story.

Our next play came from Poland. Written by Slawomir Mrozek, translated by Nicholas Bethell, adapted by Tom Stoppard and directed by Wilfred Harrison, *Tango* was a strange mixture of tragedy and the absurd. Ken Binge gave an excellent performance as Arthur, the apparently only normal human being in the whole play. Some people appeared to find the whole thing a bit incomprehensible but the majority seemed to be impressed if a trifle bemused. The production was of great significance to me for a personal reason; realisation that I would have to take action about my increasingly painful left hip and increasingly obvious limp, even with a 'lift' in my shoe. Came the fatal performance when I made an entrance closely followed by Ken Binge. As we argued I had to turn and try to leave the scene with 'my son' blocking my way and refusing to let me exit. Ken's plotted move was to put his hands on my shoulders as I approached him again to try to leave. I stepped back and, unwittingly, put my full weight onto my left hip. What happened in the next few minutes I am not quite sure. I was conscious only of blinding pain. Luckily it seems there was a chair close at hand and I managed to sit on it. How to describe the situation is difficult. I could see Ken, I could see the stage lights and the audience. My head was 'ringing' with pain and I could see Ken speaking to me – by then probably having to ad lib furiously as I could not utter a line. I doubt if I could have even remembered a line. After what seemed to me to be hours I began to hear him again, managed to mutter something and get off stage.

Poor Ken, not knowing what on earth I was doing, quite rightly thought I'd simply left him high and dry. How I finished the play I'm not sure but I made an appointment next morning to consult my doctor. Eventually I got the whole story pieced together, making of course profuse apologies to Ken who quite rightly was not exactly pleased at what had happened. The role of Arthur was difficult enough without having fellow actors 'dry' at crucial moments of the play. The episode, I gather, was nowhere near as long as I had imagined it to be but it was most certainly a grim warning that action was needed.

Without going into detail I'll say only that eventually an appointment was made with a specialist for later in the year. The outcome of all this, in February 1982, is where you started this narrative. In the meantime work had to go on and Father still had to be cared for. At least we all now knew just what the problem was and here I must pay a tribute to my fellow actors and stage manager, Ron Kiddell, who in subsequent productions all went out of their way to held me and ease my progress through each of the coming plays.

To end the season we had a play from Belgium set in France and, of course, played in English. It was a fitting end to an international season. It was a farce by Herwig Hensen, the British premiere of *His Majesty's Grenadier* set in 1815. Having heard of Napoleon's escape from Elba an ex-soldier, Henri Gendebien, gets out his old uniform and firearms to prepare for his Emperor's return to France. It is a play which eventually becomes a treatise on the futility of war. Wilfred slotted perfectly into the leading role and I had an enjoyable role as Monsieur Rampart, the over-fussy headmaster. For my incarceration in the cupboard under the stairs stage management even provided a seat for me! Directed by Felicity it enabled the *Bolton Chronicle* to headline the review, 'Season ends on a high note'.

During the summer break I was able to take some minor roles in a radio drama-documentary called *The Spencers of Althrop*, tracing the history and some of the famous ancestors of the year's coming royal bride. Trevor Hill produced it for BBC Radio in Manchester. Also in Manchester I appeared as clerk of the court in an episode of the Granada TV series *Ladykillers* featuring Christopher Cazanove and Helen Cherry.

For myself and fellow regular Octagon actor, Richard Wardale, there was an early return from our break to join a cast, mainly from the TAP company, to take part in the Bolton festival. The theme for 1981 was the first Lord Leverhulme, the king of soap – not an easy subject for a full-stage drama-documentary with music. The *Daily Express* described the piece, written by Charles Petry, as 'top-heavy with established fact: long on achievement, short on drama.' In one scene, a 1920s dance hall complete with some nifty choreography by Ken Binge, I avoided the Terpsichorean part by appearing, somewhat in the style of Noël Coward in a silk dressing gown complete with cigarette holder, and an old-fashioned megaphone to continue from a gallery some of the factual speeches above the music and hectic activity on the stage below. Another press quote read, 'There are few actors who could wring urgency or pathos from lines like "I have been thinking a good deal about soap recently".' Martin Reeve, playing Leverhulme, was I think as enthusiastic in the role as the play would allow.

The Shakespearean season for 1961 began with a lively and colourful presentation, directed by John Pickles, of *The Comedy of Errors*. My by now pronounced limp was, perhaps, fairly acceptable in the character of the old man, Eagon. Despite long and careful rehearsal the pain still caused me to have a rather nasty 'dry' in his long, long speech at the opening of the play on the first night. The two Dromeos and the two Antipholus' extracted much humour from their predicaments in the hands of Peter Joyce and William Ilkley, and Ken Binge and Robert Barrett respectively. Although it was not one of Shakespeare's longer plays, John ensured that none of the humour was missed.

Next on the list was a not terribly well received production of *Coriolanus*. As Manquius Agrippa I made good use of a stout black walking stick. The stairs to different levels of a typical Octagon Shakespeare set were becoming a real difficulty.

To follow the heavy drama was the always enjoyable *Twelfth Night*. In Peter Fairchild's colourful and very formal setting, Lindsay Blackwell as Maria, Ken Binge as Sir Andrew and I as Sir Toby were able to create fun in equally colourful costumes; so did Martin Cosgriff as a star-spangled Feste. The *Bolton Evening News* thought it 'one of the best we have seen from the Octagon's crop of Shakespeare productions.' Another publication found it 'over the top in comic scenes and ploddingly prosaic in-between.' Take your choice!

The dark November nights soon gave way to 2nd December, the opening night of *Hansel and Gretel*. Joyce Wentworth had a very busy show 'doubling' the unkind mother and the witch. Lindsay Blackwell and Ken Binge were totally delightful and believable as Hansel and Gretel and they soon got on friendly terms with the younger members of the audience. I was heavily disguised in a long flowing robe, a conical hat, green make-up and a large nose and 'twas said of me in one review, 'Colin Bean's wizard of the forest is quite superb with the audience never knowing where he is going to appear from next.' Another wrote, 'For though the wizard played by Colin Bean and the witch played by Joyce Wentworth are as scary a couple as you would care to meet in the forest you can always stop believing in them if you want to. The author, Wilfred Harrison, has given you that much leeway.'

Jolyon Coomb's direction gave the production pace, three very funny soldiers (Martin Reeve, Michael Powell-Jones and John Goodram), magic ('Britain's first free-fall pigeon whose descent from the "gods" is spectacular to say the least') and total auditorium involvement.

For the wizard this was achieved not without a little difficulty and discomfort. My hip was now becoming very painful and my sudden appearances in different parts of the building were not exactly easily achieved. Apart from having to remember at which entrance I was supposed to appear next, the Octagon's stairs up and down to the various levels took their toll, particularly on two-performance days. A mild shock came one day, as I waited in the shadows on a promontory fairly high up in the auditorium ready to step forward as my spotlight came on. I felt someone tug at my sleeve, as a very loud young voice, recognising me despite my heavy disguise, piped up to general amusement, 'Hey, you're in *Dad's Army*, aren't you!'

In January Wigan Little Theatre, obviously pleased with their production of *Babes in the Wood*, now presented my version of *Aladdin*, the one I'd presented in Ayr as *A Lad and his Lamp*. Having a much larger cast and more resources than I had had in Scotland this production was more spectacular than mine had been. Margaret Shannon gave it a lively, musical and colourful production.

1981 had seen an international season. This year the Octagon presented a Lancashire season. The plays scheduled for February, March and April were Walter Greenwood's *Too Clever For Love*, Stanley Houghton's *Hindle Wakes* and Peter Whelan's *The Accrington Pals*. My involvement was to play pub landlord Tom Holroyd – which was a blessing. By this time I was walking only with great difficulty. Stage manager Ron Kiddell constantly had my walking sticks ready for me just offstage and John Pickles directed the action of the play so that most of my time was spent behind the bar, upon which I could lean for support.

For *Hindle Wakes* I was to be in the director's seat again. Having set and rehearsed *Wakes* and played *Too Clever* for two weeks I was suddenly surprised, mid-rehearsal on the Thursday afternoon, by an important phone call. In normal circumstances receiving private phone calls during rehearsal is not only a waste of everyone's time but, in my mind, somewhat discourteous to one's fellow actors. This summons to the phone, however, came from the office with the description 'Urgent'.

Wrightington Hospital (the home of hip replacement and joint surgery) were on the line. Owing to a cancellation on Mr Wroblewski's list, could I now be ready to be admitted the following Monday? This necessitated some rapid thinking. I could not of course simply say 'Yes' without consulting with the management and I was appearing in a play and directing the next. Quandary. The sister at the hospital was understanding but insisted that I must let them know within the next half-hour whether or not I could undertake admission. I lurched upstairs to the director's office and asked to see Wilfred as a matter of importance had cropped up. Wilfred's immediate reaction was, 'Take the opportunity. Get it done.'

Swift decisions were made. I should finish my rehearsals the next day and the Friday and then leave my directing script and notes to be taken over by Felicity Taylor. David Williams was, fortunately for us, not working at the time and was able to come to see *Too Clever For Love* and, with some swift hard work, was able to take over my role of Tom Holdroyd on the Monday as I went into 'dock'. The stage manager's comments you read at the start of this tome; the decorated stout stick for *The Wizard of the Forest* had exhausted the theatre's collection of walking sticks and ideas on how to make them work differently. So that was me *hors de combat* for a few weeks.

Arrangements for the continual care of Father had to be undertaken. Our GP was notified and friends and neighbours Ann and Brian Nicolson kindly took on even more help and assistance. They had been an invaluable help to me and to Father for more than twelve months. With me 'in dock' they nobly undertook increased responsibility for which I shall always be grateful. As the saying goes 'it was a load off my mind', which was apparently a necessary preparation before the operation could be undertaken.

I'm told that in the recovery ward after my operation my main concern was to find out how the first night of *Hindle Wakes* had gone. Subsequent press reports showed that it was well received and friends from the Octagon reassured me of this when they visited me later.

Following my time in hospital I was required to convalesce for some weeks. This, the specialist pointed out, couldn't be undertaken at home with Father requiring attention. The Nicolsons carried on with their sterling work whilst I stayed in the home of stage manager Ron in Bolton for three weeks. It was very satisfying for me to be able to catch after all the final performances of *Wakes*.

After a couple of weeks of recuperation and exercise I felt ready for work again and so went into the Octagon daily. As happens in so many theatres, a pile of plays sent in by hopeful authors had built up on the director's desk. In an effort to clear this backlog I was asked by Wilfred to take, read and comment on some of them. At least I felt I was involved again. One of these plays was by Phil Melling who, purely coincidentally, happened to be the son of my next door neighbours in Wigan. The play was what one might call a strong black comedy – no pun intended – called *The Day of the African*. The subject was Rugby league football and even a non-sportsman like me knew that Bolton was not a rugby town but I felt that the play was too good to be ignored. In returning the script I suggested to the author that he should send it to a small company in Wigan – fast making a reputation for themselves with original productions of out of the ordinary plays. In 1985 the Willpower Company gave *The Day of the African* its premiere at Wigan's Mill at the Pier Theatre.

The *Accrington Pals* ran from 6th April until 1st May and April had two dramatic happenings as far as I was concerned. On my birthday came the shock news that Arthur Lowe, who with his wife, Joan Cooper, was on tour in R.C. Sheriff's *Home At Seven*, had had a heart attack in the theatre dressing room in Birmingham between matinée and evening performances on the 14th and died in the early hours of the 15th. It was a sad loss of a wonderful actor.

Drama closer to home came on 30th April. Richard Wardale, playing CSM Rivers in *Accrington Pals*, suffered a heart attack and was rushed into hospital with one performance on the Saturday evening still to do. This regional premiere of what is now regarded as a major play had played to excellent audiences and the final performance was well booked up. By now I was walking without my supportive crutches and so took up the request to read the important part of the Company Sergeant Major for the final performance.

I spent most of the night reading the script, having been present at an earlier performance. On the Saturday morning all the members of the cast who had scenes with CSM Rivers came in to a special rehearsal to go through the role with me. After a very sparse and swift lunch – I really could not eat more than half a sandwich – wardrobe mistress Mary Horan fitted me out with an army greatcoat and cap plus Richard's webbing equipment. Because I had to have the script with me – the part was far too long to attempt to learn it in the time available – we dispensed with the rifle and some other accoutrements. To say I was nervous as publicity officer Stanley Whittaker addressed the audience before the performance, was putting it mildly to say the least.

After the performance, which under the circumstances went with very few hitches, Wilfred was kind enough to comment that one outstanding moment for him was to see me, on my first entrance, march smartly onto the stage with no hint of my former limp and look of pain on my face. He probably appreciated that internally I was 'shaking like a leaf'. The members of the cast were marvellous, adapting if I happened to be in a wrong position and, particularly John Pickles, for guiding me through the battlefield scene – complete with a script in my hand. In the bar after the show some patrons were kind enough to comment that, after a short while, they were not consciously aware that I was reading the part.

Richard's indisposition meant also that I was required to undertake, at short notice, his role in the next play, Eduardo da Filippo's comedy *Filumena*. The fairly small part of Nocella was compatible with my carrying papers as a solicitor so a quick glance at some prompt notes hopefully went unnoticed.

Already 1982 was flashing by. *Filumena* closed on 29th May to be followed on the 1st June by the opening of the sombre Ernst Toller Play *The Blind Goddess* (not to be confused with Patrick Hastings' play of the same name which I had done with the Court Players in the past). Instead of being an Italian, as I was in the Hastings play, I now had three German roles – the president of the court, a prisoner and an official. There was plenty of variety to keep me busy in what proved to be a heavy Teutonic drama which, even with notable performances by Ken Binge, Lesia Melnik and others was according to the *Guardian*, 'not a barrel of laughs'. Alas, even the setting of 'bare boards, boring benches and minimal properties bathed in half-light' couldn't provide any levity. Fortunately we had the levity of

Feydeau's farce *The Birdwatcher* (translated by Richard Cotterell) to follow, in which I think we all 'had a ball'. Beautifully costumed and in very attractive sets designed by Peter Fairchild, this again was our 'end-of-term romp' before the summer break.

Chapter Thirty-Eight

The Octagon's seventh Shakespeare season opened with the star-crossed lovers, *Romeo and Juliet* under Felicity Taylor's direction. The various press reviewers referred to it as 'fast moving tragedy', 'stirring' and the *Manchester Evening News* noted particularly that 'The fights are arranged [by Derek Ware] with gusto and many exits and entrances make full use of both stage and auditorium to provide a multidirectional interest.' Carol Holt's Juliet and Nigel Cooke's Romeo were performances praised on all sides and I added a bit of weight at the beginning and the end as Escalus, Prince of Verona.

Next came the Scottish drama. A cameo portrayal of the drunken porter claimed favourable comment from one paper for Douglas Paul, but apart from that I'm afraid this was not judged amongst our successes. Even my triple roles of King Duncan, First Murderer and the Scottish Doctor, despite my varied make-ups, didn't help much.

Judged completely differently was the final production of the season, *Love's Labour Lost*. The guest director was Ian Judge, an associate director of the Royal Shakespeare Company. On the lawn of an ivy-clad Oxbridge university, firmly set in the 1920s, this production proved to be a great success. Ian had brought Fiona Shaw and Michael Ross with him to give outstanding performances, as Rosaline and Berowne, with John Pickles and I quietly going about our academic reflections and reciting the 'Twhit, to-wo' poem in 'the backyard concert' at the end, in the roles of the

Reverend Sir Nathaniel and pedant Holofernes; an enjoyable experience. At one point John retrieved and expertly returned a stray ball rolling across the lawn from an offstage cricket match. Ken Binge's young King of Navarre, Tim Hall's Constable Dull and Martin Reeve's Costard were also highly spoken of under headlines such as 'Shakespearean Success' and 'Exceptionally Brilliant'. For all of us a delightful month of colour and comedy.

Meanwhile rehearsals were in full spate for Charles Petry's festive season attraction *Jack and Jill and the Magic Secret*. For this somewhat 'wordy' but nevertheless colourful play one or two of us had to endure some discomfort in costumes which, even in December, were to say the least warm. I was generously padded (even with my natural avoirdupois) as King Bulbus IX but our main sympathies had to be with Ken Binge, Martin Reeve and Douglas Paul as the three loveable but heavily costumed bundicats. By the interval I think all three went for a quick shower while their furry costumes were dried out. And they were doing this, often twice a day, from 1st December until 22nd January. Children in the audience took great delight in being asked to perform such tasks as helping the magician with his tricks, which often went wrong, an inventor with weird mechanical creations ditto and, more importantly, helping Jack and Jill to get through the forest. Felicity's direction gave us full rations of magical effects, bangs, flashing lights and puffs of smoke which the youngsters adored and, I'm told, even surprised some adults.

Again Wigan Little Theatre had approached me about their pantomime, my object being to try to help them save money on expensive royalties. This year I lent them my *Dick Whittington and his Wonderful Cat*. Directed by Margaret Shannon, with friend Colin Hurst repeating his notable Alderman Fitzwarren and a large, augmented cast, I'm happy to say that it enjoyed success with full houses, again being more lavishly produced than had been possible on my limited means at the Linacre Theatre in 1976.

By this time my father's condition had deteriorated to the point where he was once again in Billinge Hospital. Besides his crippling arthritis which confined him to a wheelchair, he had for the past few years had to cope also with a colostomy bypass and at eighty-six he no longer had the strength or stamina to resist any further.

On the afternoon of 23rd January I visited him and he had been moved to a single side room to remove him from the noise and bustle of the main ward. In the early hours of the following morning I received the phone call from the hospital which told me he had died quietly at 3 a.m.

The Octagon, very understandingly and sympathetically, gave me some time off for I'd already started rehearsals on a very complicated project, Alan Ayckbourn's *Sisterly Feelings*. My brother Kenneth came up to Wigan as soon as he received the news and together we got through all the procedures required and made funeral arrangements. As we both had work commitments we appreciated the help and cooperation of our solicitor and the undertaker. The funeral would take place in about five or six days' time. Meanwhile back at work, I experienced some emotional difficulty in rehearsing my role as Dr Ralph Matthews in Ayckbourn's jigsaw of sisterly plays. The doctor explains to his family in each play how significant the grassy hillside upon which they are about to picnic was to his lately deceased wife and himself. At times, I'm afraid, my personal sorrow intruded and I was very grateful for my understanding fellow actors.

Sisterly Feelings was not due to open until 8th February but even without my own personal circumstances the play required intensive, detailed and concentrated rehearsal. Not wishing to write a treatise on this quite amazing and fascinating work, I'll say only that in typical Ayckbourn fashion the plays – for there are more than one – are not as straightforward as they may seem. Further action in the saga of family and friends normally depends on the toss of a coin at the end of the first scene. Following that there are alternative Scenes Two and Three which can be played before coming to Scene Four common to all the plays.

For this production it was decided that for clarity and audience convenience, we would present *Abigail's Story* and *Dorcas' Story* alternately week by week except for the final week when we did three days of each story.

For the actors Scene Two is extremely confusing and complicated because it is virtually two versions of the same picnic. Memories of rehearsing with plates clearly labelled with which sandwiches were which, and indeed sometimes recalling by one's position on the grassy hillside which version we were doing, are still very clear to me. For this production another lady with whom I've had the great pleasure of working on radio joined us to play an irrepressible Rita, the delightfully talented Paula Tillbrook who can have a rehearsal room full of actors rolling about with laughter merely by describing how she got to the theatre.

Paula was to stay with us for the next production, another meeting with *Saturday Night at the Crown*. Shades of Scarborough 1960. Paula provided an admirable and constantly hilarious interpretation of the role Greenwood had created for Thora Hird – the all-knowing, constantly gossiping Ada Thorpe. John Pickles directed the production and played Ada's silent husband, Herbert. It was change time for me. Instead of Sam Cross, the part I'd played before, I was cast as the leader of the two 'corner men' (as Thora always referred to us), the more verbose Charlie Butler – husband to one of 'that lot upstairs' who were deeply involved in an acrimonious funeral party. This time there were no Black and White Minstrels on the last night!

After *The Crown* it was time to get back into serious mood which, for some, was difficult to accept, in view of the fact that Granada TV's *Brass* had been let loose on the world. 'Trouble at t'Mill' plays became hard to accept in serious vein after several satirical efforts had been presented to the public. In its original production some sixty years earlier *Dealing in Futures* had been unfortunate in that Galsworthy's *Strife* on more or less the same subject had reached London before this Brighouse drama. Alas, also some of the younger members of our audiences found the circumstances of the play and the manner of speech hard to accept seriously. A line such as, 'Women's business is to find t'baggin' fer t'childer when they're clemmin,' was originally acceptable in this slice of Lancashire life at the turn of the century but was perhaps hard to appreciate in the later years of the century.

By now in the rehearsal room I, as Simon Spettigue, was chasing a beskirted Martin Reeves as Lord Babs in what proved to be a highly successful production of *Charlie's Aunt* directed by Wilfred with ingenious trellis-like revolving set-pieces by Peter Fairchild. This was a well-paced, highly comical presentation of the famous old farce. One reviewer started off, 'No matter how many times you've seen that popular play *Charlie's Aunt* rest assured you won't be bored by the Bolton Octagon version.' Martin captured that essential ingredient of the play, as indeed Brandon Thomas himself points out in one of his comments on this familiar favourite, that one must never forget the trousers under the skirts and poor Fancourt Babberley's embarrassingly curious situation. Unlike some interpretations, Martin's was not an exercise in transvestism or serious female impersonation. The frocks were not allowed to disguise his lordship's predicament.

From the first page you'll remember that the specialist who had carried out my miraculous hip replacement

operation attended a performance and as I chased the false
Donna Lucia (from Brazil, where the nuts come from) Mr
Wroblewski, I'm told, covered his eyes and enquired, 'Has
he made it?' Happily I got through all this hectic activity
with no ill effects.

Variety was certainly the essence of the Octagon season
for the following play was Terence Rattigan's powerful and
absorbing drama *The Deep Blue Sea*. Comments such as
'The Octagon Theatre have once again proved their
versatility' and *'The Deep Blue Sea* is a big hit' were very
encouraging to all concerned. Jenny Lee and Ken Binge
played the leading roles superbly. I was the somewhat
mysterious Mr Miller, a bookmaker's assistant formerly a
doctor before being struck off the panel, who is able to
guide Hester Collyer (Jenny Lee) back to a knowledge of
her own worth – a deeply satisfying and interesting role. It
was also to be my last for the current season as I was not
required for the final play, Clifford Odets' *Rocket to the
Moon*. This allowed my brother and I to get away to
Newcastle-upon-Tyne and carry out our late father's wish
that his ashes be returned to his beloved Tyneside.

A television engagement took me back to Granada TV
during the break and enabled me to be the foreman of the
jury in one of their *Crown Court* series. In one rehearsal
recess I was able to have an interesting talk with the veteran
actor Andrew Cruikshank, who was playing the judge in
this case. Mr Cruikshank had originated the part of Dr
Matthews in *Sisterly Feelings*, and it was fascinating to hear
of some of the occurrences in the West End production
when at some performances the play did actually proceed
according to the spin of the coin at the end of Scene One.
When I pointed out that we'd had enough trouble coping
with two versions even when we knew which storyline we
were following, he very kindly reminded me that they of

course had had a much longer rehearsal period and 'try-out' dates before reaching London.

For the eighth Octagon Shakespeare season I was virtually back where I started. However, in this production of *The Merchant of Venice* I assumed the roles of Tubal and the Duke of Venice. With a setting and costumes one might describe as Edwardian, Felicity Taylor didn't allow the play to drag and Terence Skelton handled the role of Shylock with great dexterity. 'A performance that bridges the centuries,' said one reviewer, seemingly surprised that this familiar Shakespeare play should prove to be 'a very entertaining evening' which, besides the drama of a trial scene, had colour and fast-flowing humour.

By now change was obviously in the air throughout the Octagon. Changes on the board of management, Wilfred to be taking a sabbatical to study theatre in Poland and staff changes were all 'in the wind'. Thus, though disappointing, it was not a shock to be called by Wilfred to his office to be told that change was indeed in the air. After this Shakespeare season there would, it appeared, be major changes in personnel and policy and that, unfortunately, there wasn't a part for me in the last play of the present season. So Stephano in *The Tempest* would mark my exit from the Octagon's resident company which in time, and in that form, was itself to disappear as new brooms swept clean. Mark Woolgar was the guest director, Wilfred played Prospero and David Hicks was a magical and mercurial Ariel. Paul Nettlefield as Trinculo, Henri Wahab as an impressive Caliban and I had a whale of a time in the drunk scenes, particularly when I assured them that 'I was man in the moon when time was!'

And now it was my time to move on, no more daily journeys on the number 559 bus and, for a while, a period of what we laughingly call 'resting', i.e. looking for work.

Chapter Thirty-Nine

With hindsight I realise that at this point I should have thought seriously about reorganising my life. Friends in London and in 'the biz' suggested strongly that I really should move back to the capital. I might even be able to pick up the progress I'd been making in the world of television which I had interrupted ten years earlier to move to Wigan. Perhaps it was a case of native roots now having grown too deep. With Father gone I now had a home of my own and this growing idea of 'going solo'. I'd made a lot of friends in the area and I had an idea also of setting myself up as a production consultant for companies and dramatic societies in the North. Besides which I was now fifty-seven years old and, I must confess, feeling the hole left in my life by the end of my Octagon connection. I began to miss life there very much indeed, with no obvious deadlines and opening nights at which to aim. In addition, commitments to local events seemed to increase, because of the youth club and various charities.

In November 1983 came the news that dear John Le Mesurier had died, or as he put it so typically in his own obituary, 'conked out'. Another *Dad's Army* veteran had made his exit upstage centre.

In 1984 I teamed up once more with my Bridgeman Productions colleagues John D. Slater and his wife Sue Clark-Williams, under the banner of their now established Bijou Theatre Company. Together, by pooling resources, we set up a costume and fancy dress hire sideline called

Performers Unlimited, hoping eventually to go into the field of representation. Bijou was at this time doing a lot of work in the field of theatre in education and I joined their newest three-hander schools' production on the history, working and everyday life of the seaside pierrot show called *Beside the Seaside*. For the festive season we also planned a touring production of John's pantomime *Aladdin* in which I would renew my acquaintance with one of my favourite dame roles, Widow Twankey.

For *Beside the Seaside*, Sue and I were joined by new recruit Steve Burton. Besides directing this show John was also rewriting *Aladdin* for a larger company and a much more elaborate production that our previous one had been.

Besides a two-week season at Wigan Linacre Theatre in January 1985, *Aladdin* did a fairly extensive tour of the North-West, including Bacup, Haslingden, Lowton, Maryport and Royton. John had designed and constructed an ingenious wooden framework and colourfully painted scenery, all of which folded up so neatly that together with extra lighting, musical equipment and costumes the whole show could travel in a transit van! Members of the cast who were car owners transported the company around. Once again the keyboard master Maurice Houghton accompanied us, with genial orchestra leader Wally McKenzie as a versatile percussionist. The red and gold costumes for the finale made a dazzling and memorable end to the show, which during its course had featured some colourful outfits designed by our *Aladdin*, Sue Clark-Williams.

Lisa Davies was a charming and tuneful Princess Badroulbador (John had even researched the actual spelling of that name from old versions of this favourite story). Instead of an emperor this version had Grant Heathcote as the Mayor of Chop-Suey East. Geoff Lanaway provided an Abanazer who could be both sinister and comical, even if he did have trouble with his turban and certain concerted dance steps. Mark Crowshaw looked and played to the full the role of the Genie.

For us this was a kind of anniversary – it was just ten years since I'd played Twankey in that first Bijou Theatre *Aladdin*. Judging by the photographs and press reports my performance hadn't changed! I still managed to get audience response to my 'How Are You Keeping?' song. 'A show worth waiting to see', a *Wigan Observer* report headlined in January 1985.

After panto came a lull, some more solo reading recitals, various charity and promotional efforts including the well-publicised opening of a furniture store in Wigan complete with the mayor and mayoress (Councillor and Mrs George Lockett) and spraying champagne. On 10th November I missed the annual remembrance Sunday parade because I had a day's 'shooting' as the Mayor of Dawley in Brian Finch's Granada TV play *Good as Gold* – a swimming drama played in and around Wigan.

For the 1985–1986 Bijou panto *Snow White*, instead of playing the dame I contented myself by designing the scenery and contributing help and advice when required. Advice and help were also called for by Bolton Little Theatre who from the 12th to the 21st December gave a lively and colourful production of my own pantomime *Babes in the Wood*. *Dad's Army* was enjoying the repeat showing of some episodes and I was involved in filming an episode of a children's TV series by Sid Waddell called *Jossy's Giants*. I was a bowler-hatted council official who, being a pompous killjoy, tried to prevent Jossy's juvenile football team from acquiring a proper field.

The gap following all this activity lasted until April 1986 and the filming of one of only two 'commercials' in which I have appeared. Based upon the 'Pinnochio' theory I sat as the boring, tedious and devious managing director at a board meeting. As I propounded more and more untruths about Southerners' wisdom in investing in North-East England (the Aycliffe and Peterlee development scheme) so my nose grew longer. It was a very long and tedious day following earlier 'fittings' of a succession of model noses. The original plaster cast of my own nose, upon which the models were constructed, suitably mounted upon a shield rather like a big-game trophy now adorns a wall in my living room.

Becoming sixty years old in April of this year, alas also made me aware of becoming somewhat less agile than I had been in the past. The old enemy, arthritis, began to make its presence felt again, this time in the lower parts of my legs. Getting on and off buses and in and out of cars gradually started to be more difficult. I tried, however, to press on regardless.

For instance, a very interesting project undertaken by the Bijou Company was a drama-semi-documentary about a noted Lancashire family, the ffarringdons of Worden, who gave the name to the play, eventually presented in the surviving barn performance auditorium of Worden Hall. Worden, near Leyland, is now a country park and arts complex housed in what were the old outbuildings of the now defunct hall. John, Sue and I had a fascinating time researching material which John finally wove into an imaginative script. Set in the housekeeper's sitting room, the play imagined conversations between the housekeeper and the newly arrived maidservant of the new wife of young Mr ffarringdon. They were joined for tea and further detailed information about Worden ('Here we call it Werden') by the butler and the estate manager. Phyllis Hart, Sue Clark-Williams, Tim Hans Smith and yours truly were the players with John as narrator. Passing references to some advertisements of the day provided lighter and often amusing moments.

After becoming vice-president of and being actively involved in the annual Wigan carnival in June, the month of July found me heading north of the border again.

A management with whom I'd never worked before approached me with a peach of a part, Sweeney Todd, the barber of Fleet Street fame. Alan Clements Productions were a highly respected touring company. At the time they were on tour with two plays, *Intent to Murder* by Leslie Sands and the costume drama *The Late Edwina Black*. A new version of the barber's tale had been written by friend Roger Tolliday and the Clements Company were about to present it and take it on tour.

However, drama offstage never seems to be far away. In *Intent to Murder* I had played the inquisitive veterinary surgeon, Mr Henderson, in the Victor Graham Production in Ayr quite a few years earlier. On the Alan Clements tour the part had been played by another Ayr Civic Theatre colleague, Michael Owen. Due to increasing ill health Michael had to relinquish the role. I was asked to play that role for two weeks while rehearsals for *Sweeney Todd* took place during the daytime. Thus, with the aid of my old script and a cassette recording of the play, I had a few days in which to brush up old Henderson before heading for Scotland. Travelling via Edinburgh in order to call in on my old pal Ron Stephen and to take part in his then current Edinburgh Hospital broadcasting programme, I arrived at the Adam Smith Theatre in Kirkcaldy in time for a quick run through my scenes for *Intent to Murder* on the Sunday evening after the set had been put up, and a full dress rehearsal the following afternoon. *Edwina Black* had been presented during the previous week. From Kirkcaldy the company moved to Darlington Civic Theatre for two weeks. Not playing in the costume drama lightened the load somewhat because Roger's *Sweeney Todd* was quite a sizeable part. In the whole play I was off stage for but a few minutes and the two-level transformation setting designed by Michael Brydon gave me problems with its various steps and staircases.

The premiere of *Sweeney Todd, the Fiendish Barber of Fleet Street* as presented by Mr Clements' Company of Touring Actors, took place at the Key Theatre, Peterborough. It is amazing how ex-Victor Graham Company friends turn up; here was a theatre whose director was none other than Tony Clayton, he of South Shields and Westcliff. For the opening night – a gala occasion – there were 'Mrs Lovatt's pies' available after the show!

The style of the production was very expansive, the full ham. As the local *Evening Telegraph* put it, 'There is enough traditional ham, largely from Colin Bean and Roger Tolliday, to feed a fair-sized wedding.' Roger was playing the part of Dr Aminidab, the owner of a nearby asylum for the insane, in which according to one review he was more suited to be an inmate. For Roger and myself it was almost the witch and the wolf from our Stratford East days. All our asides to the audience had no pretence about them; they were given the full treatment by Phillipa Ritchie as Tobias Ragg (Todd's apprentice), Michael Brydon as the hero, Mark Ingestrie and June Gray as a very prim and proper fiancée of the hero, Miss Joanna Oakley.

Two very strong, old-style, melodramatic performances were contributed by Terence Denville as John Parmine and Renee Bourne-Webb as the pie-making, oven-prone Mrs Lovatt. A number of our audiences really entered into the spirit of the show by booing and hissing the villains, cheering the hero and making commiserating sighs and comments for the heroine. It was a happy company and an enjoyable experience. The tour visited the Devonshire Park Theatre, Eastbourne, the Theatre Royal, Hanley, the Prince's Hall, Aldershot and the Pomegranate Theatre,

Chesterfield. A further, final date was played in 1987 at the Huddersfield Arts Centre.

A particular performance of this 'bloodcurdling drama' (*vide* publicity) was memorable in that in one scene in my barber's shop on the upper level of our multiple set I had Terry Denville in the chair, ready to be 'shaved'. As we talked in that ingratiating manner of Todd and customers I moved over to my side table to discover that, although the cut-throat razor, comb, hairbrush and scissors were set in their usual places, there was no shaving brush or bowl of lather. An integral part of this particular scene was the great play made of my efforts to start lathering as John Parmine' rabbited on about his life as a soldier. Looking offstage to the stage manager's prompt corner, I tried to indicate 'no lather'. With a look of shock on his face the stage manager vanished. I started to ad lib about not being a moment while I went to the kitchen for 'a bowl of special lather' which I kept for special customers.

As I've said before, one doesn't with intent leave another actor on stage alone. Terry, bless his heart, grasped the significance of my sudden change of conversation and started to ad lib with what proved to be quite a lengthy diatribe upon the subject of people he'd met during his service in the army as if oblivious to my presence. I, meanwhile, started down the offstage steps to find the missing bowl and brush to be met by the stage manager full of apology and furiously whipping up the soapy froth – which should have been done much earlier to allow it to set – with the shaving brush in the bowl. Naturally it was not nearly ready for use but poor Terry was still in the chair, on his own, going on and on about his life in the army. I got back onto the set as quickly as my painful knees would allow me to mount the steps again, rushed straight in, applied the very wet and runny mixture which was suppose to be a 'fluffy foam' and dispatched my victim to the cellar as quickly as I could. Alas, this was the performance which was being recorded on video so somewhere in the archives is the full embarrassing saga of the barber with no lather.

The actual chair was a mechanical contraption which had apparently been used in the West End musical of *Sweeney Todd*. After my machinations with a cunningly devised cut-throat razor which emitted 'Kensington gore' along its cutting edge and the victim's throat as I squeezed the special handle – shades of Julius Caesar – I had to swivel the chair and then operate a lever on the side. This action caused the sections of this fiendish piece of furniture to flatten out at an angle and thus become part of the slide by which the 'bodies' were sent down to the cellar. A number of times I trapped my finger in this devilish device in operation but, thankfully, only once did it fail completely. Luckily it was the last 'customer' before the interval, during which the fault was corrected. Somehow, however, there seemed to be something unconventional about Sweeney having to heave his victim up in a kind of fireman's lift to send him cellarward.

Another abiding memory will always be of Sweeney breaking into song as he pushed Mrs Lovatt into her own pie-baking oven, 'Abide with me, fast falls the eventide / In goes the one, the one who'd be my bride.'

Chapter Forty

At this time walking was getting more difficult and climbing and descending stairs painful. My GP suggested that, as I was now living alone, a smaller house on one level would be worth consideration.

In 1987 a water burst in the loft and a break-in also helped me to decide that it was time to move. After viewing one or two places my application to Wigan Metro Council was successful in gaining for me the small, well-planned, third-floor flat which I now occupy. The desk in the window, which affords me a view over a busy part of Wigan to the green fields and trees of urban countryside in the direction of Orrell and Upholland, is from where this saga emanates.

After my short holiday in Scotland, Edinburgh, Glasgow and the Inner Hebrides out of the proceeds of the house sale, life again became an interesting mixture of engagements. There were some considerable periods of 'resting' and the dole office got to know me quite well until November. On 5th November I was able to get to London to fulfil an invitation to a testimonial lunch in honour of David Croft OBE at which just about everyone who had ever worked with him was present. Actors of *Dad's Army*, *'Allo 'Allo*, *The Gnomes of Dulwich*, *Hi-De-Hi*, *Are You Being Served* and the prospective *You Rang M'Lord?* mixed with, seemingly most of the cast, secretaries, fellow directors and camera crew members, with whom he had been associated.

It was a great occasion and I still feel honoured to have been there.

Subsequent to that event came another TV engagement. For the penultimate episode of their popular series, *Hi-De-Hi*, Jimmy and David had written a hilarious episode about the wedding of chief yellowcoat, Gladys. The actual wedding service was to be shot at Lawford church in a remote part of Essex. *Dad's Army* vicar, Frank Williams, was to become a cleric again to perform the ceremony while, in the absence of the late and sadly missed Edward Sinclair, I was asked to play the part of the verger. After much discussion it was agreed that I should not, as some-one had suggested, try to do an imitation of Ted Sinclair's unique *Dad's Army* verger. I, for one, was strongly opposed to the idea. In the eyes and minds of the majority nobody else could be that particular church official. The character I developed obviously met with the director's approval. With my hair parted in the middle and plastered down and my heart-rending pleas of, 'No confetti, please,' I still managed to get myself locked out of the church, on cue, and have to get the vicar to let me in. ('Oh you silly man!')

On 15th November it was back to Edinburgh, in pro-fessional capacity this time, to make another appearance in my guise of Winston Churchill. This was for the official opening, by the Right Honourable Lord Lyell, of a new headquarters of the prominent Scottish public relations organisation, Dunseath Stephen Partnership. Partner Robin Dunseath had written a witty and amusing mock Churchil-lian speech for the occasion, old tomadachi Ron Stephen, being my director/stage manager for this impressive event at 5 Castle Terrace, almost below the ancient fortress itself.

The Christmas season brought on another attack of pantomime, again with friends of the Bijou Theatre Company, and John D. Slater's version of *Babes in the Wood*. I did not feel that my increasing difficulty of movement was really suitable for playing the dame; one doesn't often see a pantomime dame leaning heavily upon a walking stick. To play Nurse Gripewater John and Sue recruited the admirable Peter Durrant. He was an excellent dame and I felt great pleasure and happiness at his assurance that my help and advice had been responsible for a lot of his success in the role. He was a sad loss to pantomime for despite many pleas Peter gave up acting for an eventually successful role as a stage and company manager and, later, a major seaside resort pier manager.

With a very talented young man fairly new to the business called Sean McKenzie, who did most of the dashing about and knockabout stage business, I formed a kind of 'baddies and goodies' duo. I was Basher, the rogue with the cudgel, and Sean was the simple Simon character Billy Gripewater. With John himself as Sheriff, Sue as Robin Hood and Lisa as Maid Marian, our tour included the Civic Theatre, Oswaldtwistle, the Longfield, Prestwich, the Linacre, Wigan, Royton Civic Theatre and, rather strangely, a ballroom in Kirkby. The panto finished in time for me to fulfil yet another Winston's Coffee House opening on a freezing cold, wet, windy day in Leigh. (At least we hadn't far to travel to this 'date'.)

Another extensive period of 'resting' allowed me to work more on my solo reading recitals and to give my talk 'Out of the Limelight' to a number of churches and organisations of different denominations. Doing my bit as vice-president of Wigan Carnival required a few days in June to find a venue for the fun fair and various competitive events. In the end, thanks to the intervention of the carnival president Mr Jimmy Collins, the after-procession events took place, under very crowded conditions (dog shows getting mixed up with bonny baby shows!), partly in the courtyard of the Mab's Cross Hotel and partly in the yard of the primary school across the road. Not ideal but we kept the carnival going.

Early July brought another request from Alan Clements Productions. A two-week date at Theatre Gwynedd had been offered to them for *Edwina Black* and *Intent to Murder*. Rather than recruit a whole new cast for just two weeks, Alan approached his previous cast members. Fortunately we were all available so a run-through and a dress rehearsal were sufficient to put both plays back on stage and receive creditable press reviews.

After the compilation and rehearsal of suitable material the full-scale reading recital *A Gradely Neet* was premiered at St Francis' Hall in Wigan on 24th September. (Admission one pound fifty including hotpot supper.)

I have endeavoured to make this two-part programme of Lancashire dialect poems and stories as varied to the eye as to the ear. On a curtained and carefully lit stage setting, I move at various points from one music stand to another. These are positioned left and right of the acting area with a high stool at one of them. The stool allows a variation of levels and relief for my painful joints from time to time. Part One of the one and three-quarter hour show goes under the title of 'The Cliffs of Lancashire', based upon the works of two Lancashire writers you've met already, Cliff Heyworth (summer season at Morecambe in 1961) and Cliff Gerrard (Wigan in 1973). As I say in my introduction to the programme, this show is my contribution to the many great efforts being made in defence of Lancashire dialect.

That word 'defence' conjured up in my mind memories of wartime. In World War Two a significant feature in the thoughts of resistance were the white cliffs of Dover. I then thought, 'That's it – cliffs!' and then of the works of my two friendly authors, both called Cliff. Both gentlemen are members of the Lancashire Authors Association and both have written for radio and television, invariably in or on the subject of Lancashire dialect and the North of England in general.

Part Two goes, with change of costume (no expense spared!), under the title of 'Lancashire Hotchpotch' during which works by the two Cliffs are augmented by poems written by friend John D. Slater and myself. Happily the premiere was noted by a couple of local papers and received a lot of praise. A tape recording of that first performance has also proved to be quite well received, particularly by North country expats living in Australia, South Africa, New Zealand and Canada. Performances of *A Gradely Neet* in a number of venues took me into December.

Bijou's pantomime *The Further Adventures of Robinson Crusoe* was hit by a dramatic development. Two days before the show was due to open two members of the cast withdrew from the company. Sue Clark-Williams (Mrs Slater) and myself were appealed to. In haste we stepped into the roles of heroine, Polly Perkins, and the baddy, Sardinus, demon king of the depths. So much for my decision to give panto a miss this year! For Sardinus I designed and carried out a sort of sea monster make-up, basically green but with a fishlike mouth and full, balletic eyes, reminiscent, I kidded myself, of some of Robert Helpmann's outstanding ballet make-ups.

My 'opposite number' in the story was the good spirit of the sea, Neptuna, played by a new Bijou member, Alison Williams. Old friends, Gill Mason, Tony Henry and Jim Marsh played principal roles and with John's ingeniously packable production we toured to Bacup, Haslingden, Oswaldtwistle and Kirkby before our final week at Wigan's Linacre Theatre. Alison and I took the 'war' between our characters to heart, even offstage. There was good-humoured controversy as to which character's face was adorned with the most sequins. However, despite the short time in which I'd had to learn the part and the fact that to move about the stage I had to rely more upon my trusty walking stick, our frontcloth cross-talk banter went down well with our young audiences. I must not deny that there several occasions upon which Alison helped me out when, unintentionally, I missed the odd sentence.

Our own friendly enjoyment of working together as a team was, I hope, reflected in review headlines such as 'Crusoe Cracker Is a Gem'. Come to think of it, a rather apt line for a company called Bijou. This example of ensemble working was to be reflected in a much bigger step into the unknown in 1989 with John's full-scale musical play *Happy Birthday Whatsisname*.

Chapter Forty-One

Following the panto came another 'rest' but further organisation was going on, which included yet another Winston Churchill engagement for Mrs Lorraine Rathbone opening another Winston's Coffee House. In the meantime I'd opened the Wigan Hospice spring fair (not as Winston Churchill) which, despite the April showers, raised £1,300 for Hospice funds.

A prestigious engagement for August was to take part in the Bolton Festival. The theme for 1989 was international friendship. On Monday 21st I delivered the celebrity lecture written by Dr Tom Dunne called 'Bolton – An Ordinary Universe'. Dr Dunne dealt with Bolton's perception of abroad and perceptions of Bolton by others both before and after the advent of the railway age. On Saturday 26th I gave a performance of *A Gradely Neet* in the Central Library auditorium. The festival programme brochure note that this was an entertainment particularly appreciated by the blind and partially sighted helped to swell a very respectably sized audience on a fine afternoon.

Preparations and rehearsals were in hand for the Bijou Theatre music and drama version of the Christmas story called *Happy Birthday Whatsisname*, words and most of the music written by John D. Slater, with musical arrangements by Tim Hans Smith. This large and complicated show was directed by me as executive director and scenery designer, and Julia Salvage as assistant director/choreographer.

Wednesday/Thursday 25th/26th October, saw another quick dash to London for an impressive book launch at the Imperial War Museum, the book in question being friend Bill Pertwee's *Dad's Army – The Making of a Television Legend*. With the later formation of 'The *Dad's Army* Appreciation Society' the book itself has become something of a legend in its own right. Affectionately referred to by members as 'the *Dad's Army* Bible' it gives a wealth of fascinating fact and information concerning the programme and all who were involved with it in any way.

Pantomime this year was to be at Blackburn for Mr Duggie Chapman but *Birthday* (or Habwin as it came to be known by cast and crew) had to come first.

> Our Father who art in Heaven
> One with the Holy Spirit and our Lord Jesus
> In Trinity complete.
> Employ our strength of purpose
> In goodwill, love and friendship,
> That our collective skills
> May make this production
> The happiest birthday of them all.
> Amen.

Whilst sitting up late one night, or rather early one morning, planning and plotting *Happy Birthday Whatsisname* this little prayer came into my mind. I told the cast about it at the next gathering we had, which was a read-through for the principals to sort out the various roles we were all to play. Every one of us, except Tim Hans Smith, had at least two parts. Tim was the voice of the archangel and didn't actually appear; besides, he had enough on his plate as musical director. The Bijou Company, and later the many young people who joined us, liked the prayer and as a result gathered before every rehearsal and later every performance, to recite it together. It was also our warm-up exercise, together with a quick rendition of 'Happy Birthday'.

This concept of the Christmas story had, I think, been in John's mind for quite some time. One of the best known stories of all time, this was an effort to put it into 'everyday' language and context, to 'flesh out' the characters so that one felt that one could relate to them in modern and ancient terms. The setting and period were really timeless, people appeared in both biblical and modern costume. The scenery consisted of interchangeable, self-standing, open wooden frames backed by neutral curtains as a cyclorama. Played on an open stage, the scenes were changed as the action proceeded by the stage manager, Bob Williams, and his crew of three in view of the audience. Dressed in their uniformly designed and coloured working outfits they became, by the finale, an integral part of the show which I intended they should be.

Bijou regulars Sean, Tony, Sue, Jim, John, Gill and myself were joined by Susie Wright and Julia Westwood to play a whole host of varied characters. Purely as an example of the range we all covered, I played one of two commercial Santa Claus figures in the opening scene, the innkeeper and an American tourist. John himself played a present-day shopkeeper, King Herod and Mustapha, a very verbose tourist guide. At one point I even had two Japanese tourists popping in and out, photographing everything in sight, including at one point the audience!

All these main characters were augmented by the Bijou young people's group, very many of whom had either appeared in Bijou pantomimes or had been attenders at the summer drama schools which have been run by John for many years. These young actors insisted that they were not 'chorus' or 'extras' as they all had parts to play. They were in three groups of approximately twenty and came from the main areas where the show would be touring, Rossendale,

Hyndburn and Wigan. This meant that each Sunday, for about six weeks before the opening, Julia, John and myself, with Tim on occasions, had to travel about this area of Lancashire rehearsing three different groups of characters, all covering a major part of the play as a whole. They were all involved in a number of complicated action scenes and musical numbers. My job was to create and direct action and motion, and to try to ensure that the three groups developed and progressed at the same rate. Julia had the responsibility of technical and Terpsichorean detail and I have to admit that on some Sundays, after going through three lots of the same scenes and actions and dealing with all the problems which arise naturally out of groups so large, we ended our day feeling somewhat shattered. How does one cope with two sisters who say, 'We can't come next Sunday, we're going to our uncle's funeral.' Well it's a change from the usual grandma I suppose! (First funerals, now the shops. Sundays will never be the same again.)

Meanwhile the professional adult artistes had been meeting voluntarily at frequent intervals to read through, discuss roles and to allow me to explore and explain direction and moves. As so often, budget ruled the financial roost and so there was allowance for only ten days of paid rehearsal prior to 27 November – the date for the gala charity opening performance. There was however a great feeling of fellowship in our group of actors. As one member put it, 'Your Habwin prayer sums it all up – that's why I'm doing this show.'

The gala premiere provided us with a double ration of first-night nerves. As well as the actual show the social side of this particular occasion took some organising. Held in aid of the Actors' Church Union and the Catholic Stage Guild we were to be graced by the presence of the Mayor of Wigan, Councillor Audrey Bennett, and the Mayor's Consort, her husband John. Fortunately we were able to leave most of the work in that direction to a group of friends, Mrs Pat Millard, Miss Joanne Watson, Mr Graham Lynn and Mr Walter Grundy, who acted as gala hosts and arranged the after-show buffet reception.

Our super souvenir programme for the show was rather like a pocket magazine and was sold in aid of the Church Urban Fund. Besides extensive information about the show and the cast it bore messages from the Archbishop of Canterbury, the Bishop of Liverpool, the President of the ACU and the General Secretary of the CSG.

Keeping up my training by Molly McArthur I had also the pleasurable task of designing and making a lot of the props used in the show, and my 'bitza' box came into full use. (Never throw anything useful away!) Gifts of gold, frankincense and myrrh were constructed from the most unlikely materials – egg boxes, foil paper off sweets and chocolate bars, string, old bits of bedspreads, curtains and other materials. Herod's very ornate wine goblet was courtesy of a Morrison's soft margarine carton mounted upon a toilet-roll centre and a number of pub drip mats. My flat, for a time, was a mixture of Aladdin's cave and the theatre school props studio.

At the reception after the premiere Graham and Walter had arranged for a birthday cake in the shape and colours of the show's poster. This was ceremoniously cut by Sue Clark-Williams and John D. Slater (Mr and Mrs Slater) and then shared out. Amongst many favourable and congratulatory comments the mayor was also interested in the prayer, at which point the entire company recited it – not a script in sight.

After Wigan and its tour to other Lancashire centres the show closed in time for John and me to start on our engagement in panto in Blackburn. *Happy Birthday Whatsisname* was a great experience, well deserving of production on a much bigger scale than the Bijou

Company could manage alone. It provides great scope for music, drama and colour with meaning – commercial managements take note!

Robinson Crusoe was Duggie Chapman's choice of subject for his production at Blackburn's King George's Hall for the 1989–1990 panto season. Topping the bill was a new young TV children's programme presenter, Mark Granger. Only twenty-two at the time this was his first venture into this type of show. Besides Pte Sponge playing the old man of the sea, he had the support of panto stalwarts such as John D. Slater as the ship's captain and my Weston-super-Mare pantomime colleague, Steve King, in the dame role as Widow Crusoe. Sean McKenzie, now known as Sean D'Arcy to avoid confusion with his singer father (also Sean), was excellent as Billy Crusoe. 'Without a doubt it is the best pantomime that has been at King George's in the past five years' was a press quote by a spokesperson in the *Lancashire Evening Post*.

Chapter Forty-Two

Early in the new year came news of the death of the remarkable Douglas Neil of whom I wrote during my Court Players days. One of the old school of actors and play directors, Douglas had successfully moved in time into television in which field he spent the rest of his working life apart from an occasional trip to Ireland where he loved to direct opera.

I became a 'tourer' again with a number of dates for my solo show *A Gradely Neet*, including a well-attended performance for the Mid-Pennine Arts Association supported by the Lancashire Authors' Association. Other performances, though not consecutive, gave my little effort good and, apparently, greatly appreciated airings in various small halls up and down the county.

In July I was approached by a company called Pendle Productions with a view to a forthcoming production and tour of Willy Russell's play *Educating Rita*. In the stage version Frank and Rita are the only characters that the audience meets and neither of them has much time to rest offstage. At the age of sixty-four and being somewhat arthritically impaired I felt that this could be the last leading (and large) role I'd play in my career. The tour I hoped would be a success and, once we'd settled into the play, an enjoyable experience. Rita was played by Blackpool-born Kathy Usherwood and we both worked very hard during our two weeks of rehearsal. Not being part of the management of Pendle Productions we of course had no knowledge of the business details and organisational arrangements being made. Sadly, alas, the 'tour' turned out eventually to be a one-week engagement.

But what an interesting week that was. Kathy and I were flown to Belfast where our stage manager met us at the Arts Theatre late on the Sunday afternoon with the construction of our set well under way. We had done an invited-audience dress rehearsal in a school hall on the Friday of the previous week, the play being in that year's English literature syllabus. Besides extensive press coverage by Belfast newspapers we were both interviewed by BBC and commercial television and radio during our week's stay – having received a warm reception and welcome on the opening night.

If proof were needed to prove the power of film and television to form many people's perception of a subject, *Educating Rita* was that proof. At first both Kathy and myself were annoyed but quickly became amused by some of the stupid questions we were asked in these interviews. One TV interviewer actually asked, 'But how do you manage the airport scenes?' Another wanted to know how we could do the suicide of Rita's all-knowing friend, Trish, if Trish didn't appear. A beauty from a so-called arts correspondent was the enquiry, 'Isn't it a bit boring being in one scene all the time?'

In the end we got exhausted by having to explain that the play came first and what they had seen on screen was adapted from the original play. 'How does it feel to be in the shoes of Julie Walters/Michael Caine? Aren't you two a bit too young and too old for the parts?' I'm sure they were referring to Kathy and me in that order! Even at home in Wigan an elderly gentleman in my local, when he heard about it all, was convinced that I was lying. 'Never! Saw it on t'telly. You're far too old!'

Despite a feeling of tension in parts of the city everyone we met was kind and hospitable. We were taken on a tour of the magnificent City Hall and St Anne's Cathedral. A member of the city council took us in his car along both the Falls and the Shankill roads, passing en route places we'd heard of only in news broadcasts – the Divis Flats and the Royal Victoria Hospital. I don't think either of us would describe that journey as 'enjoyable' but it certainly has given subsequent news bulletins much more significance. One got used during the week to having bags searched as we went into big stores and public buildings and leaving parcels at the reception area. On our final Saturday we were able to witness a very long Orange Lodge procession through the city centre with to us the unusual sight of two helicopters constantly hovering overhead.

After our final performance we – Kathy, S.M. Neil and myself – enjoyed hospitality in the theatre bar before being taken back to our digs to prepare for the morrow's mid-morning flight back to Liverpool Airport.

November found me involved with the Houghtan Weavers and comedian Harry Pemberton in Wigan, contributing to the evening of *Children in Need*, for which our town's total, collected or pledged at the Orwell Inn at the Wigan Pier, was a respectable £60,000.

By now I had been winkled out again by my friends, the Bijou Theatre Company despite my pleas of 'old age and arthritis'. I was blatantly tempted by being offered my favourite pantomime dame, Widow Twankey. Yes, they were to revive the colourful *Aladdin*, this time with Gill Mason as the hero, Sue having 'retired' from being a principal boy. The short tour took us to previous venues in the Hyndburn and Rossendale areas. The company went out of their way to accommodate my increasing lack of pantomime agility and ability. Out of necessity my normal number of costume changes was severely reduced and a small dressing room was curtained off for me at the side of the stage; the whole gang couldn't have been kinder.

Interspersed were a further Winston Churchill appearance and two *A Gradely Neet* performances. In March began an association with another project in Wigan which absorbed a great deal of my interest in art. Local painter/teacher Maureen Gulley moved Wigan's only independent art gallery-cum-studio from first-floor premises in Market Street to a much more suitable ground-floor individual building called the Coach House, just off a main road near to the town centre. My association with the Coach House Gallery was as a member, an artist and later as consultant on performing arts, for this was a gallery of all kinds of art. Maureen ran regular classes for painters and one also had the opportunity to see, and buy, works in pottery and stained glass. My miniature calligraphic pieces called 'Initial Efforts' were, as the name implied, decorated initial letters, suitably framed. Some exquisite hand-made jewellery inside the Coach House contrasted with other metalwork – large metal exhibits out in the yard. The main gallery gave an intimate setting for some small recitals and divertissements, usually accompanied by a snack buffet and wine. Sadly, perhaps, it was too ambitious. The Coach House Gallery didn't have a very long life. By the end of 1992 it had closed.

In April of 1991 I had reached the age for state retirement pension. In the autumn of that year I had also been on one of my biennial visits to the hip clinic at Wrightington Hospital for my 'MOT' on my 1982 replacement. Further examination confirmed that arthritis was indeed present in my knee joints and showed signs of affecting my right hip. Developments would have to be awaited and noted. The replacement of the right hip took place early in 1996 after a long and painful development.

Professionally I tended now to work mainly in advisory roles. Besides being production consultant to the Bijou Theatre Company I fulfilled a similar role with a new arrival on the thespian scene, the Two-Faced Theatre Company. This small company, formed by former Bijou player Jim Marsh, engaged me to direct their first production, a comedy about actors written by Jim called *In The Business*. Later in the year Jim appeared with Bijou again in the pantomime for the 1991–1992 season, *Red Riding Hood*, for which I again acted in an advisory capacity.

An event followed which was to have a significant effect upon the rest of my professional life, even though the event was a charity do. On 18th December I appeared as guest artiste at a Christmas concert held in the Halewood Sports Centre in Barncroft Road, Halewood. Called *Star Over Barncroft* it featured local church choirs and musicians, the Knowsley Singers and the gospel choir of the Church of Christ Apostolic. My contributions were two ten-minute 'spots', selected items from my own seasonal recital, *A Christmas Stocking*. Compering the concert was the most charming and accomplished young lady from Ireland, Clare Bowles, presenter of BBC Radio Merseyside's then current daily afternoon chat and music show. Besides being an enthusiastic compere Clare was well to the fore when it came to the singing of carols. After all, she and her two sisters formed the popular singing group 'She Three'.

She expressed great interest in the items I presented and in my *Dad's Army* career, the outcome being an invitation to be the guest one coming afternoon on the *Clare Bowles Show*. Having been heard on the internal relay system at Radio Merseyside in Liverpool, I was invited by Jenny Collins, the producer/presenter of the BBC North West programme *Write Now* to read a couple of Lancashire dialect stories.

For the pantomime season 1992/1993 the Bijou Company were back at Wigan's Linacre Theatre after a break. Again I helped John design and direct a traditional family show, this time *Jack and the Beanstalk*. This year's hero was Denise Baglow a by now seasoned Bijou player.

Besides being compere at a couple of banquet-style dinners, the early part of 1993 was taken up with the preparation and rehearsal of another 'first' for me – a one-person play. Having played around with the idea for quite a long time, as I remember, John finally put into script form his one-woman play *Mrs Moses*. The eponymous lady was to be played by Denise, the work designed by John and myself and interpreted and directed by me.

This was to be an intriguing period of discovery, and proof that one is never too old to learn. The script was good, tight, dramatic, amiable and not without the odd touch of humour. For almost two hours Mrs Moses would chat to us, her audience, outside the family tent as she packed up their household belongings, yet again, for what she hoped would be the last stage of her husband-led journey out of Egypt to the Promised Land. From the finished result one got a clear and explicit picture of the life and times in which she and Mr Moses lived. I discovered how different working on a one-person play is when compared with a multicast show. There needs to be much more discussion and give and take between actor and director. In a larger cast someone has to make the final decision on any problem and that is, ultimately, the director's responsibility for good or bad. Or, as we say, 'Someone has to take the can back!' Besides the absorbing interest of staging this play I was gaining valuable experience for a further venture into the field of solo-cast drama in the future.

The Radio Merseyside production of *Write Now* was a firmly established feature of BBC Radio Northwest before

I joined the team of readers. One of my very first readings was Wigan author Tom Simm's *Vocal by Tom Occleshaw*, a funny story with a nice twist in the tail. This was soon to be followed by an hilarious story by Nick Baty (under his nom de plume Nicholas Garrick) called *Slab Cake and Old Lace*. When I read the story I commented to the producer, Jenny Collins, that this story really needed the voice of Alan Bennett. Jenny hastily pointed out that her budget wouldn't run to such an extent so I'd have to do my best.

After the story was heard 'on air' I was contacted by Nick Baty who was kind enough to say that he had originally suggested that he envisaged Alan Bennett as the reader. His further comment was that he was highly delighted with my reading of it.

Thus started another artistic and professional friendship which has continued and I've had the pleasure of reading further stories by Nicholas Garrick on *Write Now*. The comical nature of that particular tale did not enhance my efforts to become known as 'One-Take Bean' but mine, I think, was not the only hardly suppressed laughter in the studio which interrupted recording!

Another occasion requiring silence – this time of the 'bite your tongue' variety – was an occasion when I was giving my talk *Out of the Limelight*. I'd been invited to address a 'ladies' afternoon' regular meeting in the presbytery of a local church. At the end of my talk, whilst enjoying a welcome cup of tea, I was approached by several ladies individually with further questions about the ACU and the CSG. Others asked me to autograph *Dad's Army* books and photographs which they'd brought or to comment about other shows in which I'd been. Finally a lady approached saying, 'I think you were at Wigan Grammar School with my husband, John So-and-so?'

Shame upon me, the name didn't ring a bell. I didn't recognise it and I was simultaneously scribbling my name onto something. With the customary (and obligatory) smile upon my face I was about to put forward the conventional remark and enquiry, 'Ah yes, of course, and how is he?' In the nick of time I remembered where I was. This was a meeting of the St John's Catholic Widows' Club!

Chapter Forty-Three

August of 1993 saw the formation by Tadge Muldoon of the *Dad's Army* Appreciation Society. There had been an earlier effort to form one by someone in Devon but the earlier attempt came to nothing after the issue of its one and only magazine newsletter. The present society goes on, having survived the sudden and tragic death of its founder, and is now under the leadership of C in C Jack Wheeler with Bill Pertwee as president. Its newsletters and the enthusiasm of one visitor from 'down under' have resulted in the formation of a branch of the society in New Zealand.

The festive season got under way with a concert staged by hospital broadcasting, Radio Wrightington, sponsored by the *Wigan Evening Post* in aid of the studio development fund. I was invited to take part as guest artiste and, in company with the Haydock (Ogden Travel) Prize Band and the Wigan Cecilian Choir, I shivered through the performance given in a cold Wigan Parish Church. The boiler, alas, had broken down and at one point one had difficulty in hearing what was happening due to the thundering rain on the church roof. Despite all this the reception was satisfyingly enthusiastic.

Again as production consultant/director, I helped Bijou Theatre stage the pantomime *Snow White*, and by the end of the year I had already recorded eighteen items for the *Write Now* programme.

Around February in 1994 another amazing and exciting theatre venture for me started – and how glad I was that I had already had some experience of directing a one-person play. Whilst on a visit to my old stamping ground, the Octagon Theatre in Bolton, I met by chance a gentleman I had met a while before, the Rev. Michael Austin, then the minister of that unique place of worship near Bolton, The Theatre Church. Michael was at that time also chaplain to the Octagon. He invited me to join him and a friend he wanted me to meet, to have a coffee and a chat. This was when I learned about Palaver Productions and the play upon which Michael and actor, Peter Moreton, were working. Called *Temptations*, the play's description held my attention completely. At this time it was still in a formative stage but had had a limited reading which had found favour with a small invited audience. I got a feeling that perhaps I was being probed for some hints and ideas and I asked to read the play script in its finished form. A couple of weeks later I was approached to direct the play. Both Michael and Peter had, apparently, decided that my reactions during our chat convinced them that I was the person to do the job.

When I received the script of this certainly unusual play I read it through carefully. After reading the last page I turned the script over and immediately read it all again. By now I was totally absorbed by this story of Jesus' forty days and nights in the wilderness. How to stage it and how to interpret it was a task of an enormity I had never faced before. The moment I finished my second reading I was on the phone to Michael to accept; an even greater thrill was to hear Michael say that both he and Peter had earnestly hoped I would 'come aboard'.

Work upon and rehearsals of *Temptations* occupied me fully, constructively and fruitfully at a time when great decisions and changes which worried me intensely were occurring within the Church of England. At first I had also worried that a talented, vibrant young actor like Peter might, when it came to actually working on the play, feel that a mistake had been made. He was in his twenties and the difference in ages, theatrical experience and methods of working could have been a terrific obstacle. Michael knew that if such should prove to be the case I would withdraw; the play itself, to me, was too important to be spoiled by disharmony and controversy. I'm so happy to say that my fears were groundless.

Working on the basis I'd discovered with *Mrs Moses*, i.e. direct, honest and straightforward discussion, made rehearsals what I'd call a hard-working, joyous experience.

The play premiered at the Theatre Church, under the banner of 'Manchester, City of Drama '94', on 29th March and after a tour went to that year's Edinburgh Festival.

Spring of 1994 found me, with now increasing difficulty, heading north again. The Dunseath Stephen Partnership, as the public relations organisers, engaged me to bring Mr Churchill to life again to open and appear at *Time of Your Life*, the Association of Retired Persons Expo '94 at the Glasgow Scottish Exhibition and Conference Centre.

Whilst in Scotland I was able to check out the venue at which *Temptations* would be playing, St Paul and St George's Church in York Place, Edinburgh.

In May I was able to get away for a few days' holiday to visit friends in the pretty village of Collingham in Nottinghamshire and, as Pte Sponge, to declare open the annual May Fayre on the delightful village green. During June another trip to London was called for – by BBC TV this time. At the old Ealing Film Studios I recorded a filmed interview with director/interviewer Alexis Giradet. A snippet from this was to be used as an item in a panel game called *Bygones*. When I saw the programme as transmitted, lo and behold who should be one of the guessing panel but my colleague from the memorable *Goldilocks* of many years ago, John Inman.

Write Now continued to occupy me for a day about once a month in the recording studio. I was even beginning to get letters of gratitude from other authors whose work I had read on the programme. Time seemed to be moving so quickly that before I realised it we had arrived at Sunday, 2nd October, and I was back in London again. This was for the unveiling of blue memorial plaques on the former homes of Arthur Lowe and John Le Mesurier.

The occasion gave me the opportunity to renew acquaintance with the surviving members of the Walmington-on-Sea Home Guard, Ian Lavender, Frank Williams, Bill Pertwee, Eric Longworth (Clive Dunn), and of course an old friend from Watford Palace days and fellow platoon member, Hugh Hastings. Dear Pamela Cundell (Mrs Fox) and Kay Beck (the late Jimmy's wife) were present as well as numerous well-known names of showbiz – Spike Milligan, Norman Wisdom, Peggy Mount, Harry Fowler and, from Coronation Street, Sue Nicolls and Peter Baldwin. At the reception in the Olympia Hilton Hotel after the ceremonies I was to meet up for the first time with a group of chaps from Kent who are *Dad's Army* buffs to the nth degree. The members of The Barmy Army Film Club, apparently inspired by *Dad's Army*, make crazy video films on military themes, their efforts all being in support of the RAF Benevolent Fund. I was to have the pleasure of meeting up with them again in 1995.

For the festive season I was again invited to be guest artiste at the Radio Wrightington Christmas concert, held earlier this year on 3rd December, and in the warmer and more congenial surroundings of the concert hall at the Mill at the Pier. At least after the performance we hadn't far to go to the bar!

On 13th December I ceremoniously declared 'Open' a theatrical exhibition staged by Wigan Heritage Service. This history of theatre in and around Wigan over the years was a most interesting and impressive display of posters, photographs and memorabilia. It was spoiled for me though by the fact that the venue, The History Shop, is at the top of a long flight of stairs with no lift. It took me an age – and no little pain – to both get up there and then down again. *Bringing the House Down*, which for the official opening included a short music hall excerpt by the Wigan Pier Acting Company, was generally declared to be an excellent exhibition.

Christmas, as is said in more elevated circles, was spent quietly at home.

Chapter Forty-Four

A very quiet Christmas day 1994 was followed by a wonderful 'family' St Stephen's day (Boxing Day) in the company of friend Nick Baty (he of *Slab Cake and Old Lace* fame), his mother Kath and their relations and friends. A truly lovely, happy day with the added bonus of meeting the author Michael Carson during tea and having him autograph the copy of his very funny book *Sucking Sherbet Lemons* which had just been given to me from under the Baty Christmas tree.

Two visits to Radio Merseyside to record more *Write Now* stories and a few 'Meet Private Sponge' and 'Out of the Limelight' talks occupied me well enough until just before Easter. My friend the Rev. Michael phoned to say that *Betrayals* was now ready for the director's attention. I was very happy to note that my suggestion had been considered regarding the title of the play; when I received the first draft it was called *Betrayed*. Luckily, besides being the author, actor and director, Michael, Peter and I could talk as good friends. They understood very well that as far as I was concerned, being 'bred and brought up' as a traditional Anglican, the last two years (and the last twelve months in particular) had been somewhat traumatic. Decisions taken by the Established Church of England had caused pain and doubt to a great many people.

The invitation just before Easter last year to direct *Temptations*, besides being of great emotional help, prompted me to suggest that if *Temptations* indicated the ever-present nature of the subject then surely *Betrayals* would be more relevant as a title than *Betrayed* which indicates the past. Again working on Michael's play, and with the same talented and creative actor, was an emotional and completely fulfilling experience, especially with Eastertide just about a week away.

After a week of hard work rehearsing at Michael's new church in Eccles, Manchester, we were scheduled to give a preview performance at the All Saints Retreat and Conference Centre at London Colney, near St Albans, owned by the RC Archdiocese of Westminster. The occasion was a weekend conference of the Methodist Church Division of Ministries Board. Our preview was to be given in the lovely high-vaulted-roof chapel on the Saturday night after the close of the day's business and dinner. Apparently the play and support for it was to be an item on the agenda for the Sunday morning before the weekend finished with lunch.

I travelled down to London Colney with Michael, Peter having taken the settings, lights and costumes direct from his home in Birmingham in the newly acquired 'Palaver Productions' transit van. Because of their quite small nature, it was conveniently possible to carry both shows in the van and still have room for a couple of passengers. On this occasion there was obviously no point in Peter coming all the way up to Wigan to collect me when he was halfway to London Colney already.

What a beautiful, quiet and peaceful place the centre is. The rooms and the food are basic, clean and good with a facilities room at the end of each corridor for late-night/early-morning tea and coffee. Ramps, showers and adapted toilets make life so much easier for us arthritics. I'd like to go again sometime.

On the Friday morning we were able to put up the small set and lighting for *Betrayals* and then have an exploratory trial of the play. Michael was a conference delegate so had to divide his time between meetings and rehearsals. For the preview he would be operating lights and music so on the Saturday we had time for a couple of run-through rehearsals and an 'as per' full costume and technical rehearsal before the audience were due into the chapel at 8.30 p.m.

As well as all the Division of Ministries delegates there were quite a number of other guests and All Saints Centre staff in the audience of some eighty or more. For over forty years I've had one particular idea and hope which, until that evening, had never been achieved. One day, I've thought so often, I hope to appear in or direct a play which will literally hold an audience spellbound.

At the final line – 'Enough! Nearly, it is finished!' – Peter stepped forward, arms uplifted in greeting. The lighting climax we had designed worked exactly as we had planned, and there in the following blackout Peter left the stage (or in this case the acting area).

The opening music was reintroduced, very quietly, and a level of subdued but 'visible-by' lighting came up. Not a soul moved. No attempt at applause, not even a cough!

Eventually the nave lights were switched on and I made my way 'backstage' to see Peter and Michael with the very few notes I had. We found ourselves conversing almost in whispers. Conscious of the sound of chairs being moved we ventured to peep into the chapel. A few had left, obviously very quietly, but most of the conference delegates were in small groups in *sotto voce* conversation. Some were simply sitting in isolation, not moving, not speaking. I must confess, not only were we three stunned and (if pride be a sin I confess to that also) elated, but we felt we'd achieved something worthwhile.

Eventually, as actors will of course, we gravitated to the very pleasant little bar they have at the centre. The first person to come to our table was one of the centre's directors, Father Michael, who said he was 'drained after such a powerful experience'. Many of the audience came to congratulate Peter upon his truly magnificent first perform-ance and Michael upon another powerful and thought-provoking script. For my own part I was thrilled that, as with *Temptations*, nobody said, 'I enjoyed that!' Love them or hate them, these companion solo-performance works of art cannot be dismissed as 'enjoyable'. In the 1995 Edinburgh Festival the two plays were to be performed on alternate evenings for two weeks at the Church Hill Theatre Studio.

And so after another emotionally exhausting Easter I was able to settle back into the routine of an occasional visit to BBC Radio Merseyside to record more *Write Now* stories and give my 'Out of the Limelight' talk to a couple of groups. Things however have a habit of not staying quiet for very long. Tadge Muldoon was soon in touch with the latest '*Dad's Army* Society' development – the very first members' meeting. As more than half the membership seemed to live in the south of the country the society organisers felt that their first meeting should be in London. But where in London? The society isn't exactly 'rolling in money'.

I suggested the Victory Services Club, Marble Arch, of which I've been a happy and well-satisfied life member for some years. The shock came when I was asked to be 'the main item on the agenda' – in other words the guinea pig – 'just to find out if it works'. Apparently an agreeable deal was done with the club for the hire of the Alamein Room, complete with its own bar and a buffet.

'Meet Private Sponge' was followed by a showing of the 'A Soldier's Farewell' episode in which 'Sponge' is fairly noticeable. After the buffet supper a more relaxed atmos-phere took over, most members getting to know each other whilst some, who had travelled quite a distance to be there, were taking their leave and all, I'm happy to record, saying how much they'd enjoyed it and asking, 'When will the next one be?' The late Tadge and his brother Pat deserved sincere congratulations upon what – for us Northern lads – was virtually a 'step in the dark in a foreign land'. Everything seemed to me to go smoothly and unlike other appreciation societies' events this didn't cost an arm and a leg, thank heavens.

I had not appeared before a live audience for quite some time but, I'm happy to say, I still had a mild attack of first-night nerves before I 'went on', as 'twere. A large, warm and interested audience, including a sizeable detachment from The Barmy Army Film Club, soon put me at my ease.

The next event, or I should say 'events', on my horizon were all connected with the fiftieth anniversary of VE day. Having earlier in the year opened an exhibition, 'Bringing the House Down' all about theatre past and present in Wigan and district, I was recalled to the History Shop to open 'Wigan at War'.

Drama was to hit Palaver Productions again in 1995. *Temptations* and *Betrayals* were both scheduled to be presented at the Edinburgh Festival when we received what, for people without Michael and Peter's determination, could have been a deathblow for the plays and the festival appearance. Just two weeks before being due to open in Scotland's capital city it came as a shock to find that Peter was contractually bound under his agreement with the Personal Management Representation, under whose aegis he worked, to take up a role in an international tour of the play *The Duchess of Malfi*. No room for manoeuvre was possible. Rehearsals for it had to start on the day Palaver Productions was due to open in Edinburgh and Peter was not under contract to the smaller firm although a partner in it.

Out of the blue came Michael's phone call, 'Colin, help!' Another young actor, Simon Iddon, had come forward to undertake a herculean task. Michael continued, 'Even as we speak Peter and Simon are in my study going through the script. Will you "come aboard" again?'

How Simon achieved just what he did in two weeks was little short of a miracle. Working through heatwave weather we were able by Saturday to give a dress rehearsal showing of *Temptations* to four discerning friends. I prompted him only twice. The next day Simon and I started working on *Betrayals*. We worked this way because I felt it would be far too confusing for Simon (and for me!) to try to work on both plays at once.

On the Wednesday of the second week another minor bombshell hit us. Michael returned from wherever he'd been away and announced that they (the whole show – Michael, Simon and two assistants) would leave for Edinburgh at the crack of dawn on the Saturday, not on the Sunday which was the impression under which Simon and I were working. We'd hoped to get the four friends back to see *Betrayals*. Apparently radio and press interviews had been arranged in Edinburgh for Saturday afternoon. With such a vast range of productions, and competition so fierce at the Edinburgh Festival, not a single chance for any publicity could be ignored. Also Simon was scheduled to record a section of one of the plays for BBC Radio Scotland's Sunday morning service for the following day.

We managed a costume and props rehearsal late on the Friday afternoon – I sat behind the set with the script so as not to disturb Simon. It was more or less a case of 'push on regardless'. I can only reiterate my admiration of Simon's efforts. Albeit with a few omissions – very few – Simon got through the text and the moves, some of them not exactly uncomplicated, without requiring prompting by me.

As I pointed out to Michael, under the circumstances the smoother and more detailed performance by the slightly older and more experienced Peter could not be expected.

After all, Peter not only had had longer to learn the plays, he was involved in the conception of them and, at points, had helped with the writing. I pleaded strongly (as I wasn't going to Edinburgh) for Simon to be given the utmost help and support and time to relax before the Monday opening.

Over the following weekend, my efforts to give up biting my nails failed miserably. On the Monday night I got a phone call to say that everything had gone smoothly for a small but obviously absorbed audience. Subsequent progress resorts and copies of reviews restored my equilibrium by proving that Mr Iddon had surpassed all expectations and given a very creditable account of both the plays and himself. As for his application for membership of the British Actors' Equity Association, as an old life member I insist on proposing him.

In May came the actual week of VE day anniversary events with exhibitions in both sections of the Metropolitan Borough, Leigh and Wigan.

After he and the mayoress had opened each exhibition (Leigh on Saturday 6th and Wigan on Tuesday 9th), I assisted His Worship the Mayor in judging the three competitions which had been organised. The best wartime costume, the best wartime recipe and the best piece or collection of wartime memorabilia. Not, I can assure you, the easiest of tasks but at least His Worship and I weren't lynched because of our decisions on either day.

Saturday 13th brought the finale of Wigan's celebrations with a town centre carnival procession in which, once more and I think maybe for the last time, I donned the Mr Churchill bald wig, cigar, bowtie and Trinity-House-type 'naval person' cap. Seated in the back of an open-top car on what fortunately turned out to be a nice afternoon, despite some of the forecasts, I was driven from one side of the town to the other at a snail's pace. Young people asked, 'Dad! Mam! Who's he supposed to be?' Older contemporaries called, 'Colin Bean, what do you think you are doing?'

I wonder if this is the point at which I should draw the tabs in to indicate the end of this act? Perhaps I should write, 'The End'. But then someone is sure to say, 'What? You! Shut up? Who Do You Think YOU ARE KIDDING!'

Appendix A

1. A Chronological List of Parts Played on Stage in Plays

2. Directing – Not Appearing

3. Variety Revue Recitals

4. Music Hall Chairman

5. Television

6. Radio

7. Films and Video Films

8. Tape Recordings

1. A Chronological List of Parts Played on Stage in Plays

(R) Repeat of a part already played in a previous production.
(D) Directed the play as well as appearing in it.
(A) Amateur production.

Wigan

1931	Shepherd, *Nativity Play* (A)
1932	Jester, *May Queen Pageant* (A)
1934	Jan the Huntsman, *Snow White and Rose Red* (A)
	Shepherd, *Nativity Play* (A)
1935	King, *Sleeping Beauty* (A)
	Magi, *Nativity Play* (A)
1937	Narrator, *Coronation* (A)
1939	Policeman, *Ye Olde Dogge* (A)
1942	Mr White, *The Monkey's Paw* (D) (A)
	Mr Slater, *The Dear Departed* (A)
	The Devil, *The Magician* (D) (A)
	The Duke, *The Invisible Duke* (A)
1943	Matthias, *The Bells* (D) (A)
	Villager, *The Sorcerer* (A)
	Ishmael, *By Thy Cross and Passion* (A)
1944	Lord Babs, *Charlie's Aunt* (D) (A)

Hippodrome, Wigan

1944	Dago, *The Face at the Window* (first professional job!)
	Butler, *Lady Windermere's Fan*

Hippodrome, Bolton

1944	Essaie Aissa, *The Creaking Chair*

Overseas (Army Service)

1944–48 Army Variety Shows
            Tommy, *The Hasty Heart*
            Touring BCOF Japan (See Appendix B)

Southport

1948   The Mayor, *The Man from the Ministry*

Bradford Civic Playhouse and Northern Children's Theatre Tours

1948   Si Crowell and Sam Craig, *Our Town* (A)
1949   Det Sgt Ramage, *Distinguished Gathering* (A)
            Henry Straker, *Man and Superman* (A)
            Camillo, *Winter's Tale* (A)
1950   Sam Gurney (Grimalkin), *Buried Treasure*
            Dr Libbard, *The Giaconda Smile* (A)
            Luke, *The Toy Princess*
            Guest, *Everyman*
            Villager, *The Recruiting Officer*
            Earl of Ross, *Macbeth*

Dewsbury Rep

1950   Charles, *The Barretts of Wimpole Street*

Bradford Civic

1950   Humphrey, *The Lady's Not for Burning* (A)
            Mio, *Winterset* (A)

York Rep

1951   'Orrid 'Orace, *Puss in Boots*

Bradford Civic and Children's Theatre Tour

1951   The Gentleman Caller, *The Glass Menagerie* (A)
        Mr Juno, *Over-Ruled* (A)
        Malkin, *The Three Toymakers*
        King Minos, *The Two Masks*

York Festival

1951   Soldier, *The York Mystery Plays*

Bradford Civic and NCT Tour

1952   Robin Lythe, *Smugglers' Bay*
        Wooden Man, *The Magic Lighter*

Skipton Rep

1952   Mortimer Brewster, *Arsenic and Old Lace*

Sheffield Repertory Co.

1952   Police Constable, *The Mortimer Touch*
        Chuck Warren, *Deep Are the Roots*
        Overseer, *The Firstborn*
1953   E.J. Lofgren, *Harvey*
        Ralph, *Winter Journey*
        Bond, *The Cathedral*
        Sydney Spooner, *Worm's Eye View*
        Dr Gathorne Wetherby, *Adam's Apple*

Court Players: Pier Theatre Hastings

1953   Adolph, *Romance*
        Joseph Lewison, *Murder in Motley*
        Julius Winterhalter, *Waters of the Moon*
        Don Lucas, *Relative Values*

Police Sgt, *Wild Horses*
Jackie Jackson, *The Deep Blue Sea*
Tex Sebastian, *My Wife's Lodger*
Gudgeon, *The Hollow*
Mahmoud Morgan, *Love Let Loose*
Det Inspector, *Full House*
Jean-Marie De Polignac, *The Tolerant Husband*
Sir Harold Raikes, *The Man in Grey*
David Mannion, *Telltale Murder*
Ronald Bradley, *The Loving Elms*
Arthur Allen, *The Fur Coat*
Rev. Horace Wimpole, *Having a Wonderful Time*
Len, *Reefer Girl*
Hubert Drew, *The Return of Peggy Atherton*
Mr Tippett, *The Gay Bachelor*
Barry Nadell, *Merely Murder*
Bosforth, *It Happened at Christmas*
Cpl. Nicholas Brayne, *Glad Tidings*

1954   Police Sgt Spedding, *Someone at the Door*
Bertoni, *The Blind Goddess*
Quartermaster Bates, *Rain*
Peter Parke, *Lady in Evidence*
Det Constable, *Age of Consent*
Eddie Sheridan, *The Man With Expensive Tastes*
Fred, *Lady Look Behind You*
Michael Pritchard, *The Orchard Walls*
John Foster, *The Bad Samaritan*
George, *The Happy Marriage*
Frank Brown, *Welcome on the Mat*
Bramwell, *Daughters of the Parsonage*
Mr Fenton, *The Listening Hills*
David Lomax, *Job for the Boy*
Peter Swithin, *The Return*

Harry Eccles, *Too Many Cooks*
Johnny Banks, *I Hold You Prisoner*
Jim Miller, *Because I Am Black*
Hubert Mallinson, *Can This Be Love?*
Mick Egan, *Manhandled*
Frank Atherton, *Simple Simon's Baby*
Digger Mcmahon, *Friendly Relations*
Ted Wills, *The Maniac*
Harry Garlish, *As Young as He Feels*
Dr Edgar Baird, *A Chance of Happiness*
Sam Jackson, *The White Sheep of the Family*
Petrovsky, *Anastasia*
Jeremy Meranton, *Meet Mr Callaghan*
Joe Piper, *It's a Boy*
Bert Gay, *The Gay Dog*
Fred, *For Better, for Worse*
Charles, The Butler, *Me and My Girl*
Mecrae, *The Dashing White Sergeant*
Dr Gortler, *I Have Been Here Before*
Robin, *On Probation*
Curly, *Pitfall*
Edwin, *Spring Model*
Brown, *The Ticking Clock*
Chuck Meredith, *Lovers' Meeting*
Det Sgt Simmons, *Angels Unaware*
Harold Barlow, *The Season's Greetings*
Fred Heslop, *Sauce for the Goose*

1955   Robert Courtland, *Ring Out the Old*
William Saxon, *Escapade*
Jan Letzarescou, *Dear Charles*
Gerry, *The Burning Glass*
Mr Webster, *Love and Learning*
Tony Hurford, *It's Never Too Late*

Olympia Theatre, Dublin

1955   Black McDonald, *Johnny Belinda*
Tony Hurford, *It's Never Too Late* (R)
Sheldon, *Random Harvest*
Teddy Brewster, *Arsenic and Old Lace*
Ong Chi Seng, *The Letter*

Sheffield Lyceum

1955   Tony Hurford, *It's Never Too Late* (R)
Godfrey Pond, *The Happiest Days of Your Life*
Inspector Haines, *Interference*
Charles, The Butler, *Me and My Girl* (R)
Jim Miller, *Because I Am Black* (R)
George, *Come Back Peter*
Henry Bennett, *What Anne Brought Home*
Al Stevens, *Women Are My Business*
Elmer, *A Bed for Two*
Robert Van Brett, *Double Door*
Ronnie Wetson, *Black Widows*
Sheldon, *The Lady of the House*
Charlie Peterson, *Sauce for the Goose*
Peter Quinn, *Black Magic*
Fred Thompson, *Is Your Honeymoon Really Necessary?*
Howell, *Telltale Murder*
Charles Grant, *The Family Upstairs*
Tony, *Beside The Seaside*
John Carteret, *Smilin' Through*
Sir Claude Amory and
Inspector Japp, *Black Coffee*
Terry Hammond, *While Parents Sleep*
Colonel Pickering, *Pygmalion*
Conn, *Lady Look Behind You*

Simon Mostyn, *Murder on the Nile*
Joe Lovejoy, *Ma's Bit o' Brass*
Richard Winters, *Jackie*

Crewe Theatre

1955   Philip Lord, *Meet The Wife*
Fred Moulson, *Poor Dad*
Bert Hawkins, *Vice in the Street*
Geoffrey Firth, *Between Ourselves*
George Sharpe, *Love on the Never-Never*

Sheffield Lyceum

1955   King Wolf, *Red Riding Hood* (and stage
director)
Black Pirate, *Peter Pan*

Tour

1956   Black Pirate, *Peter Pan*

Hippodrome, Stockton-on-Tees

1956   Ronald Baker, *Mad About Men*
Barry Carrington, *Widow's Might*

Sheffield Lyceum

1956   Prestwick, *It's a Small World*
Richard Appleby MP, *Caesar's Wife*
The Duke, *Worm's Eye View*
Gilbert Hawkins, *Vice in the Streets*
Nigel Fleming, *Love on the Never-Never*
Barry Carrington, *Widow's Might* (R)

Princes Theatre, Bradford

1956   Keith Salesby, *Lucky Strike*
            Frank Barrett, *The Shadow of Doubt*
            Dr Sheppard, *Alibi*

Sheffield Lyceum

1956   Ben Wrackley, *Out of the Frying Pan*
            George Fairweather, *Sweet Fanny Adams*
            Morgan, *Reluctant Heroes*
            Uncle Nat Henshaw, *Apple-Pie Order*
            Leonard Mallinson, *Can This Be Love?*
            Police Inspector, *Deep in the Wood*
            Charles Pentwick, *Love's a Luxury*
            Chief Det Commissioner Kelly, *On the Spot*
            Joe Truman, *The Cure for Love*
            Lord Elwood, *Wild Goose Chase*
            Capt. Hastings OBE, *Peril at End House*
            Alf Hall, *The Love Match*
            Jack Haydock, *The Hour and the Woman*
            Humphrey Millar, *All For Mary*
            Bill Brown, *Relations the Best Apart*
            Larkin, *The Bachelor Father*
            Norman Greenslade, *The Striptease Murder*
            Charlie Brown, *Keeping Up With the Jones*

Scala Theatre, London and Tour

1956   Black Pirate, *Peter Pan* (R)

Summer Season, Ayr

Civic Theatre, Ayr
Butlin's Camp, Ayr, Wed. and Thurs.

1957 Weeks, *High Temperature*
   Danny, *Night Must Fall*
   Humphrey Millar, *All For Mary* (R)
   Heathcliff, *Wuthering Heights*
   Charles Wikler, *The Cat and the Canary*
   Alaric, *Peg O' My Heart* (D)
   Gregory, *Reluctant Heroes*
   Smith, *Murder on the Nile* (D)
   Albert, *Small Hotel*
   Herr Feldmann, *Autumn Crocus* (D)
   Porter, *Worm's Eye View*
   Colonel Pickering, *Pygmalion* (R)
   Bill Harrington, *The Patsy*
   David, *The Silver Cord*
   Sir Lancelot Spratt, *Doctor In the House* (D)

Pavilion, South Shields

1957 Danny, *Night Must Fall* (R)
   Sir Lancelot Spratt, *Doctor In The House* (D) (R)
   Smith *Murder, On The Nile* (D) (R)
   Humphrey Millar, *All for Mary* (R)
   Inspector Rough, *Gaslight* (D)
   Albert, *Small Hotel* (R)
   Oliver Costello and Inspector Lord, *Spider's Web*
   Bill Snibson, *Me and My Girl* (Co-D)
   Tom Hammond, *Dead on Nine*
   Terry, *Peg O' My Heart* (D)
   Doctor Glanville, *Night Was Our Friend*
   Harry Fleming, *Love On the Never-Never* (D)
   Sabbath, *The House of Jeffreys* (D)
   Howard, *Love in a Mist* (D)

Tynemouth Rep, Theatre

1958 Adam Yorke, *Traffic*

Sam Ryan, *Trouble at Number 13*
Rod, *Summer of the Seventeenth Doll*
Nicolai Szapary, *Give Me Yesterday*
Joe Harris, *The Poltergeist*
Esteban El Duco De Santaguand, *The Marquise*
Thomas Swinley, *The Happy Man*
Cliff Lewis, *Look Back in Anger*
Baxter, *Subway in the Sky*
Edgar Fraser, *Green Waters*
David Gold, *Ghost Squad*
Inspector Gordon, *Double Image*

Civic Theatre, Ayr

1958   Godfrey Pond, *The Happiest Days of Your Life* (R)
       Baxter, *Subway in the Sky* (R)
       Lord Babs, *Charlie's Aunt* (D) (R)
       Colonel Forbes, *House by the Lake* (D)
       Jimmy Jinks, *Baby Mine* (D)
       Terry Muller, *The Man Who Changed His Name* (D)
       Elwood P. Dowd, *Harvey* (D)
       Oliver Costello and Inspector Lord, *Spider's Web*
       (D) (R)
       Joe Piper, *It's a Boy* (with music) (D) (R)
       Fred Phipps, *Dry Rot* (D)
       Doctor Sloper, *The Heiress* (D)
1958   Thomas Royde, *Towards Zero* (D)
       Doctor Knott, *My Wife's Family* (D)
       John Goronwy Jones, *The Corn Is Green* (D)
       Robert Popjoy, *Bob's Your Uncle* (with music) (D)

Sheffield Lyceum Theatre

1958   Howard Marsh, *Piccadilly Alibi*
       Cool Kelly, *It's a Wise Child*

Captain Gruber, *Goldilocks and the Three Bears*
(Stage Director and 'Dame' Understudy)

Empire Theatre, Cleethorpes

1959   Peter Thornton, *Proof Before Murder*
Lord Quinton, *Stolen Waters*
Joe Scotswood, *Lock-Out on Love (Love Locked Out)*
Richard Paplin, *Secret Lives*

Hippodrome, Stockton-on-Tees

1959   Rev. Hardy Bronte, *The Tattooed Lady* (D)
Father, *Power Without Glory* (D)
Hugh Woodward, *No Concern of Mine* (D)
Steve Walker, *Teddy Boy* (D)

Civic Theatre, Ayr

1959   Count Skriczevinsky, *Flare Path*
Fred Tutt, *Cup of Kindness*
Geoffrey Carroll, *The Two Mrs Carrolls*
Sam Pecker, *Quiet Weekend*
Sir Claude Amory and Inspector Japp, *Black Coffee* (D) (R)
Porter, *Waggonload of Monkeys*
1959   Bill Walker, *Major Barbara*
Lt-Gen. Sir Ralph Cornwall, *Who Goes There?* (D)
Yaun Sing, *The Chinese Bungalow*
Lord Elwood, *Wild Goose Chase* (D) (R)
Dr Sheppard, *Alibi* (R)
Joe Tilney, *The Bride and the Bachelor*
Mr Van Daan, *The Diary of Anne Frank* (D)
Albert Grimshaw, *Friends and Neighbours*

Theatre Outlook, Liverpool and Tour

1959   Fabrizio, *Mine Hostess Mirandina*
       Pianist, *How He Lied to Her Husband*

Empire, Edinburgh

1960   Joe Scotswood, *Love Locked Out* (R)

Arcadia, Scarborough: Summer Season

1960   Sam Cross, *Saturday Night at the Crown*

Commercial Tour

1960   Geoffrey Lang, *Home in Three*

Garrick Theatre, Southport and Tour

1960   Grab (of Smash and Grab), *Cinderella*
1961   Martin Bryden, *Forbidden Flesh*
       Alan Vincent, *A Girl Called Sadie*

Alhambra, Morecambe: Summer season

1961   Andy Siddlethwaite, *Love Locked Out*

Empire, Newcastle-upon-Tyne

1961   Albert Grimshaw, *Friends And Neighbours* (R)

Grand Theatre, Bolton

1961   Vizier, *Aladdin*

Palace Theatre, Watford

1962   Basil Clutterbuck, *Hot and Cold in All Rooms*
Inspector Battle, *Towards Zero*
Alderman Knebworth, *Hocus Pocus*
Andre Aaron, *The Shadow Witness*
Richard Greatham, *Hay Fever*
Rev. Arthur Sexton Hifflish, *The Devil Was Sick*
Crab, *Simple Spyman*
Charles Barcher, *The Big Killing*
Inspector Jones, *Murder By Accident*
Baron De Charoncay, *Don't Listen Ladies!*
Paul, *Time to Speak*
Hilary Fairfield, *A Bill of Divorcement*
Rollo Ewbank, *Cup and Saucer*
Sam Goulansky, *The Amorous Prawn*
Sam Cross, *Saturday Night at the Crown* (R)
Hornbeam, *Doctor at Sea*
Claude, *George And Margaret*
Trenchard, *After my Fashion*
Thomas Swinley, *The Happy Man* (R)
The Nobleman, *The Man With a Load of Mischief*
Jan Letzarescou, *Dear Charles* (R)
Richard Wyndham, *The Holly and the Ivy*
Leopold Wilkes, *Open Verdict*
Bruce Banning, *Young Wives' Tale*
Black McDonald, *Johnny Belinda* (R)
Det Inspector Ogden, *Verdict*

1963   Ugly Sister Chlorodine, *Cinderella*
Reginald Kinsale, *Photo Finish*
Gilbert Crane, *Joy Of Living*
Inspector Davies, *Alibi*
Wilson, *Dear Delinquent*
Ben Brooks, *The Telescope*
Dr Alan Frost, *Signpost to Murder*

Henry Portal, *The Blue Boost*
Dr Kendalthe, *The Seventh Veil*
Oscar Ritter, *Miss Pell Is Missing*

Civic Theatre, Ayr

1963   Philip, *The Little Hut*
Charles Barcher, *The Big Killing* (D) (R)
Watkyn, *Plaintiff In a Pretty Hat*
Alec Barnes, *A Touch of Class* (D)
Easter, *Doctor at Sea*
Wilf Pearson, *Beside the Seaside*
Dr Alan Frost, *Signpost to Murder* (D) (R)
Byron Winkler, *Affairs of State*
Claude Vole, *Who's Your Father?*
Joe Harris, *The Poltergeist* (D) (R)

Palace Theatre, Watford

1963   Mr Ames, *Amateur Means Lover*
Mr Baker, *Come Blow Your Horn*
James Roberts, *How Are You Johnnie?*
Michael Starkwedder, *The Unexpected Guest*
King Arthur, *The Long Sunset*
Charlie England, *Norman*
Alfred Bunting, *The Lodger*
The Intruder, *See How They Run*
Widow Twankey, *Aladdin*

Tour – Bristol, Birmingham, Liverpool, Newcastle-upon-Tyne, Oxford

1964   Selsey Man, Harry, Lord Boxington and
Deputy Alfred P. Doolittle, *My Fair Lady*

Theatre Royal, Newcastle

1965   Alfred P. Doolittle, *My Fair Lady*

Palace Theatre, Watford

1965   Nurse Daisy Dogood, *Babes in the Wood*

Intimate Theatre, Palmers Green

1966   Richard Fraser, *Green Waters*
           Lloyd Kent, *A Whiskey Business*
           Mr Crispin, *The Man with Red Hair*
           Kevin, *Poker Session*

Palace Theatre, Watford

1966   Gower, *Henry V*
           The Common Man, *A Man for All Seasons*
           Harold Makepiece, *Semi-Detached*

Civic Theatre, Ayr

1966   Ludlow *Fresh Fields* (inc. Cummock Festival)
           Sir Wilfred Jennings, *Out of Thin Air*
           Benjy, *Beth*
           Lewis, *The Shot in Question*
           Tim, *The Girl who Couldn't Quite*
           Mr Franks, *The Man* (D)
           Capt. Biggar, *Come On Jeeves!*
           Giles Lacy, *Rebecca*
           Richard Marshall, *Busybody* (D)
           Casper Darde, *Captain Carvallo*
           Beecham, *The Reluctant Peer* (D)
           Dr Rank, *A Doll's House*
           Mr Baker, *Come Blow Your Horn* (D) (R)

Mr Henderson, *Intent to Murder*
Paul, *Fools Rush In*
Dr Bradman *Blithe Spirit* (D)

Palace Theatre, Kilmarnock

1966   Victor Prynne, *Private Lives*
        The Gentleman Caller, *Glass Menagerie* (D) (R)
        Ricard, *Rattle of a Simple Man* (D)

Intimate Theatre, Palmers Green

1966   The Common Man, *A Man for All Seasons* (R)
        Det Supt Slade, *The Man Outside*
        Sir John Holt, *A Friend Indeed*

Gaiety Theatre, Ayr

1967   Nurse Biddy Boddy, *Robin Hood and the Babes in the Wood*

Intimate Theatre, Palmers Green

1967   Henry, *The Anniversary*

Pavilion Theatre, Torquay: Summer Season

1968   Willie Beattie, *Wedding Fever*

Civic Theatre, Ayr

1968   Widow Twankey, *A Lad an' His Lamp* (D)

Theatre Royal, Stratford East

1969   King Wolf, *Red Riding Hood*

Palace Theatre, Watford

1970   Mother Goose, *Mother Goose* (D)

National Tour

1971   Mr Bogusian, *Fiddlers Five*

Wimbledon Theatre

1971   Doctor Lomond, *The Ringer*
            Bernard Lockwood, *Uproar in the House*
            Sir Charles Jasper, *A Murder Has Been Arranged*

Palace Theatre, Watford

1972   Dame Durden, *Jack and the Beanstalk*

Theatre Royal, Bury St Edmunds

1972   Ugly Sister Gertrude, *Cinderella*

King's Head, Islington

1973   Williams, *The Grave*

Wigan Festival and Tour

1973   Tom Hardacre, *Foreign Air*

Playhouse Theatre, Weston-super-Mare

1973   Queen Wilhelmina, *Puss in Boots*

Wigan and District Touring (Bijou Theatre Co.)

1974   Dame Notalotova, *The Golden Apple*
            Charlie Barlow, *Let t'Play Begin* (D)

Tom Hardacre, *Foreign Air* (R)

Widow Twankey, *Aladdin* (D) (R)

Wigan and District

1975	Nurse Daisy Dogood, *Babes in the Wood* (D) (R)
1976	Sarah the Cook, *Dick Whittington and his Wonderful Cat* (D)
1977	Edward Hardacre, *Can We Come In?* (D) (A)
	Walter Monckton, *Crown Matrimonial* (A)
1978	Penelope Stamp, *Jack the Giant Killer* (D)
	The Inquisitor, *St Joan* (A)

Octagon Theatre, Bolton

1978	Gratiano, *The Merchant of Venice*
	Casca Titinius, *Julius Caesar*
	Archidamus and Old Shepherd, *Winter's Tale*
1979	Frederick A.T.T.I., *Beauty and the Beast*
	Sir George Crofts, *Mrs Warren's Profession*
	George Riley, *Enter a Free Man*
	Ephraim Barlow, *The Northerners*
	Sir Lucius O'Trigger, *The Rivals*
	Duff, *The Old Country*
	Pistol, *Henry V*
	Duke of Albany, *King Lear*
	Dogberry, *Much Ado About Nothing*
1980	King Harold, *Jack and the Beanstalk*
	The General, *The Queen and the Rebels*
1980	Mr Wilcox, *The Merry-Go-Round*
	Bilton, *Major Barbara*
	The Duke of Ayr and Stirling, *While the Sun Shines*
	Earl of Worcester and the Sheriff, *Henry IV (Part 1)*
	Baptista Ninda, *The Taming of the Shrew*
	Gentleman, Caius Lucius and Sicilius Leonatus, *Cymbeline*

1981	Pedlar and King Fulbert, *The Golden Goose* (Co-D)
	Harry Lancaster, *The Cure for Love*
	Keleman, *The Wolf*
	Stomil, *Tango*
	Jean Rampart, *His Majesty's Grenadiers*
	James Lever, Bank Manager, Crompton and Mayor of Bolton, *Leverhulme*
	Egeon, *Comedy of Errors*
	Menenius Agrippa, *Coriolanus*
	Sir Toby Belch, *Twelfth Night*
	The Wizard of the Forest, *Hansel and Gretel*
1982	Tom Holroyd, *Too Clever For Love*
	Nocella, *Filumena*
	President of the Court,
	5th Juryman, Prisoner and Pompous Official, *Blind Goddess*
	Inspector Bridois, *The Birdwatcher* (Feydeau's *M. Chasse*)
	Escalus, Prince of Verona, *Romeo and Juliet*
	King Duncan, 1st Murderer and Scottish Doctor, *Macbeth*
	Holofernes, *Love's Labour Lost*
1983	King Bulbus IXth, *Jack and Jill and the Magic Secret*
	Ralph, *Sisterly Feelings*
	Charlie Butler, *Saturday Night at the Crown*
	John Bunting JP, *Dealing in Futures*
	Stephen Spettigue, *Charlie's Aunt*
	Mr Muller, *The Deep Blue Sea*
	Tubal and The Duke of Venice, *The Merchant of Venice*
	Stephano, *The Tempest*

Wigan and Touring: Bijou Theatre Co.

1984   Widow Twankey, *Aladdin and His Wonderful Lamp*
1986   Mr Foster, *The ffarringdons of Worden*

Kirkaldy and Darlington

1986   Michael Henderson, *Intent to Murder* (R)

Key Theatre, Peterborough

1986   Sweeney Todd, *Sweeney Todd the Fiendish Barber of Fleet Street*

Worden Hall

Mr Foster, *The ffarringdons of Worden* (R)

Theatre Royal Hanley (Alan Clement Productions) Tour

Devonshire Park, Eastbourne, Princes, Aldershot, Pomegranate, Chesterfield, Arts Centre, Huddersfield

1986–87 Sweeney Todd, *Sweeney Todd the Fiendish Barber of Fleet Street*

Bijou Theatre Co. Tour

Oswaldtwistle, Prestwich, Wigan, Royton, Kirkby

1987–88 Basher, *Babes in the Wood*

Theatre Gwynedd, Bangor (Alan Clement Productions)

1988   Michael Henderson, *Intent to Murder*

Bijou Theatre Co., Tour

Bacup, Haslingden, Oswaldtwistle, Wigan

1988   Sardinus, *The Further Adventures of Robinson Crusoe*

Blackburn, Wigan, Bacup, Rawtenstall, Oswaldtwistle,
Kirkby

1989   Father Christmas 1, Mr Wineburg and
            Reuben the Innkeeper, *Happy Birthday*
            Whatsisname (D)

King George's Hall, Blackburn

1990   Old man of the Sea, *Robinson Crusoe* (Duggie
            Chapman Production)

Civic Arts Centre, Belfast (Pendle Productions)

1990   Frank, *Educating Rita*

Bijou Theatre Tour

Bacup, Haslingden, Oswaldtwistle

1990   Widow Twankey, *Aladdin*

2. Directing – Not Appearing

1957   *Candida*
         Blithe Spirit

1959   *Single Simon's Baby*

1963   *Dangerous Corner*

1977   *In Jubilation* (Silver Jubilee Concert Compilation)

1978   *Flowering Cherry* (A)

1979   *Good Morning Bill*, Octagon Theatre, Bolton
         Come On! Give Us All a Laugh (Theatre
         Appreciation Programme)

1980   *The Linden Tree*

1981   *A View from the Bridge*

1982   *Hindle Wakes* (Co-directed With Felicity Taylor)

1992   *In the Business*, (Two-Faced Theatre Co.)
         Jack and the Beanstalk (Bijou Theatre Co.)

1993   *Mrs Moses* (One-woman Play, Bijou Theatre Co.)
         Snow White (Bijou Theatre Co.)

1994   *Temptations*, Theatre Church and Edinburgh
         Festival (One-man play, Palaver Productions)

1995   *Betrayals* (One-man play, Palaver Productions),
         Conference Centre, London Colney and
         Edinburgh Festival

3. Variety Revue Recitals

1957   *Children's Christmas Pud*, Pavilion, South Shields

1967   Compere and Feed, *Easter Parade*, Gaiety, Ayr
Compere and Feed, *Spring '67*, Pavilion, Glasgow
Compere and Feed, *Calum's Ceilidh*, Edinburgh,
tour of Highlands and Islands and tour of
Orkneys and Shetlands
Narrator, *Peter and the Wolf* with North London
Symphonia

1975   Wigan Metro Community Shows
One-Man Show, *How Do!*
Duo Show, *Words and Music*
The End of the Pier Show
St George and the Dragon
Narrator, *The Christmas Story*
Narrator, *St Michael's Christmas Story*

1980   Octagon Theatre (TAP Productions)
The Plays of D.H. Lawrence
The History of Music Hall

1984   Bijou Theatre TIE
Beside the Seaside

1986   Solo Reading Recitals
The Cliffs of Lancashire
The Great Magonagal
A Gradely Neet (Premiere: St Francis, Kitt Green,
Wigan)

1989   Bolton Festival '89
Celebrity Lecture and *A Gradely Neet*

1990   *A Gradely Neet*, Saltmine
           A Gradely Neet, Sutton, St Helens
           A Gradely Neet, Rossendale
           Servants of Masters, Coach House Gallery

1992   *Christmas Concert*
           Star Over Barncroft, Halewood Carol Concert

1993   *Christmas Concert* (Radio Wrightington/*Evening Post*), Wigan Parish Church

1994   *Christmas Concert*
           The Concert Hall (Radio Wrightington/*Evening Post*), The Mill at the Pier

1995   *A Gradely Neet*, The Waterwheel, Wigan

4. Music Hall Chairman

1966   *A Victorian Evening*, Palace, Watford
        The Intimate Music Hall, Palmers Green

1972   Four weekly programmes of *The Best of British Music Hall*, Westcliff-on-Sea

1973   *The Tramshed Music Hall*, Woolwich
        Dinner Music Hall, Sherrington Hotel
        Those Were the Days, Bijou Music Hall (Tour)

1976   *Chairman Sponge: The Goode Olde Days*
        Two weeks, King's Theatre, Edinburgh

1977   *Chairman Sponge Pub Night*

1978   *An Evening at the Music Hall*, Wigan (A)

1981   *The Mayor's Charity Music Hall*, Wigan (A)

1985   *Palace Hall Days*, Wigan (A)

1986   *Olde Tyme Music Hall*, Worden Hall

5. Television

(Speaking Roles, early 'extra' work not included)

1961   Yeoman, *Richard The Lionheart*

1963   Mr Cooper (antiques dealer), *Z Cars*

1966   Det Sgt Parsons, *No Hiding Place*

1968–77 Private Sponge in twenty-eight episodes of *Dad's Army*

1969   Beethoven, *Gnomes Of Dulwich*
        Police Inspector, *Gnomes Of Dulwich*
        Detective, *Gnomes Of Dulwich*
        Bystander, *Broaden Your Mind*
        Prison Inmate, *Gold Robbers*
        Policeman, *Harry Worth Show*
        Policeman, three episodes of *Liver Birds*
        Policeman, two episodes of *The Goodies*
        Knight, *The Goodies*
        Lord Russell, two episodes of *The First Churchills*

1970   Centurion, *Up Pompeii*
        Policeman, *Liver Birds*

1971   Dirty Mackintosh Man, *Now Take My Wife*

1972   Soap Box Orator, *Liver Birds*
        Scared Visitor, *His Lordship Entertains*
        Indian Chief, *Scott on Language*

1973   Aged newseller, *Elementary My Dear Watson*
        Various Characters in thirteen episodes of *Michael Bentine Time*
        Leatherette Gloves, *Are You Being Served?*

1976   Vicar, *Potter's Picture Palace*
        Loud Supporter, *Fallen Hero*

1978   Vicar, *Potter's Picture Palace* (two episodes)

1980   Robinson, *Cousin Phyllis*
        Policeman, *Cribb*

1981   Henry Lancaster (excerpt from *The Cure for Love*)
        Clerk of the Court, *The Ladykillers*

1983   Foreman of the Jury, *Crown Court*

1985   Pompous official, *Jossy's Giants*
        His Worship the Mayor, *Good as Gold*

1986   Chairman, Commercial ad for the Aycliffe and Peterlee Development Corp.

1988   Verger, 'Wedding Bells' episode of *Hi-De-Hi*

1994   Interviewed for panel game, *Bygones*

6. Radio

1947   Plays, Sketches, Readings (Radio WLKS Kure, Japan)

1973–82   Intermittent Service with Radio Wrightington Hospital Broadcasting (Sunday morning magazine type programme with John Mather 'spinning the discs')

1976   Alderman Muleford in episode one and Sniffy Smith (Investigator) in five episodes of *Festival At Farbridge* (BBC Radio 4)

1977   Grandad, *A Springtime Disappointment* (Radio Leeds)
Incident at Agadir (Documentary)
Best Seller Robinson Crusoe (BBC Radio 4)
Shipwreck (two episodes)

1978   Patmore and three other characters in *Heaven and Charing Cross* (BBC Radio 4)
Organ Grinder and other characters, *Fame Is the Spur* (BBC Radio 4)

1979   Mr Lowe and Mr Hobbs, *The Hornblower Story* (BBC Radio 4)

1981   Samuel Pepys and Lord Brougham, *The Spencers Of Althrop* (BBC Radio 4)

1993   BBC Radio Merseyside
Mr Bliss QC, *Murder on the High Seas*
Stories and Poems for *Write Now* (BBC Radio North)

March   *The Maestro*
         Vocal by Tom Occleshaw
         Silence (Poem)
         The Broom Cupboard
         The Old Bull
         Nothing Lasts Forever
May   *Penance*
         Slab Cake and Old Lace
         Quest (Poem)
June   'Thought for the Day', June 7th to 11th in
         Morning Merseyside
July   *The Boots*
         Remember, Remember
Sept.   *Penny Points*
         A Do At The Prims
         The Little Gem
         Th'owd Baths (poem)
         Five items on 'Thought for the Day'
         Morning Merseyside
Dec.   *One Night in Winter*
         Christmas Poem

1994

January *Bags O'Coal*
         The Shark's Tale
         George, DIY (poem)
April   *Lanzarote Night Game*
         Jacob
         The Black Hole
July   *Seven Seas*
         Milk of Kindness
         Last Tango in Rochdale
Sept.   *Waiting*
         When the Cat's Away
         Country Matters

Passed Over
Aunt Ellen
Oct.   *Christmas Carols*
Something to Sing About
Library Gardens

1995

January *Nineteen Forty-Eight*
Uncle Ned
A Man of Many Parts
April   *The Extra Cup*
The Rent Collector
A Wonderful Life
June   *Straight as a Die*
Spring Madness
Concert (poem)
Between You And Me (poem)
Nov.   *The Catch*
Plastic Surgery
Brass Band Played Tiddly Om Pom Pom
The Maggies

7. Films and Video Films

1949   Knocker-up, *Up For T'cup*

1970   Platoon member, *Dad's Army*

1985   Customer, *The Path to Flotation (TSB)*

1993   Interview for *Bygones* programme

8. Tape Recordings – Bijou Tapes, Wigan

1986 *The King and the Donkey*
   How Do!
   The Voice of His Age
   The ffarringdons of Worden

1988 *A Gradely Neet*

1989 *Happy Birthday Whatsisname*

1993 Onwards (not on Bijou Tapes)
   All *Write Now* stories (For private use, BBC and
   T. Simm)
   Radio Wrightington's Christmas Concert

1994–95 More *Write Now* stories

Appendix B

1. Extract From *The Gen*, BCOF Magazine, Kure, Japan

2. 'I Toured Japan', BCOF Magazine, Kure, Japan

3. A Commendation

(From *The Gen*, the magazine of the BCOF Combined Education and Hobbies Centre, 11th October, 1946, Kure, Japan)

The Hasty Heart
(They say that sorrow is born in the Hasty Heart)

John Patrick's whimsical wartime play was given its Oriental premiere at the Theatre Royal, Kure, by the Little Theatre players on 6th October.

Packed houses gave the play an enthusiastic reception, proving that there is a demand hereabouts for flesh and blood entertainment as a relief from canned show and sound.

Outstanding feature to this playgoer was that the characters seemed real. One has met such people here and there in the course of the war-torn years.

A play which calls for a British General Hospital Sister, an Englishman, an Australian, a New Zealander, an American and a Scot should not be hard to cast in the BCOF area, but narrow the field down to the Kure Base area and an element of luck must be admitted. Luck favoured producer George Welsh in the advent of Capt. D. McKenna of US Military Government who takes the part of 'Yank'. It also took a turn when Sister Margaret Roberts walked into and so perfectly filled the role of 'Margaret'.

The Basuto 'Blossom' is not the sort of part to be eagerly sought after by an aspiring actor. Cpl. Joe Collins compels admiration through undertaking the arduous task of blacking-up considerable portions of his anatomy nightly and the even more arduous task of removing the blacking. He only, with the exception of actor/producer George Welsh, who took the part of the C.O. of the hospital, 'Cobwebs', was required to impersonate a character and, speaking no lines, did so with intelligence and vigour.

The rest of the cast gave Patrick's lines their own natural accent and with the force and fervour of their own personalities made the play as realistic as its somewhat over-emphasised theme and too broad slapstick element would permit.

Playgoers will find it hard to believe that LAC Ron Stephen had no previous theatrical experience before joining the Base Drama Group. His portrayal of the dour young Scot, who 'did not make friends: period' was very good indeed. He lived the part, he made every line tell, carrying himself with confidence and poise, complete master of the role. One had the feeling either he was made for the part or the part was made for him.

Some of the best scenes in the play were the exchanges between 'Lachie' and 'Yank', both humorous and vehement. Capt. McKenna made the part of 'Yank' live with all his good-humoured wit, generosity and underlying firmness of purpose. Margaret Roberts lent the role of 'Sister Margaret' all the sincerity, beauty and grace playwright Patrick could have dreamed and acted with perfect sympathy throughout.

Some of the audience brought their boxing-match manners with them and, even in the most poignant passages, the majority were made to squirm by the remarks of morons and the laughter of fools.

Colin Bean, Jack McNaughton, Ron Deer and Pat O'Carrigan made up the balance of an excellent cast and appeared to revel in their respective roles. *The Gen* offers congratulations to George Welsh and his players for the first-class entertainment which was repeated at the Rex Theatre, Point Camp. If certain difficulties involving the release of key personnel can be overcome the Little Theatre Players will go on tour of the BCOF area.

(From *The Gen* the magazine of the BCOF Combined Education and Hobbies Centre, 18th November, 1946, Kure, Japan)

I Have Just Toured Japan
By Colin Bean (The Little Theatre Players)

Yes. I have just toured Japan, and what a tour! We passed from place to place so quickly that we hardly had time to find out where we were before it was time to move on again.

When it became known that the company might tour for a period the difficulties to be faced became immense and so discouraging that at one stage it was debated whether it was worthwhile taking the show out so that the boys in the areas outside Base would have a chance to see the play. Most members of the cast had great difficulty in getting released from their various units for the tour.

Everywhere we performed we were well received by our audiences and the play was greatly appreciated. There were one or two personnel and staging difficulties at a couple of places.

I sincerely hope that none of my readers are under the impression that touring Japan with a show is fun and games. Most of the time quite the reverse is true. A typical schedule to which we worked, owing to the very short time allowed to us for the tour, was rise about 04.30 hours, wake some poor Unit Cook out of his bed to provide us with early breakfast, go to our next stop, arriving about lunch-time, put up our own scenery after unloading it from the train and transport – not all venues were beside railway lines – play that evening and pull down the set the same night, pack it into the train, have a meal – possibly – and fall into bed about 01 or 02.00 hours and be up again to catch our train at 05.00 hours. The inevitable happened, of course. We soon got restless and upset, however, troubles were either quickly or lengthily ironed out and we struggled on. By sheer struggling we were able to wipe out the doubts expressed by various transportation authorities including my own – Movement Control – about our ability to keep to such a strenuous timetable.

Incidents, both happy and otherwise, occurred on the tour and now that it is over I wish to think only of the happy ones. However, one cannot easily forget a five hour wait at Takamatsu and pushing scenery into a baggage coach at midnight, or sleeping on the floor of a second-class coach on the journey from Tokyo to Iwakuni. Time and date were things we forgot. I can recollect only that at a number of points on the journey there was a lack of Japanese assistance for our baggage, due either to Sunday-no-worku or a Japanese National Holiday!

If plays are to be presented regularly and even the most outlandish units are to see them then it is obvious that the only solution lies in a permanent Base Unit formed purposely to do that job and no other. Our 'flying' visit to Shikoku pleased the Dorsets at Gomen although only half of them were able to see the show because of our one-night stand. On the other hand, I think it caused some annoyance at the HQs of the Camerons, who had so kindly provided and maintained Lachie's kilt and other uniform items; and the Welsh Fusiliers – for we were not given time to visit them all.

Back in Kure and the show goes on, locally – HMS Commonwealth (Kure Naval Base), 34 Brigade's theatre, Kaitachi Area and rumours of diversions to Miho, Kobe and, perhaps, a return visit to Tokyo.

On behalf of the cast I wish to express the thanks of the Little Theatre Players to George Welsh, our producer/director and to Bill McDermott, our hard-working and 'ever-ready' Stage Manager.

I think I may conclude by saying the Motto of the whole company, throughout the tour, was that old stock phrase – 'The things we do for the sake of the ART!'

C.B.

SHEFFIELD COURT PRODUCTIONS

Registered Office
DENMARK HOUSE
71/72 Piccadilly
London W1

Directors
H. Hanson
P.B. Watkins

Secretary
F.T. Heath

August 1956

To whom it may concern

MR COLIN BEAN, who has worked continuously for our organisation for five years, and with myself for the past three, has asked me for a recommendation and this I am most happy to supply.

As an artist he has played everything from light comedy to heavy character. In the latter he is extremely successful for he has a most forceful personality, a great power of projection and is most adept and painstaking with his make-ups. Many of these have been exceptional.

As a person, he is a joy to have in the theatre. He is never temperamental and always receives, and embodies in his performance every point of production. He gives willingly, and always of his time. He spends freely of his salary to ensure his correctness in appearance.

Always he has been willing to assist in all departments – no task has ever been beneath him, and while he is engaged as an artist his marked ability with props and stage decor has always been of the utmost help.

I have never known him late in the theatre and his discipline, and his behaviour, I must commend completely. If there were more young men like him in the profession I hasten to say that many pitfalls would be avoided.

If this commendation seems fulsome it is only because it is one of those rare occasions when I am happy to recommend someone without any qualifications. This young man has the theatre in his blood and, with that little piece of good fortune which everyone needs, he should certainly make his mark in his chosen line of work.

Yours faithfully

(Signed) *DOUGLAS NEIL*

General Manager

EMPIRE

HYLDA BAKER

LYCEUM

COLIN BEAN in
"Piccadilly Alibi"